On Warmer Tides

The Genesis and History of Italy's First World War Naval Commandos

Matthew C. Hall

Helion & Company

Helion & Company Limited
Unit 8 Amherst Business Centre
Budbrooke Road
Warwick
CV34 5WE
England
Tel. 01926 499 619
Email: info@helion.co.uk
Website: www.helion.co.uk
Twitter: @helionbooks
Visit our blog at blog.helion.co.uk

Published by Helion & Company 2023
Designed and typeset by Mach 3 Solutions (www.mach3solutions.co.uk)
Cover designed by Paul Hewitt, Battlefield Design (www.battlefield-design.co.uk)

Text © Matthew C. Hall
Images © as individually credited
Maps open source

Front cover: Italian MAS (*Motobarca Armata Società Veneziana Automobili Navali*) c.1917-18.
(Open source)

ISBN 978-1-915113-71-9

British Library Cataloguing-in-Publication Data.
A catalogue record for this book is available from the British Library.

For details of other military history titles published by Helion & Company Limited contact
the above address or visit our website: http://www.helion.co.uk.

We always welcome receipt of book proposals from prospective authors.

Contents

List of Illustrations

List of Maps

Acknowledgements

I would like to thank Mr Davide Trabucco at the A.S.M. in Modena for allowing me to study their library of documents on the Italian military and for putting me on to this story. I would also like to thank the Gallica Project in France, started by the *Bibliothèque Nationale de France* in 1997, for their vast collection of documents. I am also especially grateful to my in-laws, Giuseppe Levoni and Anna-Maria Parotta, for allowing me to stay in Italy to conduct the work; and to my fiancée, Chiara Levoni, without whom I would never have come to know Italy enough to write this book. Lastly, a mention should go to my late grandfather, whose love of history and vast collection of works turned me on to history as a child. It should also be remarked that I thank the men of the MAS units whose fearless dedication to the former Italian Kingdom provided the subject matter for this book.

Introduction

The Italian coastline is a place of stunning beauty; to say anything else would be to mislead any prospective traveller. Unlike the Italian landmass, its shores are not in the main dominated by towering cliffs, while its tides are calm as a result of its passive beaches and its waters are crystal clear. Given that Italy's land borders are rather limited, it is this boundary between sea and land which gives the country its largest frontier. Coming in at over 7,000km, it faces territories traditionally inhabited by enemies of the multitude of Italianate states, that have faded in and out of existence throughout time. To the south stands the endless deserts of the Maghreb, to the west lays the oft tumultuous lands of Hispania and in the east the exotic, and frequently hostile, Balkan landmass. The latter is a place which, as the reader will discover, is host to a littoral space far more volatile than anything found down the Italic boot. But it was during a summer a year ago, whilst holidaying with the Italian side of my family, that the idea for this book began to gestate in my then sun-soaked mind. Sitting quietly on the rocks of the Adriatic, gazing out towards the one-time Italian protectorate of Albania, it occurred to me that given the country's profound maritime heritage, why had so little been written on the matter. Wandering through the Mediterranean nation's many nautical museums, and dining with my family there, revealed a national obsession with the seas, the degree to which I formerly had no idea. When I returned to the inland city of Modena, deep in northern Italy's Po delta, my curiosity was further inflamed by an unforeseen introduction to Mr Davide Trabucco, a member of a small team of dedicated volunteer curators at a modest military museum and library run by the *Associazione Studi Militari*'s (ASM) chapter in Emilia-Romagna. It is an institute whose facilities I used for this book to great effect, and to whom I will forever be grateful. I became firm friends with Davide, and over drinks one evening he put me on to a story which provided the animus for the creation of this book.

The story in question concerned an operation conducted by the *Regia Marina*'s MAS (*motoscafo armato silurante*, or torpedo-armed motorboat) units during the First World War. This unit was entirely unknown to me; I, like many within the community of naval historians, believed that Italy's naval special forces had their birth during the Second World War. Davide's retelling of the 'Raid on Bakar Bay' made for thrilling listening as he recounted a tale of derring-do across the choppy waters of the eastern Adriatic. The tale further entrenched in my mind the feeling that Italy's naval history was woefully underexplored. Unfortunately, this did not come as a surprise, Italian military history as a whole being sadly under-visited. With this in mind, it is a history which I have done my utmost to represent accurately in this book. Interestingly, the foe of the Italian state throughout the first half-century of its existence – the Habsburg Empire – seemed to have had an equally inadequate treatment of its military; in particular its navy, the *K.u.K. Kreigsmarine*, a body which through my research I found was clearly more than a match for the *Regia Marina*, and indeed frequently bested its Italian counterpart. It soon became clear to me that understanding these two maritime forces was crucial to allowing the reader to comprehend the actions of the MAS boats. Why did their commando operations target what they did? How did their torpedoes sink the Habsburgs' armoured goliaths of the waves, such as the SMS *Viribus Unitis*? And why was such a pioneering idea tried in the first place? To answer these probing questions, this work digs deep into the bureaucratic and political background of both states and their respective navies as they tried to build up war-worthy forces. As a result, a truly fascinating picture comes into view of 19th-century into early 20th-century politics, in both the Italian nation and the Habsburg Empire, and forms this work's inimitable context.

Yet the organisational battles that brought the MAS units into existence were framed against the backdrop of the Industrial Revolution, a phenomenon whose motors turn in the background of every decision detailed in this book. Indeed, without the Industrial Revolution the concept of sailor-commandos utilising fast-moving vessels equipped with man-portable explosives would be unthinkable. There had been such men before: pirates from the Caribbean to the Baltic had long used crews of hardened men armed with cutlasses, axes and other vicious tools to surprise enemy ships moored in the dead of night. The panoply of indigenous societies inhabiting the banks of the Amazon River rowed silent canoes to bring bloody vengeance to neighbouring river bound villages, before disappearing into its malarial waters. But this millennia-old form of aquatic confrontation could not survive the evolution of shipbuilding that the end of the medieval period ushered in. Cannons by the tens began to be incorporated into the sides of vessels, naval firepower allowed ships to bombard the shore from afar and consequently sea battles now consisted of long-range slugging matches. Increasing range gave rise to battles in the open ocean, and by the 17th century the idea of commandos attacking from small vessels had faded into history. The Industrial Revolution changed everything, and as it reached its zenith in mainland Europe during the latter half of the 19th and earlier part of the 20th centuries, new fuels, new materials and new thoughts raced into the military sphere. As the world crashed into the 1900s, small boats ceased to concern themselves with the speed constraints imposed on them by muscle and bone. Destructive power was no longer confined to the blade, bludgeon or simple black powder alone, and for good reason. At the same time as the barriers to small-squad, high-speed, high-destruction units were being peeled back, a rationale arose for the existence of such units. By the dawn of the 20th century, the rickety experimental ironclad vessels of the previous 50 years had evolved into solid battleships: vessels which bristled with guns, with armour inches thick and capable of travelling across the globe for gun duels lasting hours at a time. However, with their size and sophistication came an insurmountable problem and a strategic weakness – their expense and value.

When Italy witnessed the commissioning of HMS *Dreadnought*, they wrestled with how to keep up with the cutting edge of both the Royal Navy and their enemies across the Adriatic. Both Rome and Vienna understood their inability to replace these vessels once they had been built. If any of these vessels on either side were to be lost, their primitive shipbuilding-economic complexes would be unable to replicate them without an immense loss of spending power. Naval planning in both societies began to treat these vessels with caution, just at the time when a mutual confrontation on the seas was becoming inevitable. For quite apart from firing shipbuilding into a different material universe, the Industrial Revolution had created a house of troubles in Europe; and none so more than in the Italian peninsula. From 1815–66, the land had been ravaged by war and revolution, as the ideologies unleashed by the twin forces of the French Revolution and rapid economic change created a fertile ground for an explosion of liberal nationalism. A single objective – to unite all Italians everywhere into one liberal and constitutional state – formulated in the womb of Italy's collective consciousness. Unfortunately for Vienna, the single target of this movement within the cultural mood of the Italic polity would be the Habsburg Empire, identified by Garibaldi's red shirt revolutionaries in the same vein as it had been by Robespierre's Jacobins – a great absolutist Satan. A monolithic shadow was now looming over the changing political space of the European continent. By the time HMS *Dreadnought* was being constructed in Portsmouth naval docks in 1905, the Italian people had fought three wars with the Habsburg Empire. A decade later, they would be on the warpath once more to liberate the last of the Italians from the empire's grip.

The main thrust of the Italian desire to wrest control over the last traces of Italianate populaces in Europe during the First World War was inevitably concentrated in its north-east. It was a battle-space dominated on its seaward side by the complicated lagoons of the Venetian Gulf and the powerful waves of the upper Adriatic, whilst being hemmed in on its landward side by the domineering peaks of the Dolomites. Because of its maritime nature, the flat plains of the far eastern Po delta presented a vulnerable front for the Italian Army as it shifted its forces to the border with the Habsburg Empire. Controlling the Adriatic became a priority between the two states, but despite pouring inordinate amounts of time, money and theorising into the use of battleships and dreadnoughts, the potential impact of their loss saw them moth-balled. Small ships fighting small actions for incremental results emerged, a state of affairs which constituted the ensuing Adriatic campaign. It was an environment in which the MAS squads would thrive and come to dominate. Yet it is a sad fact of history that the exploits of the MAS boats and their contribution to the Adriatic campaign have, prior to this book, mostly been ignored. Yet without their creation, the concept of today's waterborne commando may not have come about. From this origin point, the frogman of the Second World War would be born. As the interwar period saw further advances in diving apparatus, by the time Italy entered the world's second global conflict in 1939, true underwater explosive-equipped commandos were possible. From the discarded ashes of the First World War's MAS squadrons would rise the now infamous MAS squadrons of Fascist Italy. Vicious, fanatical and led by the towering fascist aristocrat, *Capitano* Junio Borghese, the MAS squadron's successor unit, Decima X, would go on to conduct operations in the Mediterranean similar to that of their First World War ancestors. Through hostile interaction with the Royal Navy, this successor unit would go on to cross-pollinate with the Royal Navy, which quickly recognised the utility of sub-aquatic commandos. Their proliferation globally followed, but without the proving actions of the MAS units and the bravery of original thinkers such as Admiral Paolo Thaon di Revel, the resurrection of these units from medieval obscurity might never have occurred. The importance of the Adriatic campaign in laying the building blocks for the future world of maritime commandos is unmatched, making the story of the MAS unit one which fully deserves to be told.

1

Claiming the Adriatic

The commencement of the First World War is one of history's greatest controversies. The most popular theories rest upon the reasoning that by 1914, a conventional conflict of some type was inevitable due to a build-up of intolerable pressure within the European state system. Furthermore, it is advocated that the pressurising forces primarily came from France and Germany, with German unification in 1871[1] and its orientation towards the Habsburg Empire ushering in the demise of France as a continental power. On the eastern front, it is commonly assumed that the Russian Tsardom and the Habsburg monarchy would also inescapably be launched into conflict, courtesy of their mutual desire to see the end of Ottoman influence and the return of Christian governance to the Balkans after nearly five centuries of Islamic rule.[2] As for the introduction into the war of the world's greatest empire since the demise of the classical world, it would be Britain's ties to Belgium via the 1839 Treaty of London,[3] and its fear of a German challenge to British thalassocracy, that would be of primary influence when the war came. What is noticeable, however, is an absence in almost all the participants to the conflict's preliminary diplomatic phase (beginning with 1908's Bosnia Crisis and ending with the 1914 invasion of Serbia by the Habsburg Empire) of ideology. Instead, alliances, international law, national honour and a vital release of pressure from the international system are to blame. Except, that is, in two cases – the Kingdom of Serbia and the Kingdom of Italy. Only in these nations was their participation in the conflict motivated by ideology alone. In both cases, that was not only nationalism but the conceptualisation of a state greater than that currently in existence. In the Serbian nationalists – encapsulated in the aims of its most extreme movement, the Black Hand – lay a desired endeavour to rebuild the legendary Serbian

1   Taylor, A.J.P., *The Habsburg Monarchy 1809–1918* (London: Penguin Publishing, 1948), p.179.
2   Glenny, M., *The Balkans 1804–2012: Nationalism, War and the Great Powers* (London: Granta Books, 2017), p.91.
3   Clark, C., *The Sleepwalkers: How Europe Went to War in 1914* (London: Penguin Publishing, 2013), pp. 306–307.

empire of Stephan Dushan,[4] and from that cause a call to seize upon a dormant late medieval claim to greatness. The Italian nationalist movement, as instrumental in bringing about the Kingdom of Italy's entrance into the war as Serbia's, sought also to strike out for a greater Italy of medieval heritage. It was a claim based not on the revanchist claims of an imaginary terrestrial Balkan empire, as was the case for the Archduke Ferdinand's fateful assassin, but on a concept of thalassocracy and ultra-marine longing. This ambition was founded on the will to enact claims on territories Rome believed to have been bequeathed to the Italian state from the ashes of the dead Venetian state that had existed from the 5th century until the 18th.[5]

The maritime space which the Italian state would seek to claim and reconquer to sate the appetites of a rabid Italian public (who by 1915 had been whipped into fever pitch, as we will see in Chapter 5) comprised some 1,346 nautical miles[6] of the Adriatic, constrained by both the eastern-facing Italian and western-facing Balkan coastlines. These two littoral zones are home to four major ethnic groups – Italians, Greeks, Albanians and Slavs – and possess three religions – Orthodoxy, Catholicism and Islam. The Italian coastline is the more picturesque of the two, comprising rolling coastal plains formed from the lowlands of the epic Apennine Mountain range. The Balkan shore – termed the Dalmatian coast – is home to some of Europe's most formi-dable cliff faces and one of its wildest mountain ranges, the Dinarics, formed some 252 million years ago.[7] Such is the extent of this alpine terrain that it consumes approxi-mately 400 miles of the Adriatic's eastern land border, encompassing almost all of the lands between Slovenia in the north and the Albanian border with Montenegro in the south. The land's karst topography has produced a pirate's paradise, filled with deep cave systems, foreboding pebbled beaches and labyrinthine coves. To make matters worse for honest sea-fearers, but to the delight of Arab corsairs of old, the shores of the Dalmatian coast are littered with rocky islands and antediluvian stacks which rise obstinately from the waves. This has historically produced waters which are violent and powerful, whipped up by biting maritime winds. The heavily fragmented nature of the Balkan coast, which these powerful aquatic rhythms career vessels towards, make the Dalmatian shores among Europe's most dangerous. The most perilous point of this nautical zone lies along the tallest part of the Dinarics, in its Albanian portion, where the Illyrian town of Orikum looks out towards the Italian commune of Otranto. The space in between these zones takes its name from the latter settlement, forming the 39 nautical mile-long Strait of Otranto. Not far north of this location, a rapid drop occurs from the Adriatic's average 200m depth, forming an abyss which stretches to 1,000m. Yet the shallower northern portion of this tumultuous seascape is no safer. Its waters lap the Istrian peninsula, whose 144 miles of coastline are as dismal and

4   Norwich, J., *A Short History of Byzantium* (London: Penguin Publishing, 1998), p.339.
5   Galibert, L., *Histoire de la République de Venise* (Paris: 1850), p.9.
6   Ivetic, E., *Storia dell'Adriatico. Un mare e La Sua Civilta* (Bologna: il Mulino, 2019).
7   Tanner, M., *Croatia: A History from the Middle Ages to the Present Day* (London: Yale University Press, 2010), p.4.

formidable as the larger Dalmatian zone to which it is attached. Unlike the southern shores though, its waters are uncomfortable and in the winter practically unnavigable. Sea ice begins to envelop its frozen coves in late autumn and terrible eastern winds batter its Italianate cities, plunging temperatures to a few degrees below zero. The water, meanwhile, descends to a hypothermia-inducing 10 degrees Celsius, forming a desolate and unforgiving aquatic realm, where operational diving would, on the face of it, be exceptionally difficult.

The waters of the Adriatic are not just climactically uncomfortable, but also historically chaotic. The Romans first discovered the anarchic nature of these waters, when in 229BC, the consul Gnaeus Fulvius Centumalus was dispatched to subjugate the pirate kingdoms of Illyria,[8] whose realms stretched from Albania to Istria, and whose Lembi[9] harassed the superhighway between the growing power of Rome and the post-Alexandrian realms of Asia. A rapid naval campaign solved the problem for a time, but with the onset of early medieval Europe the issue of piracy returned. In the 6th century, the Slavs broke into the Balkans, travelling in an immense migratory bloc.[10] Before long, preying on the weakness of the Roman Empire – now based in Constantinople – the tribal formations settling along the Dalmatian coast began to raid the Imperial shipping lanes between a nascent Venice and the remaining Roman Empire.[11] The issue with Slav buccaneers would extend into the 10th century, and would overlap with yet another influx of Adriatic-bound pirates, this time coming from the newly constituted Islamic Empire, stretching by the commencement of the 9th century from Iraq to northern Spain. But by 809, the authority of the Abbasid Empire – with its capital in Baghdad – had begun to wither.[12] A subsequent collapse in the empire's authority led to political destabilisation in Syria and the Levant too. An increase in wandering Arab adventurers and pirate lords is consequently documented in this period, with a force of Andalusian Muslims conquering Crete in 824 and transforming it into a pirate haven.[13] With Sicily having been conquered in a similar manner four years previously, this turned the Mediterranean into an unstable lake, and from that the Adriatic collapsed into chaos. Although this situation was eventually rectified with the rise of Italian naval power through the Middle Ages, the gradual conquest of the Balkans by the Ottoman Turks – from 1371's Battle of Maritsa up until the Ottoman failure to storm Vienna in 1683 – reintroduced maritime anarchy. The return of piracy, this time focused around Istria, served to hammer home the insecurity of the Adriatic and its proclivity to generate bands of sea raiders. This time it was

8   Holland, T., *Rubicon: The Triumph and Tragedy of the Roman Republic* (London: Abacus, 2004), p.165.
9   D'Amato, R., *Republican Roman Warships 509-27BC* (Oxford: Osprey Publishing, 2015), p.13.
10   Norwich, J., *A Short History of Byzantium*, p.86.
11   Musarra, A., *Medioevo Marinaro: Prendere il Mare Nell'Italia Medievale* (Bologna: Il Mulino, 2021), p.22.
12   Mansfield, P., *A History of the Middle East* (London: Penguin Publishing, 1991), pp.17–18.
13   Norwich, J., *A Short History of Byzantium*, p.134.

in the form of the Uskoks, whose highly organised intelligence network, and ferocious anti-Turkic sentiment allowed them to sunder the sea's vital trade lanes.[14] Today, this insecure piratical tradition is carried forth by Croat and Albanian middlemen, whose shaky vessels transport undocumented peoples into the grizzly hands of the Sicilian *Cosa Nostra*, Napoli's *Cammora* or the dreaded *'Ndrangheta* of Calabria.[15]

The waters of the Adriatic may therefore seem to be a rather curious waterway for the 19th-century Italian Kingdom to wish to claim: difficult to utilise on its eastern side, historically anarchic and sandwiched between the barbarous world of the Balkans and the civilisation of the Italian peninsula. But to the Italian nationalist movement of the mid to late 19th century, it was not so much what their prospective territory comprised, more the sense of them not being 'whole' without what they believed was rightfully theirs. As we will see throughout this book, it was this feeling that propelled the Italian state to make the maritime decisions that it did from 1915–18. Yet why, we may ask, was the pull to dominate the Adriatic quite as powerful as it would turn out to be upon Italian unification in 1861? The answer lies in the fog of classical civilisation's 5th-century collapse, a period on which the Italian nationalists would pin an almost mythological reverence.

By Ancient Decree

Of all the territorial claims of the cause for a unified state formed by and for the Italian people, that espoused for the Dalmatian coast, Istria and indeed the Adriatic Sea itself is perhaps the strangest. The Italian nationalist movement which would frame the later construction of the Italian state was, in essence, an offshoot of the ideals of the French Revolution of 1789. In particular, they took to heart the third article of the Universal Declaration of the Rights of Man, that *Le principe de toute Souverainete reside essentiellement dans la Nation. Nul corps, nul individu ne peut exercer d'autorite qui n'en émane expressément ;*[16] or that the principal of all sovereignty resided inside the nation. The nation was understood as an ethno-linguistic concept of an ethnically exclusive territory, whose decisions were taken by the people as a single body and then executed by a government which respected this nation of people's wishes. It was on this principle that a plethora of Italian nationalist groups – the Red Shirts, Young Italians, Carbonari – sought to best reflect the aims of the French Revolution that they so admired.[17] The question which was to haunt the Italian Kingdom up until its termination in 1946 was the boundaries to which the finished Italian nation would comprise.

---

14 Morris, J., *The Venetian Empire: A Sea Voyage* (London: Penguin Publishing, 1990), pp.162–163.
15 Saviano, R., *Gomorrah* (London: Picador, 2019).
16 Davidson, J., *The French Revolution: From Enlightenment to Tyranny* (London: Profile Books, 2017), p.261.
17 Pecout, G., *Il Lungo Risorgimento: La Nascita dell'Italia Contemporanea 1770–1922* (Torino: Bruno Mondadori, 1997), p.17.

For some, the establishment of a state encompassing the whole peninsula was merely a stepping stone. To fully unite the Italian people in this vision would necessarily mean conquering any lands where Italians lived in significant numbers. Yet within that, a second qualification lurked, that being the age of the Italian population residing in a territory targeted for unification. The date of Italian occupation had to rest somewhere in the mists of time, sufficient to sate the rather ambiguous criterion which we might call authenticity. For the mainstream Italian nationalist movement, their presence in the Italian peninsula – and their domination of that space – was legitimised by an ancient past, namely the process concluded by Roman arms at the end of the Second Punic War (218–201 BC)[18] which had involved the Latin tribes inhabiting the hills of Rome (a city founded in the 8th century BC) subjugating the confines of modern Italy. But for the extreme wings of the Italian nationalist movement in the decades leading up to the First World War, it was in Rome's fall that they found justification for their extra-peninsular claims on both the Adriatic Sea and the Balkan coastline.

In AD 410, the Visigoths breached the Istrian frontier and broke into late-Roman Italy,[19] King Alaric I subsequently marching into the Eternal City and bringing an end to Roman power in the West. Although the empire in the West would take another 20 years to finally collapse, the insecurity and chaos that the unchecked advance of the Germans had engendered in the Italian peninsula sent refugees in all directions. Over the following decades, a concentration of ethnic Romans (although it is likely not all were Latins) developed on the network of islands which congregate along the mouths of the Po, Adige, Brenta, Piave and Tagliamento rivers.[20] The coming apocalypse consolidated these peoples and forced them to ally with one another, 16 March 421 being given as the date for the foundation of their common community.[21] Facilitated by the building of a network of bridges, the polity today known as Venice was thus born. The inhabitants of this desperate refuge from the empire's collapse continued to live according to the old Roman ways, eschewing the evolving feudal society on the mainland. This retention of habits generated an otherness among the refugees themselves and would see the foundation of a separate, durable 'Italian' identity. It is remarkable that this weak band of poorly organised island statelets, haunted by the coming of the Germans, managed to survive let alone become the engine for the enduring generation of territorial claims.

But it was Venice's defiance in the face of the Mediterranean world's new rulers which would characterise its first triumphs in the foundation of an Italian realm outside of the peninsular confines of its brother Italics. In 810, the new ruler of the Western world – Emperor Charlemagne I – sent his son against Venice, but Pepin,

18   Goldsworthy, A., *The Fall of Carthage: The Punic Wars 265–146 BC* (London: Weidenfeld & Nicolson, 2003), pp.141–328.
19   Collins, R., *Early Medieval Europe: 300-1000* (London: Palgrave, 1999), p.61.
20   Galibert, L., *Historie de la République de Venise*. p.16.
21   Musatti, E., *Storia d'un Lembo di Terra: Venezia ed i Veneziani* (Padova: 1882), p.34.

the king of Italy, failed to bring it to heel,[22] in doing so conceding the lagoon-based metropolis its independence. Renouncing the claims of any Frankish ruler to its islands, over the following two centuries the Venetian Republic – founded by and continually espousing Roman values of civic organisation – would form an association of Latin city states spreading from Istria down to Albania. This proto-Venetian Empire encompassed Trieste, Pirano, D'Isola, D'Emone, de Rovigno, de Numago, Zara, Salona, Sebenigo, Spalatro, Traou, None, Almisa and Ragusa. By the end of the 10th century, the Adriatic islands of Coronata, Pago, Ossero, Lissa, Brazza, Arbo and Cherso had joined this Italian-led association. From that point onwards, by dint of their Italianate populations, Roman municipal traditions and indirect rule by Venice's *podestats*, these cities and their hinterland would be considered authentically Latin. Although Venetian power here would wane from the arrival of the Ottoman Turks in the 14th century up to the end of the Republic in 1797, the Italian populations that their dominion had given birth to would endure until 1915. This in turn allowed the more extreme wing of Italian nationalist thought to lay claim to the cities and hinterlands in which these Italian populations continued to live.

A Contested Inheritance

Although the Franks, and by extension their German successors, had abandoned their claims to Venice in 810,[23] the city's expansion into Dalmatia and Istria brought it unwanted attention from another source. At the beginning of the 9th century, the arrival of the Bulgars had demolished the Avar confederation, kicking them out of the Carpathian basin. In their wake, Almos Arpad led the Magyars from their homes east of the Ural mountains and north of the Danube. Upon their arrival in the Balkans, they, like the Avars, were humiliated by the Bulgars, forcing the Magyars to migrated again westwards into the newly vacated Carpathian basin. In 1001, after an epic centuries-long confrontation with the Holy Roman Empire's ruling Ottonian dynasty, the Magyars settled and under King Stephen I (ruled 1000–1038) converted to Catholicism, forming the Hungarian Kingdom.[24] This act brought them into the Catholic system of states, and more importantly Christendom's legal and international traditions – revolving around dynasties and territorial claims inherited through the ages. The Venetians and the Italians of Istria had already come into confrontation with the Magyars and their settlement just east of the Istrian peninsula became a cause for concern. In 899, the Hungarian horde had attempted to expand southwards, only stopped in their endeavours by Venice's lagoons, which frustrated their attempt

---

22   Collins, R., *Early Medieval Europe: 300-1000*, pp.184–287.
23   Wilson, P., *The Holy Roman Empire: A Thousand Years of Europe's History* (London: Penguin Publishing, 2016), p.189.
24   Engel, P., *The Realm of St Stephen: A History of Medieval Hungary, 895-1526* (London: Continuum International Publishing Group, 2005), pp.8–25.

to conquer the city and subjugate north-eastern Italy. Luckily for the Venetian-aligned Italian city-states of Istria and northern Dalmatia, upon admission to the feudal system of states the descendants of Arpad had to be able to operate within the ecclesiastical claims system. Thus, hunger for land was no longer a motivation in relations between the two ethnic groups. If the Magyars wanted to expand south and from there to contest Italianate claims to Dalmatia, they would have to do so legally.

Istrian-Italian respite did not last long though. In 925, the Croat portion of the great Slavic confederation – which had made its way through the Balkans in the late 6th century – formed a united state under their monarch, King Tomislav Trpimirovic (925–928).[25] This entity received legal recognition from the papacy in the same year upon their abandonment of Arianism for the Catholic faith. Although the details of this kingdom are largely lost to time and have been twisted to fit the fluctuating narratives of Croat nationalism, what is certain is that its borders stretched as far north as Slovenia and as far south as Montenegro, encompassing the whole of the Dalmatian coastline and most of the western Balkans. The Croats are reported to have consolidated their grip on the Istrian mainland into thee 11th century, although the continued existence of the Italianate cities of the coastline would suggest that they surrounded the Italian cities rather than subjugated them. By dint of these conquests, at the dawn of the reign of King Petar Kresimir (1058–1074) the Croatian claim to Istria and the Dalmatian coast was a secure one, recognised by the Papacy within the confines of international law. However, the death of Kresimir in 1074 led to an *interregnum* in which the Tripartite Kingdom of Croatia – taking its name from the unification of Dalmatia, Slavonia and Croatia – collapsed into anarchy. After 30 years of chaos, the Croat nobility invited King Koloman I of Hungary to restore order to the land, resulting in the Pacta Conventa in 1102.[26] This act put an end to the Croatian kingdom and saw its territorial claims to Istria and Dalmatia (lands also claimed by Venice) pass into the hands of the Hungarian state, under the crown of St Stephen, where it would rest until the formation of Yugoslavia in 1918.[27]

The Hungarian state which resulted from the Pacta Conventa thus encompassed a large part of the northern Balkans and the whole of Carpathia. In the 16th century, however, the Hungarians would lose their statehood and upper-Balkan dominion in the face of the Ottoman Turks. In 1371, after a century of conflict and change in the political composition of the Balkans, and in the wake of 1204's sack of Constantinople by Italian arms, an immense Slavic host was destroyed at the Battle of Maritsa.[28] The Ottoman Turks, whose forces so roundly beat them, found themselves invulnerable in their invasion of Europe, and by 1391 the ascendant Asian power had created

25 Bellamy, A., *The Formation of Croatian National Identity: A Centuries-Old Dream* (New York: Manchester University Press, 2003), pp.35–36.
26 Tanner, M., *Croatia: A History from the Middle Ages to the Present Day*, p.14.
27 Taylor, A.J.P., *The Struggle for Mastery in Europe: 1848–1918* (Oxford: Oxford University Press, 1954), p.548.
28 Engel, P., *The Realm of St Stephen*, pp.157–174.

a vast realm encompassing Dalmatia, Bosnia, Serbia, Croatia, Greece, Albania and Montenegro.[29] In 1453, the victorious Ottoman Turks marched into Constantinople and ended Roman civilisation forever, sealing the fate of the southern Slavs and by the 16th century the Magyars too. In 1526, as a last-ditch attempt to prevent the Ottomans from breaking into Eastern Europe, a vast Christian army led by the Hungarian warlord John Huyundi brought the Turks to battle on a dust-riddled August day on the plains of Mohacs. The failure to stop the Turkish onslaught there led to the deaths of vast numbers of Hungarian nobility and, more importantly, King Louis of Hungary. Without a ruling line, the Kingdom of Hungary – encompassing the Dalmatian territories granted to it via the House of Arpad's seizure of Croatia – passed into the hands of the Habsburg dynasty. From 1526 until its dissolution in 1918, the imperium forged by the Habsburg line would come to include the whole of the Hungarian Kingdom, including its Croat portion. Thus, the Venetian-aligned Italian cities of Dalmatia and Istria became surrounded by the Early Modern world's premier continental power – the Habsburg Empire. This cast Dalmatia, Istria and Venice's Balkan maritime empire into the vortex of great power politics – an unpredictable place at best.

French Fury

Straddling the Italian border with Slovenia, Campoformido is a quiet place, far from the Italian state's economic dynamos in the north-east Po basin. On the surface, the place is rather unremarkable, and if one visited it without being informed of its remarkable place in 19th-century history, you would not pay it a second thought. Like most Italian locales, the focal point would seem to be its rather unremarkable church – the Church of St Maria of Purification. Beneath its perfect banality, however, lies ground upon which men of epic significance walked. On a crisp autumn day in 1797, soldiers dressed in the dark blue and white of the French Revolutionary Army mingled with the opulently decorated forces of the House of Habsburg. Zealous Jacobites cast clouds of breath into the chilly sub-alpine air and starving Magyar horses wandered the town's small streets, looking for a meal. The presence of a legion of officials from two forces whose mutual hatred was a bitter one had been called to this place to codify a new relationship between the Habsburg monarchy and the First French Republic. Until May of that year, the commune and its surroundings had been the sovereign territory of the Italian-ruled state of Venice, whose doges had ruled most of the eastern Po Valley since a series of staggering victories against their fellow Italian powers during the 14th and 15th centuries. Nevertheless, that spring had seen all their work undone as the torch of the liberal world revolution burned across the state's near-medieval power structures. That fire had caused a vicious backlash from

29   Mansfield, P., *A History of the Middle East*, p.27.

the territory's nationalists zealots, whose appeal to the Italian state's historic greatness had resulted in a mass call to arms in the countryside of what was once called
Terra-Firma. The French retaliation had been swift and brutal, and the Army of Italy
– commanded by the future emperor Napoleon Bonaparte – had seen the uprisings
as being undertaken with the tacit support of the Venetian doges.[30] By 12 May 1797,
Ludovico Manin, the last doge of Venice, abolished the ruling council and ended the
Venetian Republic and its maritime empire across the Adriatic.[31] The Italian ultra-
marine cities which had been under its protection on both the Dalmatian and Istrian
coast were now naked to the world; primarily to the Habsburgs.

Despite their anger towards the Venetians, the forces of the French Revolution were
not in Italy to collapse Italian claims to overseas greatness. The ruling Directory in Paris
had been drawn there by lucid visions of a quick victory against their nemesis – the
Habsburg monarchy.[32] To the fathers of France's revolutionary philosophy – Robespierre,
Diderot and Voltaire – the Habsburgs represented the horrors of a feudal Europe that
they sought to replace with their vision of utopia. It had, after all been the Habsburg
monarchy which had been responsible for the early attempt to defeat the revolution
in 1792, when a pan-German army comprised of Habsburg and Prussian forces had
advanced on France's eastern border.[33] It had been the Habsburg dynasty from where
had come the ill-fated Marie Antoinette, and it had been on the connections that she
had to the Habsburg ruler, Emperor Francis II, that King Louis XVI (1745–93) had
relied when orchestrating his would-be rescue in 1792. This act of immense aggression
on behalf of the German powers had been defeated at the battles of Valmy and Jemappes
by the former royalist and hardened war veteran, Charles Francois Dumouriez. The
failure to achieve Paris's capitulation had shifted the balance of the anti-revolutionary
forces, and by 1796 the French were steaming through Italy on their way to Vienna –
hoping as they did so to bypass the Habsburg heartlands in Germany. It was in this
campaign that Napoleon Bonaparte unleashed upon the Habsburgs a lightning-fast
dart across northern Italy which would see the latter defeated at almost every turn.[34]

The resolution of the figurehead for European feudalism seemed unbroken, but
when the first snows fell in Slovenia along the Julian Alps in October 1797 – sepa-
rating Italy from the Habsburg Empire – the Habsburgs, unable to link their two
field forces, came to Campoformido to sue for a truce. Using Doge Ludovico Manin's
private villa,[35] the two sides gathered around the grandiose building's fires, sheltering

30   Ardant, E., *Campagnes des Français: en Italie, en Egypte, en Hollande, en Allemagne, en
     Prusse, en Pologne, en Espagne, en Russie, en Saxe: Histoire Complete des Guerres de La France*
     (Limoges: 1887), pp.57–82.
31   Galibert, L., *Histoire de la République de Venise*, p.542.
32   Roberts, A., *Napoleon the Great* (London: Penguin Publishing, 2015), p.74.
33   Barnes-Fremont, G., *The French Revolutionary Wars* (Oxford: Osprey Publishing, 2001),
     pp.132–144.
34   Roberts, A., *Napoleon the Great*, p.549.
35   Galibert, L., *Histoire de la République de Venise*.

a single Italian people, a single Italian blood. But for Italy's noble houses, so anxious to return to their palaces in Modena, Firenze, Roma, Parma, Torino and Napoli, these concepts were impossible to grasp. Only one exception existed, a noble house which would now propel the Italian people towards their post-Napoleonic destiny – the House of Savoy.[43]

To witness the birth of 'nationality' as one people bonded together by ethno-cultural-linguistic relativity, combined with a mutual collective pain, is but one ingredient to the resurrection of the Italian people's claims abroad. For to have a nation, or a unified people, one must create a geographical limit of the authority unto which they can legitimately claim their right to exercise said authority. The Italian theorists of the 19th century who pondered on reunification, such as Giuseppe Mazzini, would seek to build a unification movement which would place all Italians into a single entity. Yet the system of formal legal claims which had previously ruled Europe had been excoriated. Venice's claims to its maritime empire across the Adriatic had been shovelled into the furnace at Formio-Campo, and then again at 1808's Treaty of Pressburg, when its lands had been temporarily incorporated into Imperial France's domains.[44] The conclusions of the Congress of Vienna had hypothetically pushed these claims even further from the reach of the Italian people – restoring Venice's imperial domains to the Habsburg Empire, vindicating Formio-Campo and officially consigning Venice's maritime claims to history. Or at least, that was the plan. On 1 July 1820, the ghosts of Napoleon's revolution rose once more from their shallow graves. That morning, among the baking heights of Avellino – some 50 miles from Napoli – a hitherto unremarkable priest named Luigi Mincini slung a battle-scarred musket over his withered shoulders and marched to the urban capital of that province. Upon arriving in Avellino itself, Lieutenant Michele Morelli of the Royal Army of the Two Sicilies, a veteran of the Napoleonic conflict and friend to Father Minicini, marched through the town's empty streets and proclaimed its loyalty to King Ferdinand IV.

On the surface, this event may seem rather unremarkable. King Ferdinand IV had been crowned monarch of both the Kingdom of Naples and its satellite state, the Kingdom of Sicily, before the French Revolution had even been an embryo, back in 1759. But it was not to his person that they were aligning themselves, but to the constitution which he had passed in 1812,[45] amid the considerable pressure that Bonaparte's European supremacy had placed upon the realms of the continent. This constitution had been modelled on the Spanish one of the same year and was aimed at putting the aims of the French Revolution into practice as the governing framework of the nation, in essence moving the Code Napoleon from a simple legal code into the DNA of the kingdom. One of these elements – the nation, harking back to Article

43   Frezet, J., *Histoire de la Maison de Savoie : Tome Troisième* (Torino: De L'Imprimerie, 1827).
44   Bouvier, F., *Bonaparte en Italie 1796* (Paris: 1899), p.662.
45   Norwich, J., *Sicily: A Short History from the Ancient Greeks to the Cosa Nostra* (London: John Murray Publishing, 2015), p.268.

Three of the Universal Declaration of the Rights of Man – lay at the heart of these documents. The hills around Napoli were soon alive with the return of revolution. The Royal Army, whose officers and soldiery had not long before marched with Napoleon across Germany, picked up the drums of ideological warfare once more. Like the civil servant class in the more advanced north, these simple southern warriors had been shaped by swimming among the embryonic fluid of the bold new world. On 9 July 1820, this force marched into Napoli under the fluttering black, red and blue flags of the liberal-nationalist Carbonarista movement.[46]

The hastily made stitches which the Habsburg monarchy had attempted to insert into Italy's swollen political map in 1815 had burst open. By March, the region of Piedmont exploded into radical violence, led by a vanguard of upper and middle-class people with deep affiliations to the liberal movement, and who had been severely discontented with the return of the House of Savoy.[47] Their objectives were identical to those of the Neapolitani who crossed into their capital four months later, but so too was their fate. After rising successfully on the 9 March, the Savoyard Army had marched into Torino and demanded their liberal constitution. In April 1820, however, this revolutionary state was put down at the Battle of Novara, and in February the following year the Neapolitan revolution also collapsed at the hands of Magyar and Austrian troops.[48] But the failure of 1820–21 mattered little. Italian liberalism, and from that the nationalism inherent in Jacobanism enshrined in Article 3 of the Universal Declaration of the Rights of Man[49] and cemented in the Code Napoleon of 1804,[50] had dug itself from its Belgian grave, where it had seemed sealed shut six years before following Napoleon's defeat at Waterloo. It was not until the summer of 1830 that Europe's vengeful absolutists understood the profundity of the French Revolution's impact. That year, France again succumbed to the pressures which had bubbled around it since the fractious restoration of the Bourbons in the wake of the French Revolutionary and Napoleonic Wars in 1815. A new liberal government headed by King Louis-Phillipe I rose in the former home of European feudalism, the monarch filled with fear and trepidation at his own people. This ushered in a new age of French revolutionism, albeit contained within the confines of the nation's natural borders. The many Italian underground societies which aimed at national unification of both peoples and ethnic Italian lands saw with intense enthusiasm the illumination of Paris into a lighthouse of liberalism in 1830. It would not be long before Italy once more sought the liberal-nationalist revolution that its quasi-Jacobin revolutionaries craved.

46   Pecout. G, *Il Lungo Risorgimento*, pp.100–109.
47   Frezet, J., *Histoire de la Maison de Savoie*, pp.618–621.
48   Bassett, R., *For God and Kaiser: The Imperial Austrian Army 1619-1918* (London: Yale University Press, 2015), p.294.
49   Davidson, J., *The French Revolution*, p.261.
50   Roberts, A., *Napoleon the Great*, pp.275–279.

and aligned himself towards constitutional liberalism. He now believed himself to be standing next to greatness, able perhaps even to emulate the great Savoyard warlord and his direct ancestor, Prince Eugene (1663–1736), the hero of Blenheim.[56]

On the same day as their invasion, the House of Savoy formally declared war on the Habsburg Empire. In doing so, the First War of Italian Independence was launched, triggering the *Risorigmento*. From its commencement, the House of Savoy was clear that the conflict signalled not just the activation of their nationalist claim to the peninsula, but also their claim to Dalmatia, Istria and the Adriatic. We can see how important this was to Torino through the rejection of the May 1848 peace offer embassy to the Savoyard king from a panicked Vienna. It was a Vienna which just so happened to be burning, as throughout that spring, the students from the *Universität Wien* had set fire to the city and began violently agitating for a liberal constitution. The Savoyard rationale for refusing terms was the desire of its monarchy, and its adjoining parliament, to retake all the lands populated by Italians in order to forge their new state.[57] Throughout March and April 1848, the Savoyards marched through Lombardy unopposed. But unfortunately for the Savoyards, the Habsburgs' Army of Italy was commanded by legendary Czech warrior *Feldmarschall* Josef Radetzky. A man of iron dedication to Vienna, Radetzky made short work of the Italians and on the British negotiated a temporary truce on 25 July.[58] Spurred on by the victories of an Italian state against the hated Habsburgs, liberal-nationalist revolutions emerged in Rome and Florence from 1848 into the next year. However, the Savoyards were finally defeated in early spring 1849, and with them the Italian dream of uniting all Italians temporarily died.[59] Its failure mattered little though, for the fact that for the first time since the Romans had walked the earth, an Italian state ruled by Italians, for Italians, had risen against another state for the sake of creating a true Italian nation, meant the inevitability of that Italian nation. When it came, as it would on 17 March 1861, the Italian state would inherit all the claims of Venice's glorious past, tied up as they were within the driving ideology of the revolutionary nation. And since all its extra-peninsular desires lay in Habsburg hands, it would be Vienna which would emerge as the Italian nation's permanent nemesis. A naval conflict between the two over the Adriatic was thus set in stone.

56   Frezet, J., *Histoire de la Maison de Savoie*, pp.660–661.
57   Pecout, G., *Il Lungo Risorgimento*, pp.133–134.
58   Bassett, R., *For God and Kaiser*, p.300.
59   Taylor, A.J.P., *The Struggle for Mastery in Europe*, p.27.

2

Into the Age of Iron and Steam, 1805-1905

On 24 November 1859, the age of wood and sail came to an abrupt end as the world's first steam-powered armoured warship, *La Gloire*, sailed out of the French port of Toulon and into the Mediterranean. There had of course been developments with steam-powered vessels prior to the launch of that vessel. Indeed, in the 1780s, experiments were underway with the objective of producing reliable steam-powered craft (see Chapter 3). *La Gloire*'s exceptionalism stemmed instead from its explicitly military nature. As such, its ground-breaking essence did not solely rest with its propulsion, equipped as it was for the first time in naval history with a hull derived from the artificial manipulation of metals. It was also a construction complemented by the emplacement of shell-firing Paixhans guns in place of round shot-firing cannonry.[1] What may seem odd to students of naval history is that its raising was a result of the French shipbuilding industry, rather than the far superior industries of the British Isles. In actuality, that the manufacturing of novel technology should come from a traditionally weaker party in a long-term thalassocratic rivalry is not too surprising. During the Seven Years' War (1756-63), Britain's Royal Navy had inflicted a dramatic defeat on the *Marine Nationale* at 1759's Battle of Quiberon Bay.[2] Fought off Brittany's southern coast, the confrontation witnessed the crushing of a large French fleet. Without a navy, France lost its ability to defend or supply its not inconsiderable, but oft forgotten, empire in North America and the Caribbean. It was upon the seizure of these now-isolated provinces that the British Empire was founded.[3] The Treaty of Paris, signed in 1763, confirmed both thalassocracy over the Atlantic to London, and Britain's legal right (ratified through treaty) to its new American territories. The smothering of French conventional naval power at Quiberon Bay served as the trigger

1   Konstam, A., *European Ironclads 1860–75: The Gloire Sparks the Great Ironclad Arms Race* (London: Osprey Publishing, 2019), p.6.
2   Rodger, N.A.M., *The Command of the Ocean: A Naval History of Britain 1649-1815* (London: Penguin Publishing, 2005), pp.282–283.
3   Anderson, F., *Crucible of War: The Seven Years' War and the Fate of the Empire in British North America* (New York: Vintage, 2001), pp.387–415.

order, maintaining their exceptionally high standards in gunnery to execute barrage upon barrage of shot into the enemy at extreme close range. Vessel after vessel in the Royal Navy's converging lines entered the fray, aware of the orders they had to carry out, the entrance of such quantities of foes leading to an increasing number of enemy surrenders. By 17:30 hours that evening, the battle had come to a close, with no British ships lost against 22 losses for the opposition. The death of Horatio Nelson on the deck of HMS *Victory* soured what had otherwise been a flawless display of cunning and ferocity on his part. French dreams of matching the Royal Navy in terms techno-logical parity were dashed. That the *Marine Nationale* could not defeat the British fleet even when they had been outnumbered and, according to every maxim of warfare, the disadvantaged party, in the long term convinced the French to find a way to gain an edge. The victory would serve to extend their competition over the seas into the indus-trial age, ushering in the ironclad era as France's designers frantically searched for a way to reduce the Royal Navy's potency against them. The *Marine Nationale* would happen upon this antidote to the Royal Navy's preponderance quite by accident. In 1855, whilst engaged in the Crimean conflict, Emperor Napoleon III witnessed the invulnerability of a force of ironclad floating artillery batteries. Impressed at their defiance against Russian shot, he found his intrigue peaked.[8]

The Third Era of Naval Warfare – Ironclads and the Battle of Lissa

The ushering in of naval warfare's third era – that of steam, iron, torpedoes and under-water warfare – could not have occurred had it not been for the *Marine Nationale*'s lead architect, Henri Dupuy de Lôme. Born near Lorient, the spiritual home of much of France's shipbuilding industry, from the start of De Lôme's career as a naval architect he had become convinced of the superiority of iron. He toured Britain's vast ship-building infrastructure in 1842, publishing his findings in the 1844 work *Memoire sur la Construction des Batiments en Fer*. In 1852, he had built France's first steam-powered military vessel, yet its armour barely rendered it a breakthrough in comparison to the advances being made in Britain. The request to build an armoured warship, though, was a different proposition altogether, and he set about his labour of love on 1 January 1857. The resulting warship – *La Gloire*, briefly alluded to at the beginning of this chapter – was at the time unrivalled even by the Royal Navy. Lamentably, his vision for an all-metal vessel was dashed by the constraints of France's inadequate industrial base, such circumstances forcing him to simply bolt armour onto a wooden frame. This armour would be formed of 4.3in.-thick plates placed in a belt around a broadside gundeck. When the vessel's armour was tested in trials against the Royal Navy's 8in. 68lb rifled muzzle-loaded guns, it was found to be fully protected.[9] When launched,

8   Konstam, A., *European Ironclads 1860–75: The Gloire*, p.5.
9   Konstam, A., *European Ironclads 1860–75: The Gloire*, p.7.

Admiral Tegetthoff at Lissa. (Belvedere Gallery of Austria)

La Gloire immediately made the Royal Navy's wooden fleet obsolete. For the first time in maritime history, the *Marine Nationale* had an advantage over the Royal Navy. But the Royal Navy could brook no challengers and retribution would prove to be swift.

When the news came to the Admiralty Building in Whitehall, the Navy's decision-making class reacted with incredible alacrity, understanding that in order to uphold the verdict of Trafalgar they had to produce their own ironclads of superior quality. The Admiralty responded to the requirement by asking the private sector to come up with suitable designs. All but two of the submissions were designs in which the prospective vessel was wholly constructed from wrought iron. It would be the job

Habsburg Admiral Wilhelm Tegetthoff. (Lithograph from the
Peter Geymayer Collection)

of Isaac Watts, the Royal Navy's chief architect, to choose which direction Britain's
ironclad journey would take. Sceptical of wholly iron vessels due to unsuccessful
experiments with such vehicles in the 1840s, the dual proposals suggesting French-
style hybrid vessels were chosen.[10] Consequently, in 1859, both HMS *Warrior* and
HMS *Black Prince* underwent the initial phases of their construction at the Ditchburn
& Mare yards in Blackwall and those at Napier on Clydeside.

When they were completed in 1861 and 1862 respectively, they were faster,
better armoured and better armed than their French equivalent. The Royal Navy's
brief sojourn into obsolescence was over. Once the colossal industrial base of the
British Isles was activated, there was no turning back; the *Marine Nationale*'s ploy
had unleashed the kraken-like power of 19th-century British maritime engineering.
HMS *Warrior*'s successor, HMS *Achilles*, was conceptualised in 1861 and improved
on its impressive capabilities by having a wholly iron 4in.-thick hull – the same as
Warrior's gundeck. This seminal vessel was then equipped with a ram at the prow.
The real breakthrough, however, came in 1863 with the succession of Kentish architect and later parliamentarian Edward Reed as the Royal Navy's chief architect. His
vision was to build on the revolutionary nature of the ironclad by stripping away
the antiquated broadside construction. Instead, he wished to place the vessel's guns
inside a central battery enclosed on all sides by armoured bulkheads 6in. thick. When

10   Konstam, A., *British Ironclads 1860–75: HMS Warrior and the Royal Navy's Black Battlefleet*
     (London: Osprey Publishing, 2018), p.6.

the vessel was completed in April 1866, its 9in. rifled muzzle-loaded guns would sit inside the world's first armoured naval turret. A further step towards the mammoth battleships of the First World War had been taken. For the ironclad to earn its spurs, however, a great test would be needed, a test in which failure was not an option and where the consequence was death among murky waters. That test would come during the maelstrom of the Third Italian War of Independence, at the Battle of Lissa – the latest episode in the new Italian state's eternal conflict with Vienna.

Off an insignificant spit of land under the dark, rain-filled skies of a July day in 1866, two fleets – the *Regia Marina* and *K.u.K. Kriegsmarine* – would battle for dominion over the Adriatic Sea. The Austrian fleet, commanded by the enigmatic Admiral Wilhelm von Tegetthoff, clashed on the open sea with a fellow aristocrat, Count Pellion di Persano, in a rule-establishing battle between mixed wooden/iron-clad fleets. The *K.u.K. Kreigsmarine* came to the contest relying on their seven-strong broadside ironclad squadron – consisting of SMS *Kaiser Max*, SMS *Prinz Eugen*, SMS *Juan d'Austria*, SMS *Drache*, SMS *Salamander*, SMS *Erzherzog Ferdinand Max* and SMS *Habsburg* – to produce a decisive victory. Of these, the *Kaiser* and *Ferdinand Max* would be central to the battle's outcome. On the Italian side, 10 ironclads were deployed: *Terribile, Formidabile, Re d'Italia, Re di Portogallo, Principe di Carignano, Regina Maria Pia, Ancona, San Martino* and *Castelfidardo*. Among the Italian vessels, it would be the *Re d'Italia* and *Affondatore* which would prove most influential. The wooden components of both fleets would, by contrast, be almost useless. The *Regia Marina* chose the battlefield. Aware of their numerical superiority – standing at a total of 34 vessels to the *K.u.K. Kriegsmarine*'s 27 – their warships were moored at the isle of Lissa, undertaking a defensive stance. The surrounding battle space is described in Maximilian Rottauscher's account of the clash, *With Tegetthoff at Lissa*, as containing "nothing but the omnipresence of roaring waves … we were covered in a dense mist as fresh showers washed over low ironclad decks".[11] His words reflected the ferocity of the seas which harassed the Dalmatian coast, enraged by the presence of that land's island-infested shores. For all their naval tradition, the usually wily Italians had positioned their fleet in a very poor spot.

The *Regia Marina* opened the battle in traditional form, with a single line stemming from their poorly placed moorings of the isle of Lissa streaming towards the Habsburg fleet. Rottauscher records: "The first Italian ships passed at speed, our forward guns went off, flashes of lightning lit the gun deck and shot after shot crashed out towards the ironclads [of the *Regia Marina*].". Battle had thus been joined. Tegetthoff, like Nelson before him, recognised the feeble nature of the enemy line and the ease with which it could be broken. Echoing the work of both Collingwood and HMS *Victory*'s legendary commander, Tegetthoff ordered his vessel – SMS *Erzherzog Ferdinand Max* – forward into the heart of the Italian line. His objective was to close in and from

---

11   Rottauscher, M., *With Tegetthoff at Lissa: The Memoirs of an Austrian Naval Officer 1861–66* (Solihull: Helion & Company Ltd, 2010).

there to ram and board the enemy vessels, ripping out the soul of the Italian force, causing confusion and disarray. Thereafter, their vessels would be easy pickings for the still-coherent Austrian force. The concept was a copy of Trafalgar, whether Tegetthoff recognised it or not, but its originality mattered little for its operation was flawless. As the battle plan demanded, SMS *Erzherzog Ferdinand Max* went in first and, through pouring rain, made contact with the Italian flagship, *Re d'Italia*, tearing the vessel in two. It immediately began sinking; such was the force of the collision that Rottauscher heard it from several miles away, stating that "there was heard a dull rumbling, as if giant fists were beating a colossal bronze door in wild confusion, ever more heavily". With the *Re d'Italia* sinking, the *Regia Marina* lost all coordination[12]. The *Re d'Italia* supposedly contained Admiral di Persano and to all intents and purposes served as the Italian flagship. As its crew headed to the depths, the Italian captains, shocked at its demise, assumed the loss of their command and control element. This speculation was in error, however, as prior to the battle – without communicating his decision to the fleet – di Persano had switched vessels to command the goliath vessel *Affondatore*.

The latter was a beast of iron that had been forged in British shipyards. Its potency was undeniable, and unfortunately for the Habsburg fleet, its preferred prey that day was the *K.u.K. Kreigsmarine*'s unarmoured frigate, SMS *Kaiser*. Coming in at 4,006 tonnes and capable of a top speed of 12 knots, with 5in.-thick armour and endowed with two 9in. rifled muzzle-loaders,[13] it was more than a match even for Tegetthoff's SMS *Erzherzog Ferdinand Max*. Admiral di Persano, though, used *Affondatore* as his personal hunting steed, and instead of rallying his rapidly decomposing force, he focused on attacking the SMS *Kaiser*, a large broadside vessel of the pre-ironclad age. Its armaments and defences fell far short of the *Affondatore*, but di Persano's was fixated on the craft. The unforeseen result of this unnecessary hunt was to attract the attention of the *K.u.K. Kreigsmarine*'s wooden fleet. Their round shot might have been impotent against the armoured hull of the *Affondatore*, but they distracted it until the SMS *Kaiser* managed to escape. Yet *Affondatore* would not be downed by the frenetic actions of the enemy wooden fleet assailing it, but by the flaws of its own construction. It had been built with an exceptionally low freeboard, and quite unexpectedly, as the SMS *Kaiser* limped away surrounded by black smoke, the waves began to lap over *Affondatore*, almost pulling it under entirely. With the *Affondatore* unable to continue, the *Regia Marina*'s vessels began to withdraw, fighting small one-on-one duels in isolation until finally, by nightfall, they had retreated to their Italian ports. The Battle of Lissa had demonstrated the futility of round shot against iron armour, something long hypothesised but never tested in war. The manoeuvrability and rapidity gained by the use of steam afforded the ability to move free of the wind. This allowed Tegetthoff to accelerate his vessel to ramming speed whilst going against a northerly wind, during a time of adverse weather, as noted in the Rottauscher account. The lessons of

12   Rottauscher, M., *With Tegetthoff at Lissa.*
13   Konstam, A., *European Ironclads 1860–75: The Gloire*, p.16.

The Whitehead Torpedo. (Eidem & Lutken Publishers)

Trafalgar – striking the centre, rather than lining up to fire vessel by vessel – had been built upon by the use of the ram, thereby maximising outcomes in close-order battle. The wooden fleets of both sides were now clearly redundant; they simply did not have the firepower nor endurance to maintain themselves amid an environment containing ironclads. As such, the outcome can be seen as a distillation of all the progress made so far in 19th-century nautical construction. From Lissa until 1905, the ironclad would become king.

Overturning the Defence – the Torpedo

The Battle of Lissa saw the triangular relationship between environment, defence and offence permanently overturned. The long domination of the triangle by the environment had always limited what man was capable of on the world's waterways. The advent of practical militarised steam power, observed so blatantly at Lissa, relegated the environment from the top consideration to the bottom. Tegetthoff's use of the ram certified the repositioning of the defence at the pyramid's peak, whilst the offence (particularly in gunnery) languished below. Given the growing ubiquity of steam-driven ironclads, the primacy of the defence would not last for long. The same year that the ironclad had its coronation as ruler of the seas, work began on the first remote guided torpedo. The prime mover of its development was a rather remarkable inventor by the name of Robert Whitehead, who wished to build an underwater explosive device capable of chasing vessels in the open water at his direction, as opposed to using unguided gunnery.[14] Whithead's belief that there was a better way to conduct vessel-on-vessel warfare had led him to produce rudimentary prototypes prior to his work

14   Cook-Branfill, R., *Torpedo: The Complete History of the World's Most Revolutionary Naval Weapon* (Barnsley: Seaforth Publishing, 2014), p.18.

of 1866. By the time that Tegetthoff was ramming his opponents in the Adriatic, Whitehead had designed his first workable attempt at a remote-control torpedo. The device was a 135kg wholly steel construction fixed with an explosive pressure-activated warhead. The more ground-breaking part was its navigation system, which involved a depth control system dependant on a water pressure plate, which when acted upon would lift the torpedo up or down. To do this, the plate was wire-attached to fins, whose movement influenced the water around the weapon to force it up and down in the water. A pre-set rudder established its course, and a two cylinder combustion engine driven by 370psi air pressure was also pre-set to allow a constant speed. A screw system drove the instrument forward.

The first client of the torpedo was the *K.u.K. Kriegsmarine*, but the disinterest of the royal family in the wake of Lissa (see Chapter 7) saw naval budgets neglected.[15] The British Royal Navy, however, was extremely interested. The invention of *La Gloire* had taken them by surprise, and their determination not to be behind another potentially warfare-changing creation was palpable. The Admiralty's powerful voice in Whitehall decision-making echoed far, and Whitehead was paid £15,000 for his design in 1871. From 1872-1905, continuous developments would be made on the weapon. Working from a formerly bankrupt factory in Rijeka on the Istrian peninsula, Whitehead tinkered on the device with a view to increasing the instrument's speed, controllability and explosive capacity. The most important of these changes was the installation of a gyroscopic navigation system in 1895, allowing for a much-improved automotive quality in conjunction with a far-augmented degree of accuracy. The last change to the torpedo before the onset of the First World War would be the introduction, in 1905, of a fuel-burning engine which worked in tandem with compressed air to vastly increase the motor speed of the screw propulsion.[16] By developing an instrument which did not rely on kinetic energy to smash through wooden hulls, a weapon came into existence which worked by detonating a powerful shaped charge on impact. This improvement in kill capacity was made even more effective by the resulting munition's underwater trajectory, which targeted vessels below the waterline, granting it a lethality magnitudes greater than gunnery. Once it hit its target, there was little that could be done to protect the vessel; its use of cutting edge explosives technologies simply sliced through iron armour as if it was butter. Even today, a vessel wounded in such a manner is often doomed. The offence now stood to overtake the defence, as the little space required for the torpedo's use, the certain manner of its *modus operandi* and its relatively small cost per unit looked to provoke an evolution in naval theory.

15   Sondhaus, L., *The Naval Policy of Austria-Hungary, 1867–1918: Navalism, Industrial Development, and the Politics of Dualism* (West Lafayette: Purdue University Press, 1994).
16   Ballantyne, I., *The Deadly Trade: The Complete History of Submarine Warfare, From Archimedes to the Present* (London: Weidenfeld & Nicolson, 2018), pp.53–56.

Decisive Battle Doctrine v. Young School – the 19th-Century Revolution in Naval Theory

The revolution in technology which delivered parity between offence and defence in the ship-to-ship actions of the ironclad age also inspired novel theoretical thinking at the strategic level. The decision-making classes within the *Regia Marina* charged with shaping naval strategy for the Italian armed forces would be greatly impacted by this new wave of maritime strategic thinking. Indeed, they would, like many navies in Europe and elsewhere, find themselves wholly in hock to the two emerging maritime schools of thought of the age: the Young School and what we might call Decisive Battle Doctrine. The former is a well-defined concept, whilst the latter is more opaque but contains a core message just as concrete as the first. Both were products of the same naval competition between France and the British Empire that narrates the whole nautical revolution of the 19th century. These two theoretical approaches to naval warfare were in essence products of post-1870 French desperation, when it had become clear that even their much-vaunted continental position had come to an end. At the heart of its woes, France saw London and its infernal continual machinations of bankers, shipbuilders and parliament. If France did not return to the waves and escape its increasing continental irrelevance, then it had to match the British Empire in tonnage to expand once more unto the world – or did it?

The Young School was born out of this question. The idea which lies at its foundations is that to control the oceans, one does not need to contest the waves with other powers. Naval battles are, according to its tenets, rather foolish affairs which cost the nations that fight them an unacceptable toll in both manpower and materiel. The school's axiomatic thought is that the concept of a single naval battle deciding who is in charge of the seas, simply through asserting some kind of ownership, is incorrect. This kind of thinking placed nations in a psychological trap whereby, for fear of being drawn into a single battle they know they cannot win, they are forced to bow to whatever power had the larger tonnage. Contests over the seas could thus never be held, and the dominant party – the Royal Navy in this case – would be permanently unchallenged. The Young School held that this 'control' was a mere trick that could be broken, if the weaker party was able to conduct a form of guerrilla warfare on the sea. This would be executed through the use of a large fleet of small vessels, whose targets would be economically vital shipping lanes. The failure to prevent their attacks would expose thalassocracy as a fraud. The raiding fleet's low infrastructure requirements, owing to the small size of the vessels composing it, would then allow it to constantly evade prosecution by larger vessels. Being unable to destroy such an elusive force and equally unable to permit unfettered molestation of the trade lanes would coerce the hitherto dominant party into negotiation. This thesis was the work of *Amiral* Theophile Aube, who in 1882 published a seminal article in the *Revue des Mondes* entitled '*La Guerre Maritime et les Ports Militaires de la France*'.[17] By

---

17   Aube, T., *La Guerre Maritime et les Ports Militaires de la France* (Paris: Revue des Deux Mondes, 1882).

the 1880s, the tools that would enable such a strategy to be possible – unarmoured fast cruisers, destroyers and torpedo boats – had been debuted. The credit for the theory's development did not purely rest with *Amiral* Aube. Before he had been born, the work of Henri-Joseph Paixhans (1783-1853) had already alluded to a similar idea. Paixhans, who had been an artillery officer during the Napoleonic Wars (1803–15), intimately understood France's immense maritime disadvantage during Britain's 'golden age'.

Paixhans had foreseen the unprecedented speed of industrial progress that would take on a life of its own in the second half of the 19th century. He believed that if France took advantage of the coming industrial age, it could put itself ahead of its Anglophone nemesis. In 1822, he put his thoughts to paper in his seminal work, *Nouvelle Force Maritime*. In Paixhans' expert opinion as an artillery officer (albeit on land), British sea power was based on the difficulty to destroy its ships. He believed that fighting equally balanced line-by-line battles, between vessels with technological parity, led usually only to pyrrhic victories.[18] His alternative was that naval campaigns would better achieve their objectives through using smaller, faster and better-armed vessels to overwhelm capital ships by sheer number. The slow, lumbering nature of capital ships would prevent them from responding, their poor manoeuvrability would forbid their escape and their guns would not be able to target boats capable of clinging to a warship's side. Although he did not go as far to forecast the torpedo, Paixhans was unintentionally describing the fundamental theory behind the invention of torpedo boats. His focus, however, was not merely to identify a way to defeat a stronger naval adversary, but to provide a cheaper alternative than large, big-ship navies. In this manner he reflected one of the prime drivers of *Amiral* Aube's arguments as to the wisdom of a small-ship focus. Unlike Paixhans though, Aube conceptualised using fast torpedo boats within his stratagem of commerce warfare. With his writings of 1882, this synthesis of two French theorists came into being with three core beliefs: firstly that small fleets were less complex and more economical; secondly that these large, small-vessel fleets could swarm larger vessels with ease, producing deadly results at a more affordable price; and thirdly that the focus of these wasp-like forces should focus on the targeting of enemy commerce. The elucidation of this synthesis on paper would infiltrate the global naval community and spark great debate within both the *Regia Marina* and *K.u.K. Kriegsmarine* in the lead up to the First World War.

The rival to the Young School would emerge from across the Atlantic within the ambitious society that had arisen on North America's eastern seaboard by the 1890s. Freed from the rule of the Georgian monarchy by 1783's Treaty of Paris,[19] the United States had, by the dawn of the 20th century, grown into a potent maritime nation.[20] By dint of its vast Atlantic seaboard, the USA had found the need for a serious, techno-

---

18   Paixhans, H., *Nouvelle Force Maritime et Application de Cette Force a Quelques Parties du Service de L'Armee de Terre* (Paris: Bachelier Libraire, 1822), pp.100–258.
19   Scott, D., *Leviathan: The Rise of Britain as a World Power* (London: Harper Press, 2013), p.455.
20   Morris, J., *History of the US Navy* (North Dighton, MA: JG Press, 2003).

logically advanced navy. It was perhaps destiny that a nation so young and so hungry for global engagement would pose a rival idea to a moribund society such as that of 19th-century France. What we will term Decisive Battle Doctrine, if only to differentiate it from what came to be called the Young School, was the work of a New Yorker, Alfred Thayer Mahan, a career naval officer who had been mothballed to Newport Naval College on Rhode Island in 1885.[21] Mahan's formidable mind had been more adept to study than to the practicalities of a modern navy, and in 1890 he would make his mark on the landscape of naval theory. His work of that year, *The Influence of Sea Power upon History: 1660–1783*, is considered one of maritime writing's classic pieces. The book's focus is on the lessons that the history of the seas provides to naval theory. His thesis within this was that domination of the seas turned on single battles, often won by remarkable individuals.[22] Furthermore, it was that individual spirit that would turn the tide, time and again. Interestingly, proof of this can be seen in the two battles this chapter has so far examined. At both Lissa and Trafalgar, Tegetthoff and Nelson demonstrated the immense power of individual leaders equipped with remarkable grit, determination and intelligence. It is worth highlighting one of the passages concerning the second pillar of his thesis – that of the importance of large fleets capable of projecting domination across the waves. The excerpt relates to the decline of the Spanish Empire, which he compellingly argues was authored by the rapid downfall of Spanish naval power. Fundamentally, he agrees here with the Young School's insinuation that thalassocracy is effectively a psychological trick on a grand scale. Without a threatening fleet, the Spanish Empire, he asserts, was unable to impose a menacing presence on the trade lanes, meaning its treasure fleets became exceedingly vulnerable. Contrary to Aube and Paixhans, however, he believed that to control the seas navies had to have a menacing aura, built on winning decisive engagements on the oceans.

Mahan would continue writing on this theme until his death, with multiple works published on the importance of historical battles in building naval supremacy. What is remarkable, and indeed a testimony to the Royal Navy's immense impact on the 19th-century world, is that both Theophile Aube and Alfred Thayer Mahan would base their principals on their strong feelings towards Britain's fleet: hatred and fear in the case of Theophile Aube, and his ideological predecessor Paixhans; admiration and respect in the case of Mahan. But these thought experiments would generate powerful ripples across the global naval sphere. Two of the navies upon which these ripples impacted greatly were relatively new and mutually hostile – Italy's *Regia Marina* and the Habsburg Empire's *K.u.K. Kriegsmarine*. Both navies would seriously engage in conversation with these influential, quasi-philosophical schools. Their battle plans, construction timetables and force conceptualisations would at one time

---

21   Mahan, A., *The Influence of Sea Power upon History: 1660–1783* (Boston: Little, Brown & Company, 1890), p.6.
22   Mahan, A., *The Influence of Sea Power upon History*, pp.17–41.

or another follow the precepts of the two schools. For the *Regia Marina*, their engagement with the Young School would lead them to commission the formation of Italy's MAS fleet; for the *K.u.K. Kriegsmarine*, the Young School would lead to the creation of the destroyer warship type. Despite this initial success, the Young School in the main would not survive the commissioning of HMS *Dreadnought* in 1905. Although exceeding the influence Aube enjoyed on the *Marine Nationale* – limited to his one-year term as Minister of the Marine – its remaining adherents would be negligible post-1905. Only in the *Regia Marina* would the concept make a post-*Dreadnought* comeback, courtesy of Admiral Paolo Thaon di Revel,[23] a man whose appointment to naval chief in 1913 brought a brief restoration for the Young School. It would be in the precepts of the Young School's tenets that di Revel would discover the rationale for the creation of Italy's naval special forces.

Dreadnoughts and Tsushima – the Dreadnought Race and a Theoretical Resolution?

By 1900, the world of naval architecture had moved from producing wooden broadside vessels equipped with belts of armour, usually around the vessel's gun deck, to wholly armoured vessels with rotating turrets. The driver of this progress, like that of the Young School v. Decisive Battle Doctrine debate and the ironclad evolution before it, was the Anglo-French race to safeguard or break the thalassocratic outcome of Trafalgar. During this period, the Royal Navy – supported by Britain's extraordinarily advanced industries – was considered the template for how to mould powerful navies. Anything it did would be mirrored across the maritime sphere within a decade. At the beginning of the 1890s, the Royal Navy turned its attention towards a series of contemporary problems related to the clumsy nature of 19th-century naval gunnery. Its prime cause of concern was the inability of naval guns to fire reliably at their maximum range. The standard British battleships of the 1890s carried four 12in. guns and 12 6in. guns. The Royal Navy's doctrine expected these enormous craft to fight at a range of 1,828 metres.[24] This ideal range had been laid down out of a desire to ensure both uniformity in the conduct of battleships in group combat, and a standardised capability across the fleet's warships. In this way it can be seen as an echo of the lined orthodoxy of the past century. The development of the torpedo soon disrupted this stagnant contemporary thinking when fighting at range, forcing a rupture with age-old tradition. With the torpedo's growing global ubiquity, the world's navies could no longer afford to be complacent when faced with them in battle. The development of anti-torpedo tactics was required lest the Young School be proven correct, and

23   Alberini, P. & Prosperini, F., *Uomini della Marina 1861–1946: Dizionario Biografico* (Roma: Ufficio Storico della Marina Militare, 2015), pp.513–515.
24   Roberts, J., *The Battleship Dreadnought* (Oxford: Osprey Publishing, 2001), p.28.

Admiral Togo Heicachiro at Tsushima, 1905. (Old Tokyo)

navies be faced with the redundancy of their larger ships. The most obvious solution was to increase the range of naval guns, so that they outranged the still-limited radius of action possessed by early 20th-century torpedoes. In turn, this would terminate the desire for range uniformity and produce warships of greater lethality owing to their ability to lay down consistently accurate firepower across a longer distance.

The problem that faced the naval engineers who sought to increase gun ranges stemmed from the incessant decrease in accuracy that came at maximal ranges. It remains the case that the key to all gunpowder warfare relies foremost on accuracy, whether it be the fire-fighting of small squads on a terrestrial battlefield or warships facing off across miles of ocean. Without accuracy, naval guns were inefficient wastes of ammunition, and more importantly time. Time spent loading ineffective weaponry was time that the enemy could use to their advantage to either escape or, by the late 19th century, bring their torpedoes into range. Ensuring the accuracy of naval guns was the responsibility of a ship's fire control system. Since the launch of the first rotating turret vessel, HMS *Monarch*, in 1869[25] and the development of the naval shell during the same decade, fire control had been carried out via the technique of spotting. Essentially, this method required the observation and recording of the destination of artillery fire via plotting their coordinates and measuring the distance between the place the munitions landed and the target. They would then incrementally adjust their guns until their rounds were consistently on target.

From 1898, the Royal Navy carried out a series of long-range firing experiments, their objective being to increase both accuracy and range, via exploiting advancements

25   Konstam, A., *British Ironclads 1860–75: HMS Warrior*, p.22.

in range-finding technology. The experiments would continue with the ascension to First Sea Lord in 1904 of Sir John Fisher, a man whose intense loyalty to the Royal Navy and sharp mind for grand strategy allowed him to shepherd it into the 20th century still able, just about, to maintain Britain's thalassocratic control over the world's seas. In 1898, from his position as Third Sea Lord, he had taken the long-range firing project under his wing and had come to understand the importance for Britain that it should be the Royal Navy that pioneered long-range gunnery. To neglect it would have been to surrender the seas to the French, or increasingly to the German Empire. After much tinkering, by 1904 the experimentation period had paid off, and on 30 May of that year an Admiralty report stated that as a result of these tests, vessels could now expect to accurately hit targets from up to 7,315 metres.[26] A year later, the naval world would witness just how important these experiments had been in producing decisive results, courtesy of the Battle of Tsushima.

War between the Russian Tsardom and the Japanese Empire had been on the cards for much of the late 19th century. Two bones of contention rested uncomfortably between the two states. The first was buried in Korea, a land that both Tokyo and Moscow eyed with equal longing; the second lay in Manchuria, another area which both entities wished to see incorporated into their respective polities.[27] Attempted mediation throughout 1903 was unsuccessful, and on the 8 February 1904, sensing war, Japan's navy – the *Nippon Kaigun* – launched a surprise attack on the Tsardom's Chinese concession at Port Arthur. From February until spring the following year, disaster upon disaster would unfold on Russia's antiquated and underprepared navy, the *Rossisky Imperatorsky Flot*. The greatest of these Tsarist failures occurred on 27 May 1905 at Tsushima. During its execution, all the tactical and technological advancements of the near half-century since Lissa would be used by the Japanese fleet. The first indication of the battle's ground-breaking nature came with the Japanese ship-to-ship communication system, which had been rendered wholly wireless.[28] Using telegram-based information-exchanging techniques, Admiral Togo Heihachiro was able to receive detailed, near-instantaneous data on the location of the enemy – one of the key components of victory in naval warfare. At 5:00 a.m., this system was used to inform him of the location of the Russian fleet. Togo sought to draw them into a trap, whereby one division would cut off their retreat from the rear whilst the remainder engaged the Russian fleet head-on.

The afternoon saw the deployment of highly accurate long-range gunnery by the Japanese fleet, engaging the Russian vessels *Souvarov* and *Osliabia*. The precise nature of the fire reduced the *Osliabia* to a smoking hulk with the first salvo. At 3:15 p.m., the Russian cruiser *Aurora* was struck in the same manner. As night drew in at 7:30

26   Roberts, J., *The Battleship Dreadnought*, p.8.
27   Taylor, A.J.P., *The Struggle for Mastery in Europe*, p.419.
28   Meunier, R., *La Guerre Russo-Japonaise historique, enseignements, par le Chef D'Escadron D'Artillerie Brevete* (Paris: Berger-Levrault Editeur, 1906), p.392.

p.m., Admiral Heihachiro pulled his forces back to set up a trap for the Russian fleet the next day. The envisaged ambush consisted of unleashing swarms of small torpedo boats, armed with the latest iteration of Whitehead's subaquatic missiles, into the Russian fleet. When these vespid-like vessels arrived in the battle space at 20:00 p.m., Heihachiro saw his opportunity and instead of waiting until nightfall, released them into the Russian fleet.[29] A 16-strong team of torpedo boats, not unlike those proposed by Paixhans in 1822,[30] surrounded the Russian fleet and three Tsarist vessels were immediately put out of action. At 02:00 a.m. the following morning, a fourth Russian vessel was sunk and the remainder subsequently fled. The action had summed up everything the 19th century was leading towards, vindicating the approaches of both the Young School and Decisive Battle Doctrine. A decisive battle had been fought, using a hybrid of torpedo boats and big-gun vessels, to prevent an enemy from leaving the battle space, whilst battleship and cruiser gunnery duels had simultaneously reduced the fighting potency of the opposition fleet. A balance between the two dominant naval philosophies had seemingly been struck, but less than a year after Tsushima, HMS *Dreadnought* would instantly render the battle's tactical verdict irrelevant.

HMS *Dreadnought* was launched at Portsmouth Dockyard in 1906,[31] and just as the ironclad *La Gloire* had done in 1859, its unveiling instantly rendered all previously constructed vessels obsolete. In doing so, the Royal Navy once again proved its right to rule the oceans. This warship, if it could still be called one, was a 6,000-tonne behemoth, faster, better-armoured and better-gunned than any vessel in the history of humankind's long engagement with the seas. Yet for all the fanfare attached to the Royal Navy's latest toy and the pride which the Admiralty had invested within its British construction, it had been an Italian – Vittorio Cuniberti – who had laid its foundations. When Cuniberti had first sketched out the concept which would ultimately lead to the construction of HMS *Dreadnought*, he had been hoping it would be picked up by the *Regia Marina*. Throughout the 1880s and 90s, the Italians had chased the formation of an immense battleship fleet in dedication to Decisive Battle Doctrine (see Chapter 6). Rome, however, had neither the industrial base nor the finances to produce Cuniberti's idealised super-ship. The Royal Navy was perhaps the only navy with the necessary industrial base and financial power to bring Cuniberti's vision to reality. When Sir John Fisher came into contact with Cuniberti's designs, he found himself unable to refuse to at least attempt to bring the remarkable Italian's design to fruition. Fisher's enthusiasm for the project, though, was not solely to bring an intriguing vessel into being.

Fisher's interest in the dreadnought proposition came from a desire to maintain the Royal Navy's lead in its rapidly advancing competition. By introducing the

29   Meunier, R., *La Guerre Russo-Japonaise historique*, p.392.
30   Paixhans, H., *Nouvelle Force Maritime*, pp.285–348.
31   Roberts, J., *The Battleship Dreadnought*, p.16.

dreadnought design, he would wipe the ironclad slate clean. Nothing could match the dreadnought if it was to be released, and he believed that its emergence would make all previous designs obsolete. The German Empire and the United States, the Royal Navy's greatest rivals for global thalassocracy by tonnage,[32] would take time to produce their own dreadnought fleets, whilst the Royal Navy would have already achieved a considerable lead. When HMS *Dreadnought* was launched in 1906, this rather risky hypothesis paid off, but before long the German Empire had engaged the British in the race for exponentially larger dreadnoughts. Nevertheless, the extortionate cost of the first generation of dreadnoughts (HMS *Dreadnought* cost £1.7 million, equivalent to £214.2 million today[33]) delayed initial worldwide uptake outside of Northern Europe. Although nothing like it had ever existed, its creation had been facilitated by maintenance of the Royal Navy's faith in Decisive Battle Doctrine. Its existence was enough to ensure the Royal Navy's projection of fear across the trade lanes, maintaining Britain's maritime power. Now all navies wished to possess their own dreadnoughts, just as they had once coveted ever-expanding ironclad fleets. It was in essence the triumph of Decisive Battle Doctrine, as all navies desired the potential to duel each other in epic dreadnought battles. The Young School, now more than ever, felt like an increasingly irrelevant position. It was into this maritime environment of super-heavy battleships, the triumph of Decisive Battle Doctrine and high industrial output, that Italy's naval special forces would come to operate. But their *modus operandi* and the vision of the man who made the unit possible – Admiral Paolo di Revel – would be the products of a final cry in favour of Aube's recently defeated Young School.

32   Crisher, B., *Power at Sea: A Naval Power Dataset 1865–2011* (Gainesville: Florida University Press, 2013), p.28.
33   Roberts, J., *The Battleship Dreadnought*, p.13.

3

The Tools of the Naval Guerrilla: Motorboats and Explosives

The theme of this book so far has been that of increasing technological progress, amid a backdrop of political tension throughout the 19th century. Chapter 1 focused on the theatre in which Italy's naval special forces would come to operate, while Chapter 2 explored the century's high-speed progress in both defensive and offensive naval technologies and theories. This chapter seeks to take a far more specific examination of a particular area – explosives and motorboats – the invention and development of which permitted the practical evolution of the Young School, ultimately providing the technological groundwork for the development of Italy's naval special forces from 1915-18. The precepts of the Young School called for lots of fast, expendable boats armed with something devastating to enable hit-and-run raids. When Paixhans and later Aube came to write on the subject, the idea still did not have the materials to make it work. The introduction of speed would be the easier element, requiring only the miniaturisation of the steam engine and then the invention of the marine petrol engine. The incorporation of explosives into fast boats, however, would prove to be a more complicated proposition. To be a part of the Young School, the small vessels to be used as weapons platforms had to mount munitions capable of sinking large armoured vessels. Since 1859, Europe's fighting fleets were increasingly composed of ironclads alone, as part of a competition to build ever-more-capable ships. An incremental expansion of armour thickness, speed and weapon calibre resulted. The increasing capacity of the new generation of metal ships to withstand explosive blasts would force the abandonment of gunpowder. For munitions on the scale needed to punch through capital ships' armour, an alternative to black powder had to be discovered. Only then could the munitions-armed fast boat come into existence.

Inventing Explosives: from China to France

The initial advent of a chemical reaction creating an explosion in a man-made manner occurred in China. Some suggestions indicate that the Chinese were using explosives in a non-military capacity as far back as AD 300, but it is far more credible that its use began in 850.[1] Legend claims that this deliberate explosion was the result of Chinese experiments in alchemy. In the mid-9th century, a Chinese proto-chemist left the world with the chemical recipe which allowed these energy-expelling events to be brought into existence. This alchemical formula was taken down during the Tang Dynasty (618–907) and details a chemical mixture which is analogous to what Europeans would come to call 'black powder'.[2] The guidelines demand a division of ingredients into portions of 75 percent saltpetre, 15 percent charcoal and 10 percent sulphur.[3] The explosive demands contained in these ancient writings would be unaltered for centuries; only the ratios would change, and even then the modifications would be minor. Given mankind's militant nature, it was not long before 'black powder' would be used by the Tang Dynasty's Song successors (960–1279) to repel the nomadic peoples of the immense Asian steppe.[4] Unsurprisingly given the relative simplicity of the chemical compound in question, China would not be the only place in which the powder came into being (albeit never as widely used). The Europeans developed their own variant some three centuries later, courtesy of English philosopher Roger Bacon (1220–92). Yet Bacon was not as successful at ensuring its inclusion into western warfare as his eastern alchemical counterparts. During his life, he published *De Nullitate Magicae* (or *On the Nullity of Magic*), which despite its decidedly occult-like name provides a hagiography of the values of the mundane over superstition.[5] Among its sceptical pages, Bacon lays out his methodology for creating flame – nitrates, sulphates and charcoal. He recommends placing this mixture down the muzzle of a cannon and lighting it. When this concoction was exposed to a flame, a controlled explosion resulted in the shape and direction of the muzzle. Unintentionally, he had undertaken the same method that has powered all projectile weaponry until the present, i.e. the application of a thermal element to an explosive composition. But it was not until the trade routes between East and West brought the knowledge of how to create firearms that the Europeans would become addicted to the lethality of gunpowder weaponry.[6]

The first European firearms that were deployed in battle were inaccurate, difficult to manufacture and unreliable. In 1339, the contest over the French throne between the House of Valois and House Plantagenet would bring gunnery into the mainstream. In 1338, King Philip VI (1293–1350) had introduced a cannon corps to the French

1   Henry, V., *Explosions et Explosives* (Paris: Berger-Levrault, 1916), p.45.
2   Akhavan, J., *The Chemistry of Explosives* (London: Royal Society of Chemistry Publishing, 2011), p.1.
3   Braddock, J., *A Memoir on Gunpowder* (London: J.M. Richardson Publishing, 1832), p.48.
4   Fairbank, J.K. & Goldman, M., *China: A New History* (Cambridge: Harvard University Press, 2006), pp.266–267.
5   Little, A., *Roger Bacon Essays* (London: Oxford University Press, 1914), pp.321–337.
6   Disney, A.R., *A History of Portugal and the Portuguese Empire: From Beginning to 1807* (Cambridge: Cambridge University Press, 2009), pp.11–25.

arsenal.[7] To this end, Henri de Famechon was tasked with setting up a cannon factory in the kingdom. In the autumn of 1339, the English monarch Edward III marched on Cambrai and laid siege to the rather insignificant town. In response, the French defenders, equipped with Famechon's cannons, repulsed the English and forced them to withdraw.[8] From that point, the cannon would become increasingly vital to victory or defeat in battle. Gunpowder was made both more reliable and more deadly in 1425 with the invention of granulation.[9] A newfound technique called for the use of heavy wheels to grind black powder's base solid fuels – nitrates, sulphates and charcoal – into a mass with much-improved cohesion, creating higher levels of chemical purity in the resulting mixture and thus increasingly powerful explosions.[10] Consequently, guns – both early muskets and cannons – became deadlier than ever. By the early 19th century, the manufacture of gunpowder had reached its qualitative zenith. In 1832, the British soldier Jon Braddock published *A Memoir on Gunpowder*, dictating best practices whilst making black powder. Braddock relates that the charcoal had to be alkali free, and both the nitrates and sulphates used in the mixture had to be bone dry. Mixing the solid components required enmeshing them so that no spaces or gaps existed between the different compounds. He testifies in his work that "stones make the best corning [granulation] equipment". The Braddock method's end product would be a round black powder cake. European gunpowder was notably better by the 1830s as their powder was the fruit of the age of industry. But why does such a specific mixture of nitrates, sulphates and charcoal provoke such a potent chemical reaction?

To answer the above question is to understand explosives themselves. Once that was understood by the industrial scientists of the pre-First World War period, freedom from black powder could be obtained. The term 'explosive' is given to any process in which a large amount of energy is suddenly released from within a containment system. The term 'explosion' refers only to that energy which is propelled outwards at the point the containment system is breached. The liberated energy either passes itself into an adjacent physical object, causing that object's destruction, or freely expands outwards into the surrounding environment in the form of a shockwave.[11] When talking about military explosives, we mean those which produce shockwaves. The principal agent in producing these waves is the rapid change in state that a solid chemical mixture is subjected to, to make it a gas or liquid. In black powder, the mix of nitrates, sulphates and charcoal is exposed to a naked flame. The chemical mixture begins to heat up and transform from solid to gas, creating super-hot gas. When placed within a container – such as a primitive grenade – this gas builds up intense heat and pressure within

7   Hennebert, E., *L'Artillerie* (Paris: Libraire Hachette, 1887), p.20.
8   Sumption, J., *Trial by Battle: The Hundred Years War, Vol. I* (London: Faber & Faber Publishing, 1990), pp.307–308.
9   Braddock, J., *A Memoir on Gunpowder* (London: J.M. Richardson Publishing, 1832), pp.50–54.
10   Steerk, M., *Guide Pratique de la Fabrication des Poudres et Saltpetres* (Paris: Librairie Scientifique Industrielle et Agricole, 1866), pp.197–199.
11   Akhavan, J., *The Chemistry of Explosives*, p.64.

reaction. The search for an appropriate trigger would begin, as nitroglycerin became the world's first two-step explosive.

An explosive may be deemed two-step if it must be made subject to an explosion in order for its explosive properties to be activated. This prior explosive is termed a 'primary' explosive.[14] Primary explosives are defined by their instability or ease of ignition – black powder falls into this category. The job of the primary explosive is to cause the detonation of the secondary explosive, in this case nitroglycerin. The interaction between primary and secondary then produces a chain reaction, which runs as follows:

1. The molecular structure of the secondary explosive is struck by the energy wave coming off the primary explosion.
2. The molecular structure of the secondary explosive reacts to the wave by losing its structure.
3. The chaotic mass of atoms resulting from the loss of structure instantaneously reforms into gas and heat.
4. Becoming this cloud changes the form of the explosive from liquid to gas and the energy contained within the liquid is released, sending out its own shockwave.

At the end of this chain, both primary and secondary explosives have emitted all the energy contained in both explosives. Being possessed of the combined force of two explosive materials then produces incomprehensively strong shockwaves, which cannot be produced by primary explosives alone. It is this unprecedented power that made nitroglycerin so impressive to military and civil engineers alike. To rectify the issue of nitroglycerin's invulnerability to flame, Nobel would begin to pack nitroglycerin with black powder in the same cartridge, so that in order to activate the nitroglycerin one would first have to light the black powder covering it.

The resulting product – the base chemical nitroglycerin with the additional black powder charge – conversely became infamous for instability, a series of explosive accidents relating to its transportation leading to widespread scepticism over its safety.[15] In 1865, an accident at the Nobel company's Krummel plant solved this issue. Whilst processing nitroglycerin there, a bottle had begun to leak through the crack in its shipping crate. The standard packing procedure had called for the space between bottles to be filled with a silica-containing material – diatomite, the same chemical which gives toothpaste its unique consistency. This puttylike material, Nobel realised, could absorb nitroglycerin into its structure and thus become an explosive material in itself. By imprinting the chemical into a solid material, the explosive would become far more stable. He christened the new paste 'dynamite',[16] and importantly for the military

14   Akhavan, J., *The Chemistry of Explosives*, p.74.
15   Molinari, E. & Quartieri, F., *Notices sur les Explosifs en Italie*, pp.135–140.
16   Henry, V., *Explosions et Explosifs*, pp.65–66.

sphere, the paste could be fitted into mines, charges, shells, torpedoes and grenades. In doing so, Nobel went one step into vastly increasing the firepower with which infantry, in particular, could be equipped. In 1900, the capacity for dynamite to be utilised in war was considerably expanded, the work on expanding the envelope of explosive utility would be largely carried out by Massachusetts-born chemist Charles Munroe. In the 1890s, Munroe had been working with nitrocellulose, a proto-explosive similar to nitroglycerin. On one occasion, a block of nitrocellulose confined within a metal container exploded prematurely, the shockwave the substance generated being transmitted in a certain geometrically constructed direction.[17] The metal container housing the nitrocellulose had letters stencilled onto its top portion, which had seemingly provided a shape which the shockwave could emerge within. This led to the realisation that shockwaves could be shaped in order to provide more precise explosive outcomes, a practice which would come to be known as shaping. Shaped explosives held an advantage in that they could force the shockwave in a single direction, allowing it to focus all its energy in one location.[18] Few protections could defend against such a manipulative use of physics, its use was recognised quickly and the shaped charge was born. As a result, militaries could benefit from shockwaves which would be channelled 100 percent towards the point of contact with the target. Total, efficient energy transferral would prove to be a decisive innovation, and in combination with the portability of dynamite, the individual soldier was now endowed with explosive power hitherto the reserve of artillery pieces and naval guns. It was a development which would prove to be particularly useful for the dark world of the commando.

The Conspirator's Choice

The Franco-Prussian War of 1870-71 would see the first use of portable two-step explosives by infantry soldiers, a military innovation which would be used to great effect by Italy's First World War nautical commandos over 40 years later. Fought as a result of the French Second Empire's attempt to overturn the conclusion of 1815's Congress of Vienna,[19] the conflict's centrepiece would be the brutal five-month siege of Paris over the freezing autumn of 1870.[20] By January 1871, the Parisians had been cut off from food, war materials, aid and – most importantly – dynamite. Makeshift factories were thrown together to produce it from boghead (a type of coal), charcoal and silica. Using the latter as a replacement for dynamite's diatomite ingredient, the French forged their own inferior variant of the world-changing explosive.[21] In

---

17 Guilbaud, T., *Les Explosifs Actuels* (Paris: Editions & Libraire, 1916), p.3.
18 Akhavan, J., *The Chemistry of Explosives*, p.5.
19 Taylor, A.J.P., *The Struggle for Mastery in Europe*, p.205.
20 Matt, F., *Le Siege de Paris* (Paris: Maison et C Éditeurs, 1871), p.1.
21 Tanera, C., *De La Dynamite et De Ses Applications Pendant le Siege de Paris* (Paris: Librairie Pour L'Art Militaire et Les Sciences, 1871), pp.10–13.

November 1870, French armies inside Paris equipped themselves with indigenous charges and attempted to break out of the city in the Buzenval forest in the city's north-west quadrant.[22] The explosives made their mark with aplomb, thick walls being blasted apart by its shockwaves. Treelines were felled by its force to make cover for advancing French lines, and later during the winter of that year its power was used to blow through the ice of the Seine, sabotaging Prussian river-borne gun batteries.

The increase in personal explosive power that dynamite had allowed was also not lost on the 19th-century's terrorists. The second half of the 1800s would see the revolutionary put down the knife and the flintlock pistol and instead opt for the bomb. In the mid-19th century, the Russian Tsardom, which had remained by far the most backward state to be considered 'European', had begun to experience unrest from a new direction. The disgruntlement of the nobleman and the starving peasant was suddenly swept away by the ravings of the university-educated 'intellectual', the poet, the writer, the politician and the journalist. These elements of the *nouveau-riche* soon became Moscow's nemesis, their genesis having lain in the vast empire's recent sociological upheavals, as a disparate intelligentsia began to discuss their state's future. An antithesis and thesis emerged and created both radicals and moderates,[23] both sections wanting to transform the moribund power structure hampering the massive state. After a decade of persuasion, these well-meaning but naïve men of learning, roughly conforming to a moderate bloc, had decidedly failed to bring the masses around to their way of thinking. In the wake of their collapse in authority within the left-wing Russian movements of the late 19th century, the radicals took the initiative and in 1878 formally adopted terrorism as their principal weapon. Their thinking was that if they could demonstrate the lack of power on behalf of the authorities to stop their attacks, then the people would rise up, now aware of the weakness of their so-called oppressors.

Three of the movements' assassinations would prove to be debut moments for the modern thrown explosive. In doing so, they would truly demonstrate the potential of these instruments for being exceptional tools for irregular warfare. In early 1880, an unknown revolutionary armed with an unnamed explosive substance sneaked into the Russian imperial residence and detonated a bomb underneath the dining room. Tsar Alexander Romanov II (1816–81) was unharmed, but he would not be for long. On the afternoon of a March day in 1881, the tsar had been taking a stroll with Polish nobleman Count Franciszek Jackowski, when at 2:15 p.m. a radical by the name of Rysakov threw a bomb of dubious construction under their carriage.[24] Luckily for the occupants, the bomb was unable to pierce the substantial protection of the carriage and a relived tsar escaped. However, his fortune was momentary: a second assassin –

---

22   Jezierski, L., *Combats et Batailles du Siege de Paris : Septembre 1870 a Janvier 1871* (Paris: Garnier Frères, 1872), pp.125–127.
23   Pipes, R., *Russia Under The Old Regime* (London: Penguin Publishing, 1974), p.274.
24   Ular, A., *La Revolution Russe: La Dynastie et La Cour, La Bureaucratie, Le Regime Witte* (Paris: Paris, 1903), pp.16–18.

Hryniewiecki – threw a second bomb at Alexander II, the delay mechanism failed, and the device detonated in mid-air, throwing the tsar to his feet and eviscerating him with the strength of the subsequent explosive shockwave. The power of the attack makes it clear that this was no black powder charge, and although the specifics are unclear, it was certainly a two-step device. Twenty-three years later, another shocking attack would take place, this time against Russia's secret police chief, Vyacheslav von Plehve (1846–1904). On a stifling summer's day in 1904, two radicals – Sazonov and Sikorski – armed themselves with pyroxyline bombs. Upon sighting von Plehve at the Varshavsky railway station in St Petersburg, they threw their bombs under his armoured car and within moments the nemesis of radicals all over Russia lay strewn across the road.[25]

One year later, the radicals targeted yet another pillar of the Russian regime's security state, Grand Duke Sergei Alexandrovic Romanov (1857–1905). Appointed the military governor of Moscow, his objective had been to crush the revolutionary intelligentsia whose over-educated minds had already motivated attempts to topple the tsar. Unfortunately for him, he had failed to eliminate the revolutionary spirit of Ivan Kaliaev, a member of the notorious Social Revolutionary Party's Combat Detachment. Kaliaev provides us with the first known use of a nitroglycerin bomb for irregular revolutionary warfare. On 4 February 1905, he ran up to the grand duke and hurled the unstable two-step explosive right into his lap. The disruption of the liquid within the casing caused it to begin its detonation chain, exploding upon impact. The consequent shockwave tore through flesh and bone, with the duke's wife's biographer commenting that "scattered all over the crimson-stained snow, lay pieces of scorched cloth, leather, the stump of a hand here and a finger there". This was the horrifying but wholly effective aftermath of a modern man-portable bomb.

On 11 June 1903, two years prior to Grand Duke Sergei's assassination, a military coup had erupted among Belgrade's Stari Dor,[26] the royal residence of King Alexander Obrenovic I and his despised wife, Queen Draga Masin. That evening, members of Serbia's ultra-nationalist, ultra-right Black Hand movement stormed their way into the palace. Copying the breaching techniques of the 1870s French Army, the conspirators affixed a dynamite charge to the couple's specially constructed oak security doors. The charge had such a phenomenal effect that this first-generation explosive blew open the barred doors, tore through the royal bodyguard hiding behind them and fused the palace electrics with the power of its blast. The disruption enabled the close-knit team of conspiratorial executioners to complete their task.

It would be from the brains of this same organization – the Black Hand – that perhaps the most infamous assassination using explosives was carried out: the murder of Archduke Franz Ferdinand. On 28 June 1914, the archduke – one of the most powerful men in the Habsburg Empire – paid a visit to Sarajevo, where he was

25   Ular, A., *La Revolution Russe*, p.19.
26   Glenny, M., *The Balkans 1804–2012*, p.299.

targeted by seven terrorists organised into two cells. The terrorists were equipped with two-step bombs, which had both primary and secondary explosives contained within them. These were activated by a delay fuse connected to percussion caps at the top of the casing.[27] When these caps were popped, heat would occur inside the container, setting off a fuse which would produce sufficient heat to trigger the primary explosive within. In this case, the fuse was set to explode after 12 seconds, slowly heating the primary explosive within that time.[28] When the archduke's car crawled towards the Cumurija Bridge in central Sarajevo, the Bosnian terrorist Muhamed Mehmedbasic popped his percussion caps and threw his bomb into the convoy. The bomb failed to kill its target, but the vast shockwave injured several and resulted in a change to the convoy's route. On the altered route, the archduke would run into Gavrilo Princip, and the subsequent well-known events set the stage for the war with whose conduct this book primarily concerns.

The sudden redundancy of black powder and the increasing pace of innovation, particularly in chemistry, ended up producing a truly phenomenal weapon; a weapon which was, as this section has demonstrated, amply fitted to the needs of infantrymen, commandos and guerrillas alike. From a naval point of view, it would not be hard to imagine the effect that these new explosives could have, even to the best-protected ironclad. Indeed, the power packed into these novel devices might prove to be just the antidote to the ironclad's thick armour. It was an idea not lost on the torpedo manufacturers of the early 20th century, and by the outbreak of the war for Italy in 1915 it was TNT (Trinitrotoluene) that was the explosive of choice for subaquatic munitions.[29] However, for nautical strategists of the Young School, the opportunities presented by the advancements in explosive technologies would require the development of an adequate delivery system. That would come in the shape of the motorboat.

The Humble Rowboat

For countless centuries, humanity navigated the globe's rivers and coastal waters by using the rowboat. The boat or launch, in maritime terminology, has traditionally been used to transport a person or small groups of people from ships to land, from ships to ships and from land to other land best accessible through water. Their uses are wide ranging, and as a category they form the ancestors of the motorboat. The first evidence for the use of boats of these sizes and designed for these aforementioned functions lays outside the Peruvian city of Lima. The site in question – El Paraiso – belongs to the Chavin culture, a forerunner to the Inca civilisation, whose

27 Hastings, M., *Catastrophe: Europe Goes to War, 1914* (London: William Collins Publishing, 2013), p.xviii.
28 Akhavan, J., *The Chemistry of Explosives*, pp.74–83.
29 Cook-Branfill, R., *Torpedo: The Complete History*, p.54.

society was wholly predicated on the ability to traverse the vast river systems of the eastern South Americas.[30] This facet of their polity was required due to the dense jungle and goliath mountain ranges which separated their cities. A dependency on single- or double-manned vessels to carry merchandise and people from one place to another soon developed. These log boat canoes appear to have proliferated across those proto-nations which straddled the Amazon, from eastern Brazil all the way to northern Ecuador. These small craft were basic, being put together with logs and leather ties. They were steered by way of what the Spanish missionary Gaspar de Carvajal described as "a series of centre mounted boards which were pushed down to shift water from one side of the boat to the other". These developments in small sub-ship vessels were mirrored in North America, with among the oldest finds in this region being in Florida. Newnan's Lake in the far north of Florida is home to a fleet of log canoes dating to at least 1000 BC. These boats, like those in eastern Latin America, predate metal, and seem to have been made by creating a seat in the middle of the craft by carving out of the wood using sharp tools.[31] This process occurred in parallel with the creation of the 'skinboat', an equally agile craft designed for small teams of people in the Pacific Northwest and among primitive cultures in Siberia. But the spark of inspiration which gave birth to these constructs was not exclusively an American affair.

If one travels nearly 7,000 miles east of the prodigious sites of El Paraiso and Newnan's Lake, one will arrive on the banks of the Euphrates River, a waterway known to laymen and experts alike as the cradle of humanity and the birthplace of civilisation. More accurately, it is the birthplace of a succession of ground-breaking societies dating as far back as 6,000 years. The series of civilisations, from a coalition of the world's first city states in Sumer around 4,000 BC down to the Babylonian Empire of 1,895–539 BC,[32] were utterly dependent on Mesopotamia's two rivers, the Euphrates and Tigris. They, like the Amerindians of the Amazon Basin, required the rivers for trade, communication or, in the case of imperial authorities, control. However, a separate tradition of construction emerged in both the East and West, with the Arabs inhabiting a land devoid of forests and the Americans populating a blessed continent replete with huge expanses of wooded areas. To this end, the Middle Easterners were forced to depend on non-arboreal constructions such as buoyed rafts and reed-built river craft. The former consisted of a combination of inflated animal skins, strapped to each other and then connected with a wooden floor. This formed a kind of primitive rigid inflatable boat (RIB), today favoured by naval commandos and waterborne authorities. Still further east, it was the Asian coracle which became the dominant form of waterway transportation.[33] Instead of the boat shape with which

30   Paine, L., *The Sea and Civilization: A Maritime History of the World* (London: Atlantic Books, 2015), p.24.
31   Paine, L., *The Sea and Civilization*, p.25.
32   Mansfield, P., *A History of the Middle East* (London: Penguin Publishing, 1991), p.3.
33   Woodgate, W., *Boating* (London: Longmans, Green & Co, 1888), p.8.

we are familiar, the coracle consisted of a bowl-shaped hull covered with a stretched animal skin for buoyancy and to keep out the water.

Despite their name, the Asian coracle has been found in different forms right across the early human world, from the river systems of Britannia to China. It is perhaps the only vessel which was buildable by a single man with very little resources, which is the likely reason for its eternal popularity, particularly among humble hunter-gatherers. By the time European empires had begun to spread across the continents, the world of small watercraft had little changed since the invention of these primitive boats thousands of years ago. In an 1888 text on the history of rowing, author W. Woodgate relates how the aboriginals of the Australian colonies still used pieces of lightwood to venture along that continent's lengthy coastline. Even today in the frozen wastelands of Greenland, far northern Canada, and the Arctic portion of Siberia, hardy peoples still use the canoe and the kayak. Yet despite the variance in manufacturing styles and materials, they all had one thing in common – they all required muscle power. For the ocean-going aspirations of industrial navies, muscle power would not be enough to transport troops to land. Nor was it sufficient to propel men from ship to ship with the increasing distance between vessels during operations as the age of steam wore on. What was needed for the navies of the 19th and 20th centuries was the first upgrade to the small-boat formula in millennia.

Dawn of the Motorboat

Like many developments, innovations and inventions studied so far in this book, the motorboat's creation was the result of the stunning scientific revolution of the late 1700s and 1800s. The first enterprise in the journey to discover an alternative to the rowboat was aimed not at providing speed for the commando or as a means for transporting men from ship to ship, but at finding a use for steam power. In August 1647, the discoverer of steam power – Denis Papin – was born in the central French town of Blois. Unfortunately for the House of Bourbon, the soon-to-be genius Papin (1647-1713) had been born a Protestant.[34] In a kingdom which had, in living memory, not just succumbed to terrible religious violence (the French Wars of Religion, 1562-98), but actively participated in Europe's largest religious conflict until that point, the Thirty Years War (1618-48).[35] It should thus come as no surprise that the young mathematician decided to leave the confines of the anti-Protestant French monarchy for the thoroughly Protestant kingdom of England. Once there, like many young immigrants, he would attempt to pursue his fortune among London's shady back alleys and

34   Figuier, L., *Les Merveilles de la Science ou Description Populaire des Inventions Modernes* (Paris: Jouvet et C. Éditeurs, 1870), p.1.
35   Wilson, P., *Europe's Tragedy: A New History of the Thirty Years' War* (London: Penguin Publishing, 2010).

polluted waterways. His journey proved fortuitous when in 1681 he was admitted to the Stuart kingdom's finest academic society, the Royal Society of England. Whilst there, he conducted an experiment whereby he sealed a copper vase with a screw lid, within which water was confined, and when heat was applied super-hot air was created within the vase. Papin noted that this cloud of hot air was not, as previously thought, created through the heating of the environment, but that it was directly caused by the heating of the water inside the vase. By disproving the long-held hypothesis of environmentally created 'hot air', he unintentionally encountered a way to create controllable clouds of hot air; in other words, steam.

When Papin wrote down what he had found, it was transmitted to the world in English and from England. In doing so, the France lost out tremendously on man's first documented meeting with steam power. Yet Papin could not initially work out what his invention meant. It was only when he put together a machine which could produce steam that he realised it could move objects, in this case a cylinder which he had affixed to the system. He hypothesised that if two of these steam-producing machines were fitted to a watercraft, then they could power the boat by moving a piston and pump to move what would later be termed a 'paddlewheel'. It with this hypothesis that the Comte D'Auxiron became enamoured. From 1770, this rather eccentric French nobleman took retirement from military service among the white-coated ranks of the Royal French Army and set about planning to put Papin's maritime ambitions into play. Two years into the project, the Auxiron Society was formed to further the concept, leading to the enlistment of the Counts of Bourdeilles and Follenay alongside the Marquis of Jouffroy.[36] By 1774, a prototype steamboat had been fitted with a twin-cylinder steam engine, but it was victim of an act of sabotage on 8 September that year and destroyed. Although the Count of Auxiron would die four years later, his brainchild dashed, his fellow aristocrats in the endeavour refused to give up so easily. It would not be until 1783 that the Count of Follenay and Marquis of Jouffroy made a breakthrough, creating the steamboat *Pyroscaphe*.[37] The vessel was 45.4m long, with paddle wheels 4m tall, and that summer it paddled up the River Saone for 15 minutes. In doing so, its invention broke the tyranny of muscle power and opened the way for thinking about new propulsion methods.

If the steamboat became the grandfather of all vessels in the coming age of steel and iron, then the electric boat was the direct father of the diesel-powered motorboat which would emerge in the 1890s. It would be the electric-powered boat, with its small propulsion assembly, that would make the non-muscle-powered canoe/kayak/launch possible. Surprisingly, given the woeful lack of innovation in the Russian Tsardom during the 19th century, it would be a St Petersburg-based scientist, Moritz von Jacobi, who would make the electric motorboat possible.[38] Prussian by birth, Moritz

36   Nansouty, M., *Les Merveilles de la Science: Moteurs* (Paris: Bovin Éditeurs, 1910), p.1.
37   Nansouty, M., *Les Merveilles de la Science: Moteurs*, p.1.
38   Nansouty, M., *Les Merveilles de la Science: Moteurs*, pp.16–17.

was among the thousands of Germanic experts, academics and professional officers imported into Russia from the 1820s onwards as part of an addiction to all things German on behalf of the Russian intelligentsia and ruling classes[39] (an alliance of interest not replicated in any other aspect of their relations). His invention, an electric boat, was based around utilising an array of electro-magnets to move a paddle wheel, since the propeller had not yet been invented. Unfortunately, the crew died in the attempt to prove his concept, fatally wounding his proposition. It would fall instead to a national of an equally failing society – the Third French Republic – to succeed where Moritz had not. Gustave Trouve was a scientist of spectacular skill whose particular contribution lay in the miniaturisation of the truly massive technologies of the day. It was his imposition of his specialism on the matter of engines that enabled him to plot the path for both outboard motors and the marine diesel engine, developments without which neither the explosive charge-equipped military diver nor the torpedo boat would have been able to exist.

On a beautiful Parisian summer's day in 1881, Trouve tested the first ever electrically powered motorboat. He had not followed the path of the steam pioneers in building enormous vessels driven by paddlewheels, with centrally housed boilers. All he had built was an electric motor, which was portable and could be fitted on any launch the client desired; it was this motor, and not the vessel it propelled, which was of importance. He had in essence uncovered the oar of the modern age, simple and able to propel far smaller boats than the sail or the steam engine had been capable of. Consequently, automatic propulsion was granted to a 5.5m-long canoe-like vessel carrying three people through the simple fitting of a 5kg motor activated by Faure-Plante accumulators on the back of the launch. The motor was attached to a state-of-the-art three-bladed propeller. This outboard motor was improved by its second iteration, which contained a four-bladed propeller system – the blades measuring 28cm – driven by Bunsen-plate batteries charged using a mix of hydrochloric and nitric acid. This second motor allowed the canoe-like vessel to which it was attached to travel 150m in 24 seconds. Being battery-powered, the speed gradually reduced so that after five hours it would take a minute to move 150m. Despite this issue, French high society was greatly impressed, and in October 1882 Trouve exhibited his electric motorboat at the French Yacht Club's annual regatta. It was an occasion where his motorboat undertook the 3,200m-long course in just 17 minutes.[40]

For prospective military use, there were hitherto unmentioned aspects of intense interest pertaining to the electric motor – its stealth and portability. On the second count, the irregular warrior would technically be able to transform any small boat into a motorboat by carrying the lightweight motor and fitting it to the back of a vessel. It would thus allow mid-mission adaptation, increasing the range of actions available. On the first count, stealth would prove to be indispensable. In 1888, the

39   Pipes, R., *Russia Under The Old Regime*, p.259.
40   Desmond, K., *Guinness Book of Motorboating*, pp.17–18.

Racing Motorboats at the 1913 races. (University of Washington)

Chinese Customs Office looked to the motorboat as an alternative to the clumsy, noisy and frequently pungent steamboat.[41] They wanted something more befitting their ambush-reliant work. Seeking to obtain a vessel capable of surprising smugglers, the Qing customs men eyed Trouve's electric motors with a deal of fascination. Its quiet nature and small size created the perfect hunting vehicle for attacking the criminal enemies of the late Qing Empire (1636-1912).

After a rocky start with steam, the move away from rowing was starting to pay dividends for the increasingly plausible concept of torpedo-equipped fast attack boats; vessels which one day would become the vehicles for Italy's MAS units. However, the benefits of stealth were short-lived as the world of micro-scale marine propulsion turned to focus on a need for speed above all else. It was a search which would immensely aid the viability of the torpedo boat. In a surprisingly rapid timeframe, the world of sub-ship boats went from gas engines by Gottlieb Daimler in 1886 and Frederick Simms in 1890 to petrol engines, debuted by French inventor Alfred Seguin in 1892. Each were the same replications of outboard motors which first broke the trend with steam under Trouve's electric motors. A year after Seguin's unveiling of the first petrol maritime motor, a German – Rudolph Diesel – unleashed his diesel engine, once again revolutionising small-boat propulsion.[42]

---

41   Desmond, K., *The Guinness Book of Motorboating: Facts, Feats and Origins* (Enfield: Guinness Superlatives Ltd, 1979), p.18.

42   Ecorchon, F., *Le Moteur Diesel et ses Derives: Traite Theorique et Pratique* (Paris: Librairie, 1929), pp.vii–x.

The roots of the diesel engine lay across the Atlantic on Rhode Island, courtesy of George Brayton, who in 1872 took a gas engine and swapped it out for petrol. Instead of pressurising gas to force an explosion to drive pistons – which in turn kick-started whatever contraption the engine was strapped to – it would be petrol that would be pressurised. In doing so, Brayton pioneered the fossil fuel-powered engine and launched the modern age of propulsion. However, the system was inefficient, and Rudolph Diesel believed he could do better. He designed his engine in 1893 and laid out his vision in his text *The Rational Thermal Motor*. In this document, he stated that his objective was to create an engine whose energy did not expand outside the system, retaining all the energy created by the explosive reaction between pressurised fuel and piston.[43] Should this be possible, he would be able to produce an engine capable of driving any attached motorised system much faster than petrol, which worked in a similar fashion but with less efficiency. After four years of tinkering with his new device, he finally finished his engine to a commercially viable standard. In the same year, he declared: "The numerous commissions of engineers and politicians around the world declared it the best motor for its superior quality."

Thanks to Diesel, by 1900 the fastest boats that had so far ever existed began to emerge. It should come as no surprise that Europe's idle nobility immediately put this fast-boat revolution to good use and commenced the sport of speedboat racing, a pastime which supercharged the development of speedboats in the decades immediately preceding the First World War. In the 1901 regatta at Nice, an oak boat fitted with a Mercedes-Daimler diesel engine achieved the first speedboat world record of 20mph, winning the race with ease.[44] The following year, it was the French vessel, the *Vitesse*, which won the regatta with a speed of 13½mph, making it the fastest speedboat of the season. By 1903, boats were being fitted with up to 35hp (horsepower) engines, with the winner being a 35hp Mercedes engine-equipped boat capable of doing 23mph. In the years leading up to 1914, competitive speedboat racing was held annually in Monaco, with ever-faster boats arriving on the scene.

By 1914, both explosives and the means to convey them – either via torpedo or by the commando's hand – had reached their pinnacle of pre-war development. In this chapter we have established how naval operatives could now get to their locations, and how, employing high explosives, they could cut through the sides of ships and fortifications like they were naught but cloth and silk. The dual developments in explosives and aquatic propulsion by 1914 had finally achieved a point whereby the Young School would be capable of reaching its full potential. Within the *Regia Marina*, one voice had witnessed these developments with great interest – Admiral Paolo Thaon di Revel. As we shall see, his enchantment with the possibilities of the nascent small boat world would allow for the birth of the *Regia Marina*'s naval special forces – the

43   Chalkley, A., *Les Moteurs Diesel Type Fixe et Type Marine* (Paris: Dunod et Pinat Éditeurs, 1919), pp.i–xv.

44   Desmond, K., *The Guinness Book of Motorboating*, p.24.

MAS squadrons. But the concept of rapid-attack torpedo-equipped vessels would not be all he was interested in, and the *Regia Marina*'s minority Young School adherents began to think about utilising divers capable of carrying ship-killing explosives. That idea, though, was a mere dream until the outbreak of the First World War.

4

From Scyllis to Fleuss & Davis – the Evolution of Diving
A Tradition of Problems

In 1931, an intense 46-year-old journalist meandered his way down the Red Sea on his way to China. The Frenchman in question, the later inspiration for the cartoon hero Tintin, Albert Londres, was never one to pass up the opportunity to write a good story. And in Arabia he found one which would provide an irresistible font of literary inspiration – the exotic pearl divers of the vast Arabian peninsula. Tragically, Londres would die on his return journey from China, but fortunately for diving history, his observations on the practices of the Arabian oyster procurers would survive him, being posthumously published in 1932. The work's subject matter is betrayed by its title, *Pecheurs de Perles* (Pearl Fishers), a commentary on the 'naked' aquanauts of the Red Sea.[1] Naked diving refers to the practice by which human participants submerge themselves beneath the waves without protection from either water pressure or the body's finite air capacity. This form of submerged exploration is that which, as we will see, has been prosecuted throughout human history as the main form of non-surface maritime activity. By the 1930s, these pearl exploiters (found from Italy to Ceylon and Arabia) had become the last remaining edifices of this millennia-old form of nautical economics. The testimonies of these dwellers of the windswept Arabian coastline rolling off the Sarawat Mountains[2] provide us with an excellent introduction to the problems facing naked divers. They were problems whose complexities would require centuries of scientific progress to work out, and when they had been, there arose the birth of modern diving, with all its military opportunities.

Pearl diving in the primitive practice elucidated above was, and is, a psychologically daring feat. Attempts by these incredible divers to master the reasonable fears that the mere prospect of their work awoke in them led to a plethora of sea shanties and chants designed to build their courage. It is within the emotional verses of these incantations that we find evidence of the litany of physiological challenges that faced them on a

1   Londres, A., *Pecheurs de Perles* (Paris: Albin Michel Editeur, 1931).
2   Lacey, R., *Inside the Kingdom* (London: Arrow, 2010), p.xiv.

daily basis. The 'Song of the Pearl Divers', in its fourth line, for example, informs us, *Qu'importe d'tre sourd puisque l'huitre ne parle pas* or "What does it matter to be deaf since the oyster does not speak". What may seem to be a humorous stanza actually alludes to a common debilitating barotrauma (injuries sustained as the result of pressure changes) and indeed to its cause. The trauma in this case is deafness and the causation is being subject to rapid change in water pressure during rapid surfacing, i.e. decompression sickness. When applied to the ear, this barometric change can rupture the delicate structure of the inner ear, and water can flood through the rupture site into the ear and deafen the diver.[3] The cutting off of one's auditory functions will often lead to vertigo and a state of unbalance, which in turn renders the diver vulnerable to his exceedingly hostile surroundings. Yet this is not all that water pressure does. A rapid change in the human body's environmental circumstances allows gas bubbles to penetrate through the human skin into the muscle tissue, from where the bubbles infiltrate the blood stream. Especially large collections of bubbles can block the blood supply to the organs, killing the diver. Additionally, the pressure itself, without any change, can exert upon man's anatomy an intense force which can lead to bruising, joint pain and crippling abdominal anguish. At certain depths, the force is even sufficient to crush metal and bend objects.[4] Through both depth compression and decompression, water pressure thus formed a ruinous force to the naked diver.

Congruous to the dangers of water pressure is an altogether more insidious peril to naked divers – the body's own air-processing capabilities. Aside from the obvious time limitations imposed upon humans by the endurance of the lungs, there lies another danger in the ingestion and retention of air. This hidden jeopardy was nudged at when the aforementioned French journalist consulted a member of a pearl diving crew upon whose vessel he was travelling. The intrepid Somali diver in question stated that once his fellow submarine fishermen returned to the surface, they often took to "walking upon the moon",[5] a phraseology which clearly hinted at the delirium experienced by those who had just ascended from particularly deep dives. Although this could partly be explained by vertigo from unbalanced ear rupturing, a second participant in the process of this 'madness' occurs through the storing of depleted air within one's respiratory system. This leads to an increase of carbon dioxide within the bloodstream, which in combination with rapid decompression sends a resurfacing diver temporarily insane. It was this restriction on how much the human body can capture good, nourishing air, in combination with water pressure, which formed the dual barriers which prevented human operations beneath the waves past a certain degree. In turn, this meant that until the Industrial Revolution, the military diver would be as constrained by his own inadequate physiology as the pearl divers of Arabia.

3   Jablonski, J., *Getting Clear on the Basics: The Fundamentals of Technical Diving* (High Springs, FL: Global Underwater Explorers, 2001), pp.86–87.
4   Jablonski, J., *Getting Clear on the Basics: The Fundamentals of Technical Diving*, pp.90–91.
5   Londres, A., *Pecheurs de Perles* (Paris: Albin Michel Editeur, 1931), pp.95–97.

The physical quandaries encountered in the 20th century by Londres' Arabs were exactly the same as those stumbled across throughout naked diving's vast history. Two prohibitive forces, then, can be seen to exist beneath the water's surface which strictly controlled the activities of the unprotected human form whilst in its murky depths: the matter of water pressure and the rather more obvious presence of a finite lung capacity, and from that the degradation of breathed air whilst inside the body. Until these problems could be explored and solved through the application of industrial science, divers would be limited to highly restrictive mission times. Nevertheless, this did not deter ambitious admirals from attempting to push the physical boundaries of what man could do whilst subject to water's hammer-like currents.

Military Diving Before the Industrial Age

The question most pertinent to the historically interested reader is why, if the mysteries of the deep were so impenetrable, did it seem prudent to attempt to utilize the subaquatic realm in battle? Military operations are risky enough without adding the axiomatically hostile subaquatic environment to the roster of perils facing the fighting man. Nevertheless, the benefits to be gained from operating in such surroundings were as obvious to the earliest admirals as they would be to the Italian Kingdom's naval high command upon their entry into the Frist World War in 1915; namely, the desire to gain an edge over a stronger enemy without the impossible requirement to match that enemy in number or quality. As we shall see in this section, the use of pre-industrial combat divers was therefore, in essence, an extension of the eternal competition between offence and defence. The aim all too often was to negate the immense defensive infrastructure of warships and coastal defences/fortresses by employing stealth to catch their prey unawares and damage them with silent methodologies. Consequently, their role throughout history was to be an aquatic guerrilla whose target, instead of personalities, fortresses and public infrastructure, was towering battleships and immense shipyards.

In the 2nd century AD, a Greek geographer writing for a knowledge-hungry Roman public stepped foot once more in his Hellenic homeland. On a poorly recorded date, this Greek – Pausanias – arrived at Euboea and trekked across the island until he reached its capital, Elateia,[6] the crowning city of the Phocians. He happened there upon a vast garden of statues. One of those statues is to a now-forgotten 5th-century BC man by the name of Scyllis, whose story even the prodigal sons of the classics faculties at Cambridge and Oxford might be hard-pressed to recall. To diving historians, however, he is of immense importance. Scyllis of Scione, to give him his proper name, was the primary protagonist of the first documented military dive, the execution

---

6   Jones, W. & Ormerod, H., *Pausanias' Description of Greece with an English Translation* (Cambridge: Harvard University Press, 1918).

of which during the Persian Wars appears in the works of Herodotus. Interestingly, not only was Scyllis supposedly the marine special forces archetype of a covertly operating sabotage specialist, but he also fits the legendary image of the commando: a treacherous, roguish individual motivated by money and a love of derring-do, something which he would share with Italy's First World War pioneers of military diving over 2,000 years later. The exploits of Scyllis are told in two formats: a fictionalized legend and then a more basic (and probably more factual) narrative version. In the legend, Scyllis of Scione and his indomitable daughter Hydna dived under the parked triremes of the Persian fleet and dragged away their anchors.[7] The invading fleet of King Xerxes I (reigned 486–465 BC), as the story went, was thus irrevocably damaged and the ruling Amphictyons of Greece granted Elateia a statue, honouring his acts.

Unfortunately, the statue of Scyllis has been lost since the Roman Emperor Nero (AD 37-68) looted Delphi, but luckily the true story has been preserved.[8] As is almost always the case, it is far more illuminating than the myth. In Herodotus' telling, King Xerxes' Persian invasion of Greece got underway in 480 BC in an attempt to fulfil his father King Darius I's dream of European conquest. To do so, the Persians had created a grand fleet. They understood that Greece's political structures, based on a collection of coastal cities, could not be subdued lest their navies overcome. In the summer of that year, the predominantly Egyptian mariners of the Persian armada defeated the Athenians – Greece's foremost sea power – at Chalkis. It is at this point we are introduced by Herodotus to Scyllis, except in this telling he is a man who hitherto had been employed by the Persians for mere coin. Here we discover the first use of ancient military divers, Herodotus writing that the task Scyllis carried out for his Zoroastrian masters was to dive the Hellespont – a place that the vast Persian army had crossed in April that year – for sunken treasure. It thus seems that the first documented use of military divers was in a recovery capacity. The second use for Scyllis is described soon after, whereby he betrayed his Persian pursers for pay providing intelligence as to the location of a wounded Persian fleet to the Greeks recovering at Chalkis.[9] In doing so, he fulfils the role of a reconnaissance diver. The third and most sought-after role of a diver – the sabotage commando – is detailed subsequently, with the aforementioned execution of a stealthy approach to the Persian fleet and the cutting of their anchors by the use of a knife. In this way, the fleet careered out of control and was put at a significant disadvantage to the smaller Greek fleet. The balance of the field was thus restored, and the Greeks were able to vanquish the Persians.

The story of Scyllis can be seen to provide maritime history with evidence that the three core uses of special forces today – reconnaissance, sabotage and recovery – had already been established by the first documented outing for nautical commandos. The

7   Crawley, R., *The History of the Peloponnesian War by Thucydides* (London: J.M. Dent & Sons, 1950), pp.58–75.

8   Bourguet, E., *Les Ruines de Delphes* (Paris: Paris, 1914), p.28.

9   Crawley, R., *The History of the Peloponnesian War by Thucydides*, pp.58–75.

politically unstable waters of the Aegean would have even more audacious uses for divers, forever pushing the limits of what they could do in a military role. On 31 December AD 192, Emperor Commodus perished in a brutal assassination, kick-starting a period of intense civil war amid the Romans. By January 193 the would-be emperor Septimus Severus looked to be the favourite, a fact cemented by his defeat of General Niger at the Battle of Issus in Asia Minor the following year. The city of Byzantium – predecessor to Constantinople – remained loyal to the Nigerines and it was not long before the Roman Navy was descending on the Bosphorus. This time it would not be the attackers who would use the plethora of creative options provided by combat divers, but the defenders. The Nigerines had been caught out without a navy (unsurprisingly due to the expense involved in acquiring one), but rather than accept their fate, combat divers deployed from Byzantium tried to seize Roman vessels. The plan demonstrated a fourth special-forces role – battlefield acquisition.[10] These proto-commandos facilitated this remarkable operation by diving down to the target vessel's waterline and hammering nails into the wooden sides. They then attached rope to these nails and dragged the ships into the harbour, sequestering them for their own use. By the end of the Classical Age then, we have seen on two separate occasions the ground-breaking operational potential of these divers, but the coming of the Dark Ages put paid to further mentions of diving commandos for over a millennia.

The Middle Ages witnessed similar operations to those detailed above, yet the next novel advancement would not arrive until the 14th century and would come in the field of sabotage. In early 1340, the House of Plantagenet was in the midst of its centuries-long struggle with the Capetian dynasty over the French throne. The French fleet had hitherto been superior, but the English navy had decided to challenge them and by 24 June both fleets faced each othr off the Belgian coast at a place called Sluys.[11] Both sides deployed military divers whose objective was to go below the water line and sabotage the wooden walls of the ships. Much in the way that modern naval commandos place bombs below the waterline of vessels, these divers drilled holes in the ships' wooden sides. Jars of incendiary Greek fire were then smashed into the drilled hole, setting the vessel on fire from below. Drills were also used to allow water to pour into the ship and thus destabilize them. Interestingly, it appears that primitive diving helmets were coming into use at the same time. They were supposedly shaped like kettles and worked by having a long spout which reached the surface, enabling the divers to ingest air whilst under the water. Here once more we see divers being engaged as saboteurs, but technological advancements had by then provided them with fire-based weaponry and the equipment to prolong their operations. The limitations of the human body and advancements in naval construction, however, would soon make those limitations insurmountable. By the reign of King Louis XIII

10   Cary, E., *Dio's Roman History in Nine Volumes* (London: William Heinemann Ltd, 1957), p.175–183.
11   Sumption, J., *Trial by Battle.*, p.264.

of France (1610-43), military divers had seemingly lost their importance,[12] having been relegated to a maintenance role in military dockyards. Military divers, despite their remarkable battlefield abilities, had fallen foul of the turning wheel of scientific progress – in particular the inexorable rise of gunpowder.

In the 14th century, cannonry appeared in Western militaries for the first time, and by the mid-1600s the evolutionary track of these extraordinary weapons had led them onto the cramped decks of Europe's navies. It would be the English who were the first to take advantage of this new way of nautical combat. During the reign of Queen Elizabeth I (1533-1603), a harnessing of on-board gun power led to a tactic whereby an attacking vessel would dart towards a target ship, before firing all its cannons before withdrawing to reload.[13] This gave birth to an English departure from the ancient mode of naval warfare – closing in and boarding. Tactics have a habit of becoming contagious, and throughout the century following Elizabeth's death, Europe's maritime forces also turned to gunnery-first warfare, as evidenced by the exponential rise in numbers of guns per vessel. In 1655, the largest English ships, the great frigates, were carrying 44 guns, but just shy of two decades later they had 72.[14] The shift from the primacy of boarding to long-distance gunnery was there to stay, and by 1700 the art of boarding had been relegated to a secondary consideration.

The prime directive of ships' captains from then until the advent of the ironclad was to maintain distance from the enemy whilst attempting to keep them in sufficient range to fire back. For divers to be effective, they had to operate near a shore facility or upon vessels. Without close support, they would not be able to surface and breathe in safety. The new emphasis on long-range warfare meant that ships were no longer just metres away from each other, stripping the diver of his short-range support network. For a diver to get close to two vessels exchanging fire in the gunnery age, he would need a rapid means of transport to cover the wide distance between rival warships, but all the technology of the day could muster was the simple rowboat. Even then, robbed of their ability to use shore facilities by the advent of open ocean combat, divers found themselves irrelevant. To continue to play a role, they would need the ability to operate independent from life support infrastructure on the surface. It would take two centuries of scientific advancement before this could take place.

Encountering Problems – the Scientific Basis for Subaquatic Dangers

By the dawn of the industrial age, sub-surface commandos had encountered laws of nature which prohibited their continued employment. Nevertheless, a series of

12   Figuier, L., *Les Merveilles de la Science ou Description Populaire des Inventions Modernes*, p.618.
13   Rodger, N.A.M., *The Safeguard of the Seas: A Naval History of Britain 6601649* (London: Penguin Publishing, 2004), p.204.
14   Rodger, N.A.M., *The Command of the Ocean*, pp.216–226.

brilliant innovators began to find ways around these restrictions. The first of these problems was water pressure. It would take a Frenchman of remarkable scientific intelligence and ability to overcome this barrier. Blaise Pascal was born in 1623 to a local judge and tax officer in central France's Auvergne-Bas province, but it was not long before his scientific mind turned to greater pursuits than taxes. In 1653, during the lengthy reign of the Sun King, Louis XIV (1643–1715), Pascal published his seminal treatise *The Equilibrium of Liquids*,[15] which laid out an analysis of his observations of liquids in a static state. He claimed that the static nature of non-moving liquids provided them with a hydrostatic balance which could only be maintained if no force was exerted upon the water. When force was applied to the static water, it came under pressure and thus started to move. This pressure was cumulative, changing with each localized imposition of force. The pressure generated by the newly introduced force was unfettered when introduced and transmitted itself without diminishing, meaning each new introduction came with the same unbridled potency. This discovery was eventually codified into Pascal's Law, which states that when a change in pressure is applied to an enclosed fluid, that pressure change is transmitted throughout the fluid without diminishing its force. The modern explanation for this law is that because the atoms of a fluid move without restriction, they can transmit their full energy without loss. When applied to natural bodies of water such as seas, oceans, lakes and rivers, the pressure, Pascal discovered, came from the atmosphere, in the form of atmospheric pressure. Science had already provided the first inkling of the workings of atmospheric pressure, not in France but in the power-house of 17th-century science, Italy.

In 1644, Evangelista Torricelli, the Florentine academic and former student of fellow Italian genius Galileo Galilei, invented the mercury barometer to measure air pressure. This creation was merely the terminal point of a longstanding inquiry into the topic. He believed, as had Aristotle, that the air in which humans moved had to have a weight, and that humans were simply living at the bottom of a massive ocean of air. It would not be until the next century that oxygen was discovered, so for the time it sufficed to be convinced that the space around mankind was not just empty. To discover its existence, Torricelli carried out experiments with air placed into a container,[16] in a line of thinking that led to the barometer, which works by balancing the weight of 'air' against the weight of a mercury column. The higher the air pressure, the higher the mercury, and vice versa. With this discovery, it was possible for later scientific thinking to unify this with Pascal's Law to understand one of the ingredients that creates water pressure within natural bodies. The pressure which was enacted on a diver was thus discovered to be the cumulative effect of both the weight of the water and the atmospheric pressure enacted upon the water. It was this system of

15   Jablonski, J., *Getting Clear on the Basics: The Fundamentals of Technical Diving.*, p.12.
16   West, J., *Torricelli and the Ocean of Air: The First Measurement of Barometric Pressure* (Bethesda: Physiology, 2013).

aquatic pressurization which had to be understood in order to properly comprehend the issue facing the divers of the industrial age.

The limitations of pressure on divers now being understood, we move to consider the matter of lung capacity and breathing as a diving restriction. To surpass these barriers, two discoveries first had to be made. The first was oxygen and its carbon dioxide opposite, and the second was the functions of the lung. The discovery of oxygen came courtesy of another Italian, Marcello Malphiaghi, who was born in Emilia-Romagna in March 1628. A remarkable biologist even considering the depth of intellectual capability of the Italian scientific circle at the time, his work on the lungs correctly deduced their function for the first time. Utilizing advances in microscope technology, Malphiagi examined both the alveoli and pulmonary capillaries. Although he did not correctly diagnose their role – that of taking carbon dioxide out of oxygen and then pumping oxygen into the blood stream – he did understand their ability to provide air to the blood.[17] A century later, this mysterious 'air', whose true nature had eluded all 17th-century Franco-Italian biologists, would finally be scientifically classified.

The deciphering of the composition of air would be both one of the most important discoveries in scientific history and one the most contentious. This should come as no surprise, as unveiling the truth that air was nothing more than nitrogen and oxygen laid the foundations for much of the industrial progress experienced in the 19th century. Nitrogen had been discovered by the Scottish doctor Daniel Rutherford in 1772, not long before the first encounter with oxygen. Its discovery came about as the result of one of Rutherford's combustive experiments, which had involved the burning of phosphorus until it petered out. The remaining substance in the burning chamber was then examined, and in doing so the isolation of nitrogen was achieved. By the end of 1772, its existence had become reported fact. Oxygen's identification was not so simple an affair, with three men – Joseph Priestley, Antoine Lavoisier and Charles Scheele – all claiming to have discovered it around roughly the same time. The Yorkshireman Joseph Priestley's debut into the oxygen controversy came courtesy of his 1772 work *Experiments on Different Kinds of Air*. Published over six volumes, the experimental tell-all detailed a series of observations on air divided into those carried out on still air, sulphur-influenced air and air subject to human respiration.[18] These experiments allowed him to divide the air into nitrous and what would later be called oxygen; in doing so he uncovered that the solid mass known as 'air' actually contained a chemical duality. He conducted a follow-up experiment, whereby he extracted nitrogen from 'air' and subjected living specimens to the remaining air minus its nitrogen. What he noticed was an increase in energy in the subjects receiving this treated 'air'. He came to the conclusion that the chemical that had been separated

---

17   West, J., *Marcello Malpighi and the Discovery of the Pulmonary Capillaries and Alveoli* (2013).
18   Declare, J., *Histoire de la Chimie* (Paris: Imprimerie Gauthier-Villars Et C., 1920), pp.119–131

from nitrogen gave life to sentient beings, and it was this as yet unnamed chemical, not nitrogen, which allowed humans to function.

Although Priestley had encountered oxygen – at a not inconsiderable risk to his own health – it would be Antoine Lavoisier who would name the chemical. Published five years after Priestley's work, the text of *On Combustion in General* ratified Priestley's discoveries and identified the bi-component nature of 'air'. In his conceptualization, these elements were labelled as vital air and lifeless air – oxygen and nitrogen. Charles Scheele navigated an earlier and different route when, in 1771, he managed to produce and identify oxygen by heating mercury oxide in combination with nitrates. When this occurred, he noted the flame increased in intensity; he labelled this intensifying ingredient 'fire air', which later turned out to be Lavoisier's oxygen. Scheele's published work on the matter coincided with Lavoisier's and so is unfortunately forgotten in the self-publicizing Frenchman's wake. Nevertheless, we now know, thanks to the early strides made by these three pioneers, that the 'air' described since the beginning of recorded history is 78 percent nitrogen and 21 percent oxygen[19]. It was found by Lavoisier that nitrogen provided no life to humans when exposed to the gas. But when breathing in nitrogen directly whilst underwater – as early experimenters with diving suits did under the auspices of breathing in 'air' – it directly contributed to decompression sickness, the condition which created the various debilitating issues afflicting Arabia's pearl divers, as noted by Albert Londres. Nitrogen causes this effect underwater due to the gas's greater efficiency at penetrating human muscle tissue. Once this penetration occurs, nitrogen floods into the body and bubbles begin to form as they come under the influence of ambient pressure changes. It would take another century for scientists to understand how to mix gases within air so as to negate the danger from this bubble formation. By the 1770s, however, the scientific mysteries which had pervaded the world of diving since the earliest times had mostly been catalogued and understood. With the discovery of these chemicals, their manipulation by mankind became possible, and from that the natural walls that confined military diving into its post-Medieval dead end began at last to seem breachable.

From Diving Bell to the Fleuss Suit – the Evolution of the Modern Diver

The modern diving suit has a long chain of ancestors. The concept which would one day spawn the diving suit has a simple idea at its core – a human submerged in water protected from pressure via a protective outer shell. The progenitor of the practical application of this concept, the diving suit, was the diving bell. It is once more from Aristotle that we derive the first verifiable entry on the topic of diving bells. Fundamentally, a diving bell is a life support chamber which operates by maintaining equal air pressure to the ambient water pressure within its walls so as to keep the water

19   Declare, J., *Histoire de la Chimie*, pp.143–148.

out.[20] At the same time, air is pumped into the chamber to allow the inhabitants to breathe, whilst the water pressure outside the bell incrementally pressurizes the air in line with increasing depth. Consequently, the air pressure inside the bell is kept equal to that of the water pressure below the bell, keeping the interior dry and filled with 'air'. In this way, diving crews using this apparatus can reach depths that their natural breathing forbids. Additionally, the bell provides vital protection against the exponential growth of external pressure and the inevitable barotraumas that result from human exposure to this. Since it is estimated that roughly only 1 percent of ancient literature survives, we cannot say for certain when diving bells first came into use, but Aristotle provides a good description as to their usage in the 4th century BC: "Divers are sometimes provided with instruments for respiration [diving bells], through which they can draw air from above the water, and thus remain a long time under sea."[21] These devices have a depth limitation which, unlike with humans, does not derive from a limited lung capacity. Instead, it is related to the amount of water which progressively leaks into the bell and destabilizes the intricate balance between internal air pressure and external water pressure.[22] These ingenious but somewhat crude devices are the direct ancestors of the early diving suits of the 20th century. It was the capability ceiling present in these diving bells, in terms of both breathing and pressure, that would lead to the rebreather and the diving helm, the next two developments in the journey to the 20th-century diving suit.

The diving bell as described above has been in existence since at least the time of Alexander the Great of Macedonia (reigned 336–323 BC). One of the stranger stories relating to the legendary monarch recounts his adventures within a diving bell. As incredible as it sounds, it does appear to have happened. Aristotle, in his book *Problems*, recounts how during the fall of Tyre during Alexander's Levantine campaign of 333–332 BC, Alexander took a glass diving bell to inspect the city's great seaward defences. Later embellishments claimed that this device was made entirely of white glass, testimony perhaps to the myths that surrounded the conqueror's astonishing life.[23] It is, however, a shame for academic and casual reader alike that the sources for the development of the diving bell before the industrial age are so scarce. It is a testimony to the remarkable paucity of evidence that only two verifiable sources attest to their medieval usage.

The first source comes from the High Middle Ages courtesy of the English Franciscan friar Roger Bacon. In his book *De Mirabili*, authored in 1250, he recounts the contemporary use of devices through which "men could walk on the bed of the ocean without harm to their bodies". The other source comes from the 16th century and is prescient of

20   Jablonski, J., *Getting Clear on the Basics: The Fundamentals of Technical Diving*, pp.12–13.
21   Hett, W.S., *Aristotle: Problems, Books XII–XXXVIII* (London: William Heineman Ltd, 1957), p.205.
22   Ballantyne, I., T*he Deadly Trade: The Complete History of Submarine Warfare*, pp.1–3.
23   George, G., *Histoire de la Grèce Depuis les Temps les Plus Recules Jusqu'à La Fin de la Generation Contemporaine d'Alexandre le Grand: Tome 5* (Brussels: A. Lacroix Verboeckhoven et Éditeurs, 1867).

the remarkable advances in knowledge which would come in the 1700s. The occurrence took place within the murky depths of the Venetian lagoons,[24] in which it is reported that in 1552 a group of Adriatic fishermen were utilizing a home-made instrument consisting of an air tank some 5 metres high and 3 metres long. The ruling senators of Venice were curious and supposedly rushed to observe the work of the men, whose dive is said to have lasted for two hours. Termed 'The Venetian', the air tank was attached to two tubes. One tube was plugged into the diver's head and the other into the water. The head-mounted tube pumped in fresh air and was connected to a surface-operated bellows, while the second tube expelled used air. These devices were the first inkling that independent, oxygen-aided diving might be an option for the future.

During the same period that oxygen was discovered – the first half of the 18th century – a series of inventors who experimented with diving bells emerged in the British Isles. These men – John Smeaton, George Rennie, Charles Spalding, Edmund Halley and the Swede Marten Triewald – progressively merged the age-old wisdom behind the diving bell with the technological improvements of the early modern era. Despite their collective work, all of them came unstuck over the issue of mobility and surface independence for the divers. During this period, the majority of diving bells were used with the intent to allow the divers inside to exit them onto the seabed or riverbed. Whilst there, they would be connected to an oxygen reservoir within the bell by a tube into a usually overburdened helmet. This method did not allow the diver any flexibility, as they were restricted by the length of tubing. Independent operations such as those involving commando divers were out of the question; the unaided commando divers of old had only been able to carry out their work because they were not inhibited by apparatus. Despite intense work on the issue, none of the inventors were able to crack the problem of how to permit surface-independent diving.

The first breakthrough in attempting to provide a more manoeuvrable variant of the diving bell for subaquatic operatives came courtesy of Breslau-born Prussian engineer Karl Henrich Klingert. He created the device from which all subsequent diving bell-independent life-support suits stem, with his 1797 invention of a suit directly connected to an air supply system on the surface.[25] Klingert thereby bypassed the use of a diving bell, providing the diver with a far less unwieldy support system that allowed him to explore his surroundings at will. The connection to the surface, rather than to a diving bell, theoretically allowed the diver to operate for as long as he liked, greatly increasing operation times. The Klingert suit was operated by the use of a large cylindrical iron helmet moulded into a domed shell that totally covered the head of the diver. The metallic nature of the helmet and its shape had two features which served to increase subaquatic operation times. Firstly, due to the durable material used, water pressure was less likely to induce barotraumas in the operator. Secondly,

24   Figuier, L., *Les Merveilles de la Science ou Description Populaire des Inventions Modernes*, p.629.
25   Figuier, L., *Les Merveilles de la Science ou Description Populaire des Inventions Modernes*, pp.635–647.

two tubes were inserted through holes bored into the helmet and were attached to the surface, allowing the intake of fresh air and the expulsion of used air. Consequently, carbon dioxide build-up was avoided and the atmosphere within the apparatus could be maintained at an acceptable level indefinitely. The adjective 'suit' is slightly misleading, as apart from the helmet, the remaining parts of the outfit only consisted of a pair of leather pants and a non-descript jacket. It was on top of this jacket that the helm rested on the user's shoulders. The practical rationale for the lack of protection below the neck was that the pressures encountered at 6–7 metres – the maximum depth at which this novel diving gear operated – did not negatively affect exceptionally sensitive areas of the body such as the inner ear.

The next step in the evolution of the diving suit would have to wait another 50 years, coming about through the agency of 19th-century Germany's archnemesis, the Second French Empire. Joseph Martin Caribol, following up the work of exceptional Anglo-German inventor Augustus Siebe, developed a phenomenal breakthrough in independent diving. His suit, which would become his namesake, was composed of two parts rather than the mono-form Klingert suit. The first part was, like Klingert's device, a metal helmet mounted on a metal shoulder plate, reinforced against water infiltration. A circular window was forged in the superstructure and protected against floating objects with an iron grill. Like previous attempts at more independent diving apparatus, this headgear involved the imposition of a twin pipe system to facilitate the exchange of spent and fresh air. An interesting development was the inclusion of a valve on the side of the helmet which the diver could adjust himself, either to admit more air or to allow the extraction of air. The Caribol suit was a significant step in the independence of divers, as it removed the necessity to communicate with surface operators. This resulted in greater autonomy for the diver when underwater. The potential danger of the helmet uncoupling from the main portion of the suit was mitigated by the use of a weight hung across the operator's chest.[26] The inclusion of this weight also aided the diver's stability whilst in the depths, keeping him rooted to the seabed and providing some protection against the locomotive power of the waves above. However, the Caribol family of underwater life support systems unfortunately continued a flaw that existed in previous suits, as it had still not broken the reliance on a surface-based air supply. Although mission times could be extended and the diver could work unmolested by the need to keep in contact with the surface, he did still rely on the surface for life-giving oxygen. What was needed for increased diver independence was the rebreather.

A rebreather is a device that undertakes the work of the various breathing tubes hitherto used to bring surface air into the diver's lungs. Instead of providing raw air into the interior of a watertight helmet, rebreathers provide air directly to the mouth. More importantly, they constantly work to recycle breathed air, nullifying the requirement for a connection between the surface and diver. This means that the

26   Figuier, L., *Les Merveilles de la Science ou Description Populaire des Inventions Modernes*, pp.637–671.

surface supply of fresh oxygen and the extraction of depleted oxygen are no longer required,[27] as this can all be accomplished by the diver whilst under the sea or river. Given the scientific progress that such an invention required, it was not until the late 1870s that one came about. The prohibitive issue facing those investigating how to recycle oxygen lay in failing to comprehend that spent air becomes not just unusable, but deadly. When humans respire, they take in air – a mixture of oxygen and nitrogen – and expel carbon dioxide. In pre-rebreather diving helmets, no distinction was made between fresh air – oxygen and nitrogen – and spent air made up of carbon dioxide. The air in diving helmets would become toxic if too much spent air built up inside. It was for this reason that all diving suit designs until the late 19th century had an extraction tube alongside the air intake tube. If they had not, then depleted air, mainly composed of expelled carbon dioxide, would form the atmosphere inside the helmet, causing in the diver madness, loss of consciousness and eventually death. Although scientists did not as yet understand the exact processes, the effects of 'bad air' were clear. The only known treatment until the late 1800s was the extraction of breathed air and its replacement with new air via the air intake tube. When the secret of how to convert 'bad air' back to 'good air' was then discovered, it permanently changed the operational capabilities of divers. To invent air recycling, however, would require the discovery of the process of oxygen depletion.

Like so much of the progress which led to the science of modern warfare, and indeed contemporary life in general, the seminal development for understanding oxygen depletion came in the mid-18th century. The scientific investigation into the matter was led by Cambridge-educated priest Stephen Hales. Through experimentation, Hales deduced that air lost its life-sustaining properties after two-and-a-half minutes, discovering this by happening upon a correlation between the heat in a room, the room's humidity and the fall in air quality.[28] The reason for this is that the more carbon dioxide there is in a room, the greater the incremental heat increase. Later examinations carried out by Hales on the effect on mortality of human concentration within interior spaces came to a similar conclusion – that shared air becomes less nourishing more quickly. Although a decade would pass before oxygen and nitrogen were identified as the components of air, the rough identification of the concept of oxygen depletion had been made. Being only one step away from a correct analysis allowed Hales to design the first ventilator in 1740, using this rudimentary understanding of oxygen content decline. In the story of the modern diver, the importance of this discovery was the first successful attempt at an elementary rebreather, due to Hales identifying that one could extract carbon dioxide from spent air if that spent air was forced through a chemical solution, leaving just oxygen and nitrogen. He found this chemical in a combination of salt and tarter, and in applying the solution

27   Vann, R., Denoble, P. *et al.*, *Rebreather Forum 3 Proceedings* (Durham: PADI, 2014).
28   Smith, I.B., 'The Impact of Stephen Hales on Medicine', *Journal of the Royal Society of Medicine*, Vol, 86 (June 1993).

to a flannel liner he created what is now called a chemical scrubber. This rudimentary solution solved, for the first time, the issue of independent breathing within a hostile chemical environment. The leap into applying this system to diving, though, would require another century-and-a-half of development.

For the world of diving – and military diving in particular – all that was needed to create the first agile surface-independent life-support system by the 1880s was a rebreather that did not require a helm to house it. The man to produce this ground-breaking system was Wiltshire born engineer Henry Fleuss. The idea of what would become the first independent breathing apparatus for divers came to Fleuss whilst he was visiting Ceylon (modern Sri Lanka) on behalf of the P&O maritime logistics firm. Whilst observing the island's pearl divers, he became obsessed with the manner in which they could free-dive without relying on surface oxygen supplies. Fleuss was eager to move the concept of surface-independent diving to Western Europe, but with the added ingredient of finding a way to enable long-duration dives.[29] The resulting synthesis would produce the capability for divers to engage in dives that had a longer possible duration and enjoy almost total autonomy from the surface. In short, he sought to create the technological space for the emergence of the modern diver. Through ingesting the work of Hales and the subsequent chemists who looked into oxygen and carbon dioxide, Fleuss came to understand that strongly alkali chemicals absorb carbon dioxide. The conclusion he arrived at was that if an individual diver could have an instrument that carried both a powerfully alkaline chemical and air, then it would allow the diver an inexhaustible reserve of clean air.

From 1878-79, Fleuss tinkered alone with his revolutionary concept until he met up with a chemist with an intense interest in toxic chemicals, Dr Benjamin Ward Richardson. In 1880, the two men demonstrated the fruit of their labour by placing a leather mask containing their proto-rebreather on a volunteer who was then sent into a chamber full of poison gas. The experiment proved a success, and in 1881 Fleuss produced the first diving suit which did not require a heavy helmet. The only vestige of the traditional heavy diving equipment of the past was the retention of weighted boots to hold the diver onto the seabed. In place of the old style of large headgear, Fleuss' apparatus consisted of a front-mounted air bag and a back-mounted alkali case, made of metal and secured with screws. A mask connected to the breathing chamber and the alkali case was then placed on the face of the diver. This created an air recycling circuit that was termed an aqualung. Two further versions of the suit were developed in 1902 and 1906, each one reducing the size of the air recycling circuit.[30] The final variant led to something very similar to that which divers use today, with a mouth-piece and nose clip in place of the leather full mask, but the diver was still unable to swim. The idea of the modern diver – unburdened by dependence on the surface, free of complicated tube systems and liberated from the constraints of metal helmets

29   Jackson, P., 'The Fleuss Apparatus', *Historical Diver*, Vol. 10, Issue 2 (2002).
30   Jackson, P., 'The Fleuss Apparatus'.

– was breathtakingly close to its apotheosis. One requirement remained – to be free of the burdensome weights which secured the diver in place but simultaneously robbed his freedom of action. Sadly for our story, the solution to this issue would emerge only in 1927 with the adoption by the Royal Navy of the Davis Submerged Escape Apparatus. Yet by 1915, the enhanced independence of divers meant the return of the military diver was only a stone's throw away.

5

The Great Opportunity of 1915
A Betrayal Foretold – the Triple Alliance

On the 30 September 1896, two men sat across the diplomatic table and discussed a single burning issue stemming from a dispute over an ancient spit of land off the North African coast. The resulting conversation was amenable to both sides, and before long French Foreign Minister Theophile Declasse and his Italian counterpart, Emilio Visconti Venosta, had agreed the Franco-Italian Accords.[1] The agreement sought to address citizenship queries relating to Italians living in Tunisia after France's shock annexation of the territory in 1881. The seizure had caused uproar in Rome, which had considerable economic interests in Tunis itself, interests which were long seen as a prelude to Italian annexation. The French blocking of Italian designs on Tunisia had been the apotheosis of a 19-year-long break between France and Italy. Once close allies, they had fallen out over the question of the Papal States – the only sovereign state aside from Italy to exist in the peninsula by 1862.[2] The Italians had held up the theocracy as an obstruction to the *Risorgimento*, believing it to be incomplete without possessing Rome. The French commitment to the Vatican dated back to the liberal mania that had spread across Europe throughout 1848. On 29 April that fateful year, Pope Pius IX declared the liberal movement as irreconcilable to the values of the Catholic Church. The reaction to his rejection of modernity had already been foreseen by Klemens von Metternich, the leading 19th–century Austrian diplomat. A year after Pius' ascension, the wily Metternich had declared that "Never [having] turned his mind towards matters of government ... [Pius] is in a net from which he no longer knows how to disentangle himself ... he will be driven out of Rome."[3]

The prophetic words of Europe's Svengali of realpolitik were later proved utterly correct. On 14 November 1848, the Holy See's first minister – Count Pellegrino

1   Fenby, J., *The History of Modern France*, p.232.
2   Pecout, G., *Il Lungo Risorgimento*, pp.197–207.
3   Norwich, J., *The Popes: A History* (London: Vintage Publishing, 2012), p.382.

Rossi – was hacked to death by the notoriously boisterous Roman mob. The imperilled pope was rescued by the daring endeavours of France's ambassador to the Vatican, Duke Eugene d'Harcourt. The rescue, authorized by Louis-Napoleon Bonaparte's administration (1848–70), was part of a desperate plea to France's concerned Catholic population, which felt grave concern stemming from their country's recent revolution of 1848. The excessively cruel secularization policies following the radical overhaul of the French state in 1789 had left painful scars in rural France. The official position of the Francophone Church, encapsulated by Lyon's Archbishop, Louis Jacques de Bonald, was one of tentative support for the second revolution, hoping to avoid the consequences of the first. The trust of the paranoid French laity would be harder to win over. The evolving question over the Papal States amidst the Italian revolutions of 1848 was seen as a perfect opportunity to set out the new republic's Christian credentials. The opening now being eyed by republican France had been formed at the beginning of the year. Unrest in Rome due to the absence of their Papal ruler had blossomed, facilitating the rise of a revolutionary republic in the city. The new state born on 9 February 1849 called itself the Roman Republic, the first such state in just under 2,000 years. Under the leadership of Italian radical Giuseppe Mazzini, the beating metropolitan heart of the Catholic faith would become a bastion of the liberal revolution (see Chapter 2).The taking of the city by heretical forces then allowed the clarion call for President Louis-Napoleon Bonaparte's *faux* anti-secular mission to be issued, driving the French towards a confrontation with the new Italian Kingdom.

On 18 April 1849, an expeditionary force of 7,000 men under Louis-Napoleon's orders left the bustling port city of Marseilles for Rome. After a brief conflict through late spring into early summer, a struggle began over Rome's formidable defences began. The last stand mounted by the Republic was in vain, however, and on 30 June the short-lived revolutionary state fell to General Nicolas Oudinot's forces. St Peter's baroque throne, which had sat vacant for nearly a year, anxiously waited for the return of its master. The chair, though, would have to wait a little longer. The upheaval of 1848–49 had thoroughly shaken Pope Pius, who requested the maintenance of a French garrison to act as his protectors. The request was granted in April 1850, and two years later the now Emperor Louis-Napoleon III formally recognized the permanent nature of the French presence. From then on, the Second French Empire (1852–70) was intimately tied to Papal defence policy. The Papacy came to regard the French military as the pinnacle of martial prowess, trusting its generals to run their armies in the stead of Italian candidates. The Frankish obsession of Papal strategists was first revealed in September 1860, when a Savoyard army marched south to dislodge the revolutionary Giuseppe Garibaldi from Napoli. Whilst they crossed through central Italy, the Savoyard King Victor Emmanuel II had subtly redirected his forces to take the remaining Papal States of Marche, Umbria and Abruzzo. The battles of Loreto, Perugia and Ancona throughout early autumn had seen the Italians grapple with significant numbers of French volunteers, including the Papal army's General Christophe de

Lamoriciere.[4] The growing anti-French feeling that these events had driven into the psychology of the Italian decision-making class could have been halted by 1864's September Convention, a negotiated settlement whereby the Franco-Papal alliance could be eased out of via the progressive withdrawal of his holiness's French bodyguards over a two-year period. Unfortunately, Garibaldi had other ideas, the early autumn of 1867 witnessing the vengeance-fuelled mustering of the Red Shirts for one more march on Rome.

The Garibaldist movement, once so noble, was becoming an anachronism. The Red Shirts and their leader had failed to understand that the Italian state was now the chief agent of the *Risorgimento*. King Victor Emmanuel II saw cooperation with France over the Papacy as a far more potent weapon than the outdated *élan* of the mass movement. The government in Torino saw the September Convention as the first step in detaching Rome from France, with a view to its bloodless assimilation. Alarmed by Garibaldi's mustering of men, a Savoyard force was sent to detain him. The firebrand's escape was perhaps inevitable, but Paris could not go back on its oath to the Papacy. On 3 November 1867, as Garibaldi approached Rome, he was halted by a French Army under General Balthazar Alban Gabrielbg. A one-sided battle evolved 10 miles from Rome, at the small town of Mentana. By the end of the day, some 1,100 Red Shirts had been cut down, against just 38 French dead. The cult of personality which surrounded Garibaldi, once fostered by the House of Savoy, now turned into an international relations nightmare.[5] The French Revolution of 1789 and the Liberal eruption which occurred after its collapse in 1815 had hammered home the message that a vibrant, fresh and dynamic public opinion now existed. Governments had been rendered impotent against waves of popular sentiment, lest they fall afoul of the regicidal radicals of the 19th century. Had the Battle of Mentana simply represented a diplomatic incident between two governments, the cracks might have been painted over. However, the intercession of an incensed, emboldened public rendered this possibility moot. The insinuation of a Franco-Papal conspiracy against the Italian Kingdom, apparently exhibited at Mentana, throughout the September campaign of 1860 and through the Papal rescue of 1848–49 fell on receptive Italian ears.

Italian hostility to the Vatican had begun long before their more recent ill-feeling towards Paris. Since the original sparking of the European liberal revolutionary epoch of 1789–1848, both the Sardinian and the successive Italian legislature had been dominated by liberal intellectualism. Senators and deputies were drawn primarily from Italy's highly developed northern metropolises, where French Jacobinism had been felt the strongest.[6] A second potent anti-Clerical strand in the Italian bicameral system – the legislative body having two chambers – hailed from ferociously anti-Catholic cities in central Italy, a series of conurbations whose citizens had only just escaped the

4   Norwich, J., *The Popes: A History*, p.395.
5   Pecout, G., *Il Lungo Risorgimento*, pp.180–185.
6   Pecout,. G., *Il Lungo Risorgimento*, p.65.

unenlightened tyranny of Papal governance. The preponderance of anti-Clerical feeling among Italy's legislators allowed for an anti-Papist legislative norm. The first Francesco Crispi administration (1887–89) exemplified this, introducing sweeping laws curtailing political freedoms and mercilessly harassing the rights of Catholic politicians.[7] The 1860s had seen the liberals displaced as a force of virulent anti-Christianity by a new atheistic wind blowing in from the East. The vanguard of this radical migratory breeze came in the dishevelled form of the Russian Mikhail Bakunin. Born in the rather obscure Tver Oblast on the eve of Napoleon's 1814 exile to Elbe, Bakunin had settled in Florence in 1864.[8] The radical Tuscan underground soon became the focus for his philosophizing. Among his more insidious musings were those regarding the Church; writing in his 1882 work *God and the State*, he eulogizes on the constricting nature of theism. Bakunin writes: "Oppressors take advantage of the religious because many religious people reconcile themselves with injustice on earth by the promise of heaven." The observation is none too original, yet it serves to illustrate the ease with which a *de facto* anti-Papal union between the old Jacobin-inspired liberal establishment and the young anti-theistic left-wing radicals could come into being. The presence of these two forces, one rising and one declining, would give Francophobia a deeper intellectual meaning than it would otherwise have had. The mis-association of the Lateran and Tuileries palaces was reinforced by the French willingness to aid the Vatican and a Vatican willingness to call for French support.

A powerful suspicion towards Parisian intentions *vis-à-vis* Papal-controlled Rome fostered an imagined union of objectives between both states. The unspoken unitary hypothesis, vented by the wild rantings of Italy's most extreme church burners, became increasingly difficult to refute by the close of the 1860s. The high-pitched screeching of extreme intellectualism would soon be vindicated in its fog of international para-noia. On 4 September 1870, Emperor Louis-Napoleon Bonaparte III surrendered in the penultimate battle of the Franco-Prussian War of 1870–71. The war, deliberately begun in July 1870 by Prussia's Machiavellian chancellor, Otto von Bismarck,[9] had seen the French troops based in Rome hastily transferred, to fuel a doomed defence against Prussia's relentless invaders. France was paralyzed by an oncoming siege of Paris, and on 20 September – a day after Prussian artillery had begun its reduction of the boulevards of Paris – Italian forces circled on a vulnerable Rome.[10] A last pre-battle appeal to the Pope was made by the 60-year-old Senator Gustavo Ponza di San Martino. Pius chose to remain defiant, replying: "I cannot respond to the questions in your letter, I cannot (either) adhere to the principles it contains … . I appeal again to god … to free Rome from every danger."[11] The resulting siege was quick and relatively

7   Cuccu, L., *Storia della Burocrazia Italiana: Dalla Riforma Cavour alle Riforme Bassanini* (L'Universale Cagliari: L'Universale, 2018), pp.25–29.
8   Leier, M., *Bakunin: The Creative Passion* (New York: Thomas Dunne Books, 2007), pp.11–13.
9   Clark, C., *Iron Kingdom: The Rise and Downfall of Prussia*, pp.550–552.
10   Taylor, A.J.P., *The Struggle for Mastery in Europe*, p.209.
11   Norwich, J., *The Popes: A History*, pp.399–400.

bloodless, the crowning glory of the Italian army that day coming with the storming of the Aurelian walls by extravagantly dressed *Bersaglieri*. By nightfall, the dazzling array of nationalities defending the Holy See flew their white flags of surrender. The terms of the capitulation were not truly formalized until 13 May the following year.[12] Apart from Roman assimilation, the matter of the Vatican's existence as a sovereign state had to be addressed. The Law of Guarantees was designed to answer this question. The Lateran and Vatican palaces would be the Papacy's only sovereign territory, and the Pope would receive a significant stipend. Crucially, the Vatican was to be allowed to operate a separate diplomatic corps, a concession which permitted it to set an independent foreign policy and a portentous decision whose implications for Franco-Italian relations were easy to foresee.

On 8 February 1871, among the rubble of a once-glorious global capital, yet another Parisian upheaval was in the works. Outraged at the indignities placed on France by the Versailles Treaty closing the Franco-Prussian conflict, radical politicians of the French left such as Louis Blanc and Felix Pyat agitated for revolution.[13] Soon, the city's militia – the National Guard – began to clash with regular soldiers and an uprising was on the cards. The revolt desired not the mock constrained outcomes of the risings of 1830 and 1848, but for a return to the anarchic *tabula rasa* of 1789. From March until 28 May, clashes burned across Paris. By the time the streets came under government control, 25,000 radicals lay dead on the city's blood-soaked pavements.[14] A French government was once again faced with the need to soothe the tempers of the country's petrified Catholics. The Third Republic, declared immediately after Napoleon III's abdication in early September, had been steered through the crisis by a cuttingly intelligent revolutionary of the old school, Adolphe Thiers. To win over the jumpy Catholics, Thiers set about a policy of reconnection with the recently emasculated Vatican. The effort was successful and in 1892 Pope Leo XIII dispatched the '*Au Mileu des Solicitudes*', an encyclical directed at the immense French flock. The Papal document spoke to a sincere desire on behalf of the Church for devout Frenchmen to cooperate with the minimalist revolution in Paris. Once again it seemed as if France and the Vatican were rekindling threatening relationships, when perceived through the prism of Roman anti-Clericalism. The dreamt-up return to the dangerous collaboration of Napoleon III was, however, semi-fictional. Of far greater concern was France's seemingly cavalier attitude to Italian claims on the world stage. The aforementioned Tunisian affair of 1881 had echoed far louder than Vatican-French *rapprochement*, which merely fuelled a grander paranoid delusion born of the Italian public consciousness.

Tunisia had been a wake-up call, adding reality to wild claims of Franco-Papal cooperation. Consequently, a search began from the newly liberated Rome for allies

12   Norwich, J., *The Popes: A History*, p.400.
13   Fenby, J., *The History of Modern France*, p.166.
14   Badsey, S., *The Franco-Prussian War 1870–1871* (Oxford: Osprey Publishing, 2003), p.4.

against an ostentatiously pro-Papal and fervently anti-Italian French state. One option stood on the banks of the River Spree, observing the plays of Wildenbruch and the operas of Wagner, while staring east to the untamed wilds of Poland. Twenty-five years ago, these unusual friends had bested a poorly led Austrian army at Koniggratz,[15] delivering for their Junkers in Berlin a famed victory. Since the breathtaking 1866 confrontation between Austria and Prussia, the fortunes of House Hohenzollern had increased exponentially. Not since the days of King Frederick II (the Great) had the fledgling Prussian power had such a run of good luck. It was under Prussian bayonets that Sedan had been stormed and France's attempts at a European restoration broken in the war of 1870–71. The space left in European politics by Paris' collapse swiftly led to German unification under the Prussian eagle. On 18 January 1871, Kaiser Wilhelm I had been declared Emperor of the Germans, bringing into existence a unitary German state.[16] The Italians had never forgotten what the Prussians had achieved for them in 1866, saving their young state from certain defeat at the hands of Austria in the aftermath of Italian defeats at Lissa and Custoza in June and July respectively. Without the Prussian success at Koniggratz on 3 July, Veneto – and with it Venezia – would have remained in Habsburg hands. The *Risorgimento* would have been permanently crippled and the ability to embark on the conquest of a greater Italy rendered unthinkable. Since their Teutonic salvation, a certain Germanophilia had emerged among the Italian intellectual classes.[17] Cultural connections were made and advancements in science, philosophy, literary forms and architecture were freely shared. Italian historian and senator Benedetto Croce attests to an intense encroachment of German thinking on Italian universities, cocooning Italy's future leaders in Germanism. The secularized world view of not just the Prussians, but many northern states which formed the backbone of the German Empire, encouraged closer cooperation too. The Germans would never contact the Pope, nor contest Italian authority in Rome, and its forces were perceived now to be as unmatched as their Prussian forbears had been. In many ways, it was a perfect ally against French ambitions.

The prospective anti-French alliance with the German Empire was inconveniently frustrated by the presence of Berlin's friendly view towards the Habsburg Empire, a state which saw the Italian Kingdom as an abhorrence. The Italian Kingdom had attempted to bury the hatchet with its former masters in the wake of the Great Eastern Crisis (1875–78), when Marco Minghetti's second administration (1873-76) perceived Austrian insecurity in the east.[18] The plan to calm tensions between the states was subsequently put on the back burner, but France's Tunisian adventure compelled Italy to act. The diplomatic fallout from this had provoked a panicked Agostino Depretis government (1881-87) to strive for

---

15   Bassett. R, *For God and Kaiser*, pp.333–349.
16   Taylor, A.J.P., *The Struggle for Mastery in Europe*, p.189.
17   Pecout, G., *Il Lungo Risorgimento*, p.197.
18   Lepre, A. & Petraccone, C., *Storia D'Italia Dall'Unita a Oggi* (Bologna: Il Mulino, 2008).

Habsburg friendship. Foolish pride made such overtures useless, and an outright refusal from Vienna was hastily issued. The Germans soon took the decision out of Habsburg Emperor Franz Josef I's hands as serious events were afoot in France. On 14 November 1881, the revanchist candidate for the French Third Republic's elections, Leon Gambetta, won a supermajority at the head of a leftist coalition. He had won a landslide victory with 411 of 545 seats through expressing exuberant promises of reconquering the Rhineland – given to Germany in 1871 – and alliances with London.[19] In Berlin, both Chancellor Bismarck and Kaiser Wilhelm I understood the danger. An ally on France's border was desperately needed. Fortunately, in 1873 Russia had left Bismarck's chief continental alliance – the Three Emperors League – over events in the Balkans. The foreign policy goals of both Vienna and St Petersburg in that region made a continuous mutual pan-European alliance an impossibility. The current pact to which Germany belonged was solely with Austria, and the gap left by Russia had to be filled. Austrian reticence up until Gambetta's election had been a previously immovable object to any deal with Rome. Yet Germany had controlled Austria's actions since removing it from the western sphere in 1866's Peace of Prague, robbing Austria of any say in German affairs. Consequently, Vienna would have no choice but to play ball with Berlin, a form of subjugation which would only increase in the countdown to the First World War.

On 20 May 1882, Italy joined the Triple Alliance at the request of Berlin.[20] The coalition principally dealt with the French menace, but the alliance's central defensive obligations also came with unforeseen strings which ran counter to Italy's grand strategy. Italy still yearned for the completion of the Greater Italy vision. For that to come true, Dalmatia, Trieste, Istria and Tyrol had to come under the control of the Savoyard kings. These longed-for Adriatic prizes, however, were wrapped up in what was called the Eastern Question, a term referring to speculation over what the eventual carve-up of the Ottoman Empire would entail. If Italy was isolated from that discussion, the Balkan chimera to which it ascribed would again slip into the hands of others, yet to retain those territories would entail fundamentally weakening Austria-Hungary. The German Empire set out to walk the tightrope of tying both diametrically opposed powers together.[21] Bismarck would do this by simply taking the Balkans out of the reach of Italian strategists. The drafting of the treaty would allow for its seamless exclusion. The primary treaty obligation relating to Italy was that it was only needed to come in to defend the German Empire against France. The anticipated requirement to aid Austria never came. The Austro-Hungarian objectives for any war in Europe lay only in the Eastern Question; excluding Italy from 'aiding' Austria would leave it without a claim to be considered in the eastern peace. Rome had

19   Fenby, J., *The History of Modern France*, p.209.
20   Taylor, A.J.P., *The Struggle for Mastery in Europe*, pp.325–346.
21   Clark, C., *Iron Kingdom: The Rise and Downfall of Prussia*, p.345.

been trapped, tied to a position in the west where it had no interest save self-defence, whilst at the same time its eastern hands had been severed. The question for Berlin was whether the Savoyard kings would make good on such an unprofitable alliance.

To War with a Sheathed Blade – the Making of Italian Neutrality

When Otto von Bismarck lobbied the Austrian emperor to accept Italy's intrusion into the Pan-German alliance, he had believed that Italian national ambition could be controlled. The blocking of the road to Vienna and the Balkan territories it yearned for left Italy with an empty space in the body politic. The disabling of this final chapter of the *Risorgimento* flowed parallel to the death of liberal nationalism.[22] By 1900, the liberal constitutionalism which had so dominated global politics in the Western world since 1815 had begun to ebb away. The same stagnation which had afflicted absolutist conservatism before 1789's storming of the Bastille now infected Italian liberalism too. The import of perilous ideas from the tyranny lying beyond the German Empire's eastern border had soon hastened Jacobinism's inexorable decline. The politicized youths who had once cried *'Viva Garibaldi, viva Italia'* now screeched *'Proletari di tutti i paesi, unitevi!'* (Proletarians of all countries, unite) with equal vigour. The Italian tricolour, once so provocative to the Austrian authorities in Venice, had been replaced by the stark red flag of organized labour. It was now Russophile philosophers in grizzly Slavic tones who prophesized doom for the established classes, in place of France's elegant rabble-rousers. The liberal order which had once seemed so fresh devolved into a repeat of the *ancien régime* dominated by fat, ranting, aged deputies and senators. Once heroes of the *Risorgimento*, their principles lay buried among bribes and mistresses. A testimony to their lethargy had been the 1882 execution of Guglielmo Oberdan in Trieste, shot by Habsburg authorities for merely showing support for the Greater Italy project. Italy's politicians did little in his name.[23] The Triple Alliance was simply too comfortable for protest.

The decline of enthusiasm for continuing the *Risorgimento* was combined with its completion being nullified by Germany. The acceptance of both truths had opened hitherto unconsidered avenues for advancing Italy's prestige among the great powers. Unfortunately, by the 1880s, the world's richest available locations had already been taken; only remote parts of Africa and the Chinese interior remained relatively untouched. East Africa currently hosted no serious competing interests, unlike North Africa, which had been found to be too contentious. The Italians had first arrived in East Africa in 1886, when a Genovese exploratory firm bought the Sultanate of Assab. By 1890, the modern territory of Eritrea had been founded as an Italian possession. To allow the Italian people to move on from the *Risorgimento* in the same way the politicians had would require a larger piece of land than a strip of hinterland opposite

22   Pecout, G., *Il Lungo Risorgimento*, pp.271–393.
23   Pecout, G., *Il Lungo Risorgimento*, pp.318–325.

Arabia. The Kingdom of Ethiopia was an obvious next step for Italy's colonial project. On 15 December 1894, the Francesco Crispi regime (1894-96) mounted a bid for conquest.[24] However, the two-year conflict proved humiliating; on 1 March 1896, four Italian generals were spectacularly defeated at the Battle of Adua. One of them, General Matteo Albertone, was even taken prisoner. The death of some 7,000 Italians was unacceptable even to the catatonic politicians in the senate and house of deputies.

The humiliation at Adua led to Crispi's resignation and ended his Pro-German government. He was replaced by Palermo native Antonio Starabba di Rudini. The Sicilian aristocrat had brought Italy's 'Historical Right' faction back into power after a 20-year absence. The cabal believed it represented the legacy of liberal nationalism which drove the *Risorgimento*. They proudly traced their lineage to Cavour – Camillo Benso, the Count of Cavour, first Prime Minister of the Kingdom of Italy – and found their origin story in the Kingdom of Piedmont-Sardinia. The faction's creation myth dictated a close orientation to France, rather than Germany, who did not share the same Napoleonic-inspired past as the Italian historical right. Realignment with Paris was made inevitable; to not do so would be to betray the party, and on 30 September 1896 the Tunis deal was hammered out. Soon after, agricultural trading was normalized and during the oppressive Parisian summer of 1902, a secret Italian neutrality agreement was signed. The duplicitous concord contained a binding promise to declare Italy neutral in case of a second Franco-German conflict. Napoleon III's 1858–64 *de facto* Franco-Italian alliance may not have been resurrected, but it was a start. When war eventually came on 28 July 1914, Rome stood in the eye of an information storm. Everyone from the Senators at the Palazzo Madama to the Deputies at Palazzo Montecitorio waited with bated breath for the verdict of Prime Minister Antonio Salandra and King Victor Emmanuel III. On 2 August, in a sauna-like session of Salandra's cabinet, the 1902 pact was honoured and a declaration of neutrality was proclaimed to the world.[25]

The fury was palpable in Vienna and Berlin, with the Chief of the German General Staff, Moltke the Younger, telling Austria's General Conrad von Hotzendorf: "Italy's felony will be revenged in history. May God now grant you victory so that later you can settle with these scoundrels."[26] His words referred to a mutual Italio-Habsburg revulsion which both states had always known would have to be sorted out, once again on the field of battle. A day later, Conrad unwittingly alluded to the circumstances which had led to Italy's expansion abroad, failure at Adua and now its return to the Balkan Question. Raging uncontrollably, he ranted: "Our future lies in the Balkans: our barrier is Italy: we must settle accounts with her." On 30 July 1914, the Russian Tsardom issued its mobilization orders. The next day, the massed ranks of German

24   Poma, S., *L'Italia in Guerra: La Grande Storia degli Italiani del Regno 1896–1943* (Cagliari: L'Universale, 2020), pp.41–52.
25   Lepre, A. & Petraccone, C., *Storia D'Italia Dall'Unita a Oggi.*
26   Herwig, H., *The First World War: Germany and Austria–Hungary, 1914–1918* (London: Arnold Publishing, 1997), p.32.

youth boarded cramped trains westward. Two days later, Germany declared war on France and the great curtain call on European global supremacy unfurled. A month later, Berlin, Paris, London, St Petersburg, Vienna and Brussels were engaged in frantic activity as Generals Kluck and Below threw a lost generation of German youth against General Lanzerac's Fifth Army to decide the fate of Paris.[27] Over 600 miles away, amid the baroque majesty of Rome's Palazzo della Consulta, foreign ministry typewriters lay silent. A legion of mobilization orders lay in the dusty drawers of forgotten cabinets, and the political elite sat to their lunches in the *faux* renaissance opulence of Rome's fine dining establishments. Lamentably for Austria, Conrad von Hotzendorf had spoken far too soon and its shameful advance into Serbia would call everything into question.

A Nemesis Broken – an Opportunity Beckons

On 12 August 1914, the Habsburg army had begun its journey from Bosnia to Belgrade. The 20th-century Austrian military was a different beast even to the one which had beaten the Italians at Custoza in 1866. Indeed, the imperial army was more divided in the summer of 1914 than at any time in its illustrious history. The establishment of what amounted to a separate Hungarian state in 1867 had granted the Magyars their own army.[28] Other nationalities soon followed, with each Diet (assembly) gaining a military force to control. The Common Army was the single central force responsible to Vienna, but fragmentation of the empire had begun to corrode even this central military structure.[29] Not satisfied with the concessions granted to it, the Hungarian Parliament insisted on the recognition of Hungarian as the realm's second language. For the Common Army, this had meant that all officers had to learn Hungarian and German to a reasonable degree. Additionally, the standard soldier had to know 80 words in German and Hungarian and a plethora of technical terms for pieces of equipment. Consequently, the command and control element had to be extraordinarily tight and continually present. The nature of the army also meant that it was based on conscription. The private soldiers and NCOs were present not due to patriotic fervour (though it was occasionally cited as a cause), but because they had to be. Prior to being press-ganged into the front line, a large proportion would never have left their home-towns. In such circumstances, the multilingual officer class assumes a disproportionate importance on the battlefield. The lack of an officer would force private soldiers and NCOs, to coordinate defence and attack with limited mutual intelligibility. The creativity otherwise available to a polyglot-led multi-ethnic force would rapidly disintegrate into predictable tactics – easily exploited by a skilled adversary.

27   Hastings, M., *Catastrophe: Europe Goes to War, 1914*, pp.159–200.
28   Taylor, A.J.P., *The Habsburg Monarchy*, p.131.
29   Bassett, R., *For God and Kaiser*, pp.365–498.

Externally, the changes to the Austrian Army were more welcome. Gone were the splendid white tunics of the line infantry, the dazzling breastplates of the cuirassier and the fabulous hats of the uhlans. The only vestige of the vainglorious age just passed were the feathered hats once sported by the jaegers – now the preserve of the Habsburg officer.[30] Modern dark blue uniforms dominated and a revolution in weaponry had made the Minié ball-firing rifles of the 19th-century Austrian Army obsolete. The rather drab-looking soldiery of the industrial age were misleading in their modesty; in their sun-soaked hands that summer, the columns of Austrian infantrymen held truly awesome degrees of firepower. The bullet and the bolt action firearm now ruled the day. The massed ranks trudging through the bone dry earth tracks of the Serbian summer came sporting a mix of Steyr M1912 and Mannlicher bolt action rifles and Rast & Gasser M1898 revolvers. Behind the relatively rapid pace of Germans, Magyars and Slavs came the innovative and supremely effective 1908-built, 8x50mmR Mannlicher-firing, toggle-delay, blowback-operated, 580 rounds per minute Schwarzlose machine gun. After traipsing through the countryside for three days, the *Vojska Kraljevine Srbije* (Serbian Royal Army) finally gave Conrad von Hotzendorf his long-awaited battle for the future of the Serbian Kingdom. The conclusion of the confrontation in the heavily wooded hills surrounding Mount Cer[31] would either cement Austria's military reputation or damage it irreparably. The 289m-tall mountain stands along a collection of similar geological structures, the highest of which reaches 400m. The territory overwhelmingly supports the defender. The preponderance of formation-breaking heights, with their restrictive wooded environment, makes continuity of command difficult. Acceptable grounds for contest by arms in such terrain are formed of isolated copses, rare clearings and occasional groves. It was poor luck for the Habsburgs, as the terrain called for close and consistent small-squad tactical supremacy if victory was to be achieved.

The Austrians took the defensive advantage and at 11.00 pm on 15 August, the two sides had their respective baptisms of fire. A merciless combat commenced, with the mosquito-infested heat of a Balkan August making everything more difficult. Lost-looking German youths fired off their rapid-fire Mannlicher rifles, utilizing its micro-delay eliminating, straight pull bolt action for a speed advantage over the M1895 Mauser-wielding Serbs. The standardized Budapest-forged rifles fired 8x50mmR Mannlicher rounds at speeds of 620m/s. Unlucky Serb fighters in the rifle's 2,000m set iron sights, received ruthless 2,042 joule impacts that sliced through flesh causing ceaseless haemorrhaging, with 25.83mm projectiles ejecting their casing for maximum force.[32] The Serbian Mauser, once manufactured by German industry, now cut down Berlin's incompetent allies in droves. Serb riflemen might have fired more slowly than their Germanic rivals, but the 2,742 joule, 700m/s, 7×75mm Mauser rounds were

30   Bassett, R., *For God and Kaiser*, pp.458–480.
31   Hastings, M., *Catastrophe: Europe Goes to War, 1914*, p.151
32   Thomas, N., *Armies in the Balkans 1914–18* (Oxford: Osprey Publishing, 2001).

anything but underwhelming. Born into a culture of resistance, martyrdom and sacrifice, Serb regulars maintained a dogged determination, retreating only when the Habsburgs' state-of-the-art Schwarzlose machine guns arrived. The 41.4kg squad support weapon would then spew 8x50mmR Mannlicher rifle rounds, at formidable speeds of up to 580 rounds per minute. The appearance of one of these guns was rendered even more deadly by its reliable nature, utilizing a toggle-delayed blowback to minimize barrel pressurization. The weapon's durability, rarely suffering accidental overheating of ammunition in the chamber, would force Serb units to call for their Maxim guns – Russian weaponry which exchanged safety for speed, achieving obscene rates of fire.[33]

The battle's claustrophobic environs made close-quarters combat a frequent affair. One account records how an axe-wielding Serbian lieutenant general engaged the 9.8in. bayonets of Magyar infantrymen in single combat.[34] Such fever-pitched fighting allowed the advancements in personal defence weaponry to be magnificently showcased. Gone were the clumsy single action revolvers seen at Lissa. Now, close combat was settled with double action revolvers and recoil-dependant handguns. The officer-to-officer clashes witnessed on Mount Cer's peaks featured M1912 9mm eight-round pistols coming into contact with robust 7.62mm Nagant M1895 revolvers in epic duels. The decisive moment across the six-day battle came with a hurricane of artillery fire. Commanded by King Peter Karadodevic I himself,[35] a complement of French-built Canon de 75 Modele 1897 guns spat out barrages of 5.3kg impact-detonating high explosive rounds. Some rounds prepared by the gun crews were set only to detonate on a timer, leading to the horrifying spectacle of steel shells violently exploding only after penetrating an enemy formation. Even more deadly were 7.24kg shrapnel shells which intentionally burst above advancing infantry,[36] each shell leading to the showering of 290 piping-hot lead balls into Austrian heads. The gun's immense 500m/s muzzle velocity added to its dreadful potency, and its 6-mile range allowed it to harry retreating formations. The Habsburg army could not withstand much more of the inferno it had entered, and on 20 August its formations were in general retreat. The victorious Serbs counted some 3,000 dead across the battlefield, the defeated Viennese a staggering, 28,000.

The path to the decimation of the Austro-Hungarians during their final retreat in December 1914 owed much to the Battle of Mount Cer. The near-mythological resistance of the Serbian army against a far larger and, on the surface, more advanced military showed the world Austria-Hungary's weakness. The disaster at Mount Cer was repeated twice more before the Habsburgs were forced to retreat actross the River Sava. By the time they had begun to withdraw, summer had passed and winter rains had deluged the river, swelling it greatly. To make matters worse, the Austro-Hungarian army was

33   Thomas, N., *Armies in the Balkans 1914–18*.
34   Bassett, R., *For God and Kaiser*, pp.458–480.
35   Hastings, M., *Catastrophe: Europe Goes to War, 1914*, pp.138–159.
36   Thomas, N., *Armies in the Balkans 1914–18*, p.87.

constantly harassed by Montenegrin partisans, whose wild reputation instilled an inca-
pacitating terror into central European conscript and Serb alike. On 15 December, the
presence of a single bridge over the overflowing Sava forced the Habsburg soldiery to
queue to cross, allowing the Montenegrin clansmen to catch up to them in force.[37] Eager
Balkan trigger fingers pressed hard on their Russian-made Mosin Nagant M1891 rifles.
The weapon, modest in Russian hands, became savage in those of the southern Slavs.
The once-restless students pressed into service from Vienna, Budapest and Prague learnt
to respect the authority of the bullet that day. Before the first Austrian trooper had even
mounted his Viennese bound train, the Russian attaché in Belgrade had written that
"The Serbs will fight like lions."[38] He was right. The Austrian pursuance of the Serbian
issue had led the Viennese elite to neglect the old enemy, whose ire was as incurable as
their ambition. Under bright midwinter skies, Italian Prime Minister Antonio Salandra
read the news of Austria's humiliating defeat with cautious glee. The Italian Kingdom
now gazed across the Adriatic with hungry eyes, asking if somewhere as unimportant as
the Serbian Kingdom could defeat Austria, why could Italy not do the same?

The Peace is Dead – Long Live the War

The death nail for Italian neutrality had not, in fact, had much to do with Italian
politics, but had instead been plotted in the dreary confines of Britain's House of
Commons. By January 1915, it had become clear that the Western Front had hope-
lessly stalled. The Germans had not expected the French to offer such intense resistance, nor had they believed that the British Army would perform so exceptionally.[39]
The Belgians had unexpectedly ended the mobile war in October 1914 when they
flooded the River Yser on the night of the 26th, whilst under intense and persistent German attacks. On the Eastern Front, the Habsburg Empire had performed
appallingly, first against the Serbs and then in Galicia against the Russians.[40] Despite
spoiling events turning the tide against the Central Powers, it was clear in London
and Paris that there would be stalemate for the near future. The British, being permanently fixated on the Empire, presented a different vision. The ever-eccentric spirit
that frequently motored British policies around the globe was on full display as the
'Eastern Lobby' began its inexorable rise in decision-making circles. Its adherents
believed that the French war would lead, eventually, to failure, and that in consequence the only way to weaken the German Empire was through attacking its allies.
    In August 1914, the relatively underfunded and underequipped Serbian Army
had pushed back a supposedly world-class force. The conclusion that the British and

37   Bassett, R., *For God and Kaiser*, pp.472–473.
38   Clark, C., *The Sleepwalkers: How Europe Went to War in 1914*, p.468.
39   Herwig, H., *The First World War: Germany and Austria-Hungary, 1914–1918*, pp.29–33.
40   Stone, N., *The Eastern Front 1914–1917* (London: Penguin Publishing, 1998), pp.70–92.

Italians had shared was that the untested strength with which the Habsburg Empire had swaggered about for half a century had been found to be an illusion. The British reasoned that if an allied force could link up with Serbia from the south, then they could jointly march on Vienna. The elimination of Austro-Hungary would follow, allowing the Russians to bring all their force to bear against Germany. After that, it was theorized that the Germans in the west would be easier to crack. It was among this same feast of ideas that the Gallipoli campaign was conceived. The hindsight so often touted around Gallipoli's launch and poor progress was not possessed by the Habsburg monarchy. The potential success of an operation around Gallipoli in order to land allied forces in Greece severely rattled Emperor Franz Josef, who hastily sent a petition to Rome to secure Italian neutrality.[41] Vienna had attempted the same overtures on 9 August, just as the war had been entering its first phase; then as now, the Austrians were profoundly reticent on territorial concessions. The Habsburg delegation of 1914, perfectly aware of Italy's actual goals, merely offered to converse on the future of Trentino, south of the Tyrol. The unwillingness to compromise on the possibility of a Greater Italy led, predictably, to the collapse of Habsburg–Savoyard mid-war negotiations. The groundwork for rehabilitating Franco-Italian relations that had been carried out by Rudini's government in 1902 would now come in handy. The resulting conversations with the *Entente Cordiale*'s plenipotentiaries were not particularly taxing, as the domestic mood in Italy had already reached an hysteria in favour of war.

The furnace which had produced such energetic warmongering among the Italians had been stoked relentlessly for 17 years. The icy winter of 1897 had provided the impetus for a period of political control and societal pressurization. The climate of apathy among the *ancien régime* that the establishment liberals had entertained in the preceding decades seemingly had no antidote. One veteran of the old guard, Sidney Sonnino, believed that he had the cure. January 1897's edition of the Italian journal *Nuova Antologia*, contained his ground-breaking thesis 'Torniamo'.[42] This provided an idealized blueprint for the return of constitutional liberalism. For the *Risorgimento*'s core values to be protected, Sonnino hypothesized, an over-powerful executive enslaved by a messianic reverence for the constitution was required. The legislature would then see itself transformed into mere window-dressing for the real power – the Prime Minister. The result would be the cutting out of the people from the decision-making process. Their popular will, he posited, was poised to destroy the liberal revolution as a result of their shift from an allegiance to liberalism over to an alliance with radical leftism. Their exclusion was necessary for liberalism to survive. The assassination of King Umberto I by the Tuscan anarchist Gaetano Bresci in July 1900 burst the fanciful bubble of complacency in which many of the liberalist establishment still resided. A need to prevent the ascension of the left was now paramount, and Sonnino's

---

41   Herwig, H., *The First World War: Germany and Austria-Hungary, 1914–1918*, pp.29–33.
42   Pecout, G., *Il Lungo Risorgimento*, p.371.

blueprint seemed flawless. A year later, the once-formidable liberal thinker Giuseppe Zanardelli was interred into the premiership.[43] Zanardelli was 77 years old by the time he was appointed, with his best days long behind him. The decaying cadence of this formerly quick-thinking writer was a sad affair, but it allowed a cunning snake to slither back into Italian political life – Giovanni Giolitti.

Giolitti had managed to carve himself a role in the interior ministry while he surreptitiously waited for Zanardelli to expire. Having entered politics in 1882 as a liberal, he quickly climbed the ladder, becoming Minister for Internal Affairs in Rudini's short-lived first administration (1891–92). When Rudini fell to the pressures of Italy's chronic instability, it had been Giolitti who succeeded him. However, the habitual intrigue in which he dabbled had proved to be his undoing, and in 1892 he became embroiled in the collapse of the Roman Bank. He left office in disgrace in 1893, but during his sojourn from politics had come to the same conclusion as Sonnino. Giolitti thus set out to make the 'Torniamo' vision a reality, building a muscular state ruled by a strong elite married to an impenetrable bureaucracy. Giolitti began expanding Italy's small bureaucracy as soon as he took office after Zanardelli's death in 1903. A profusion of new posts were created and forced upon the provinces, regional civil services were given control over electricity, gas and water supplies, the rail sector was nationalized in 1905 and in 1907 the telephones followed suit. As the legal profession increasingly dominated the civil service, the routes through this labyrinthine citadel of paperwork became ever more difficult to traverse. By the dawn of war in the summer of 1914, the cost of the Italian civil service had increased to 566.9 million lira, compared to 171.5 million lira before Giolitti's premiership.[44] Every action and every policy was prosecuted with a view to excluding the anxious working classes of northern Italy's industrialized throng. Yet the obsession with taking power out of the hands of the people instilled within Giolitti a cold and unprincipled approach to politics. Gone were emotive appeals to the Garibaldine ideal, the Mazzini conceptualization of a free united Italy or Rudini's sentimental *rapprochement* with France. This freezing of popular politics had severely destabilizing consequences. Giolittism had delegitimized all routes for progress, either for the left or the right, and violence was becoming the only outlet. As voices across Italy were muted by bureaucratic dominance, uncontrollable popular frustration had begun to build.

The adventures which Italy had embarked upon across the African continent in a vain attempt to sate its Balkan hunger had generated a radical expansionist groundswell. The imperialist experiment now waited in the wings to give the tired liberal nationalism which inspired the *Risorgimento* a pristine futuristic makeover. Fresh from yet another expedition, the Italian people had turned away from the mundanity of life under Giolitti's grey bureaucrats towards the swashbuckling bravery of the Turkish War. Fought between September 1911 and October 1912, the escapist reporting of

43   Lepre, A. & Petraccone, C., *Storia D'Italia Dall'Unita a Oggi*.
44   Cuccu, L., *Storia della Burocrazia Italiana*, p.35.

the conflict allowed young Italians to fantasize about their place in the world.[45] The obliteration of the Turkish fleet at Qouz Bay, the grizzly vengeance carried out by Italian troops at the Mechiya Oasis and the heroic deeds of Italian marines on the beaches of Tripoli set fire to the nation's imagination. The war occurred within a slipstream of new nationalism sparked by a 1911 publication by Professor Luigi Valli entitled *Cos' e Il Nazionalismo e Cosa Vuole* (what is nationalism and what does it want). The work dismantled the liberal nationalism predicated on the Universal Declaration of the Rights of Man Article 3, and instead defined nationalism as "a supreme love of the motherland and the will to propel it to power in the world around it".[46] The work had found a home in the minds of the shapers of the Italian Nationalist Association (ANI). The Italio-Turkish War supplied the ANI with eager volunteers, and between 1912 and 1914 the construction of a new, radical, supremacist and expansionist nationalist party began to take place. Taking advantage of Giolitti's stagnant politics and a severe curtailing of left-wing influence in government affairs, the nationalists began to present an exciting alternative to a muted, boring political ecosystem.

The dawn of 1913 ushered in yet another economic crisis in the unlucky kingdom, with a light being shone on the inequality which had existed since Italy's formulation in March 1861. The economic crisis of 1913, though, was different to any that had come before it. The legislature may have become increasingly pointless, but organized labour and the diffusion of political parties had continued apace.[47] The left had benefited considerably from these developments, and with an economic crisis devouring the land, only a single event need take place for the fire of revolution to burn. On the first Sunday of June 1914, the anniversary had taken place of the Albertine Statute, which had created modern liberal Italy. The left had hijacked the celebrations and turned them into demonstrations, which spiralled into rioting, kicking off '*La Settimana Rossa*' ('The Red Week'). Uprisings followed in Ancona, Ravenna, Forli, Fabriano, Jesi and Parma. The northern manufacturing powerhouses of Milan, Bologna, Alessandria, Cremona and the Reggio-Emilia region were all home to hotbeds of communist agitation. The government began to see the rifles, nooses and guillotines on the horizon and anxiously prepared for the fight. Luckily for the man himself, a series of political manoeuvres had already seen Giolitti fall. Antonio Salandra had succeeded him immediately after, taking the mantle on 25 March 1914. The mess of Red Week was as much a reaction to over a decade of the restrictive sidelining of the people's will as it had been about economic hardship. Ultimately, Red Week came to nothing, save to give an ominous foretaste of what was to come.

From the point of Salandra's refusal to join the First World War up until the signature of the Treaty of London – formally attaching Italy to the *Entente Cordiale* – powerful

45   Poma, S., *L'Italia in Guerra*, p.59.
46   Pecout, G., *Il Lungo Risorgimento*, p.389.
47   Colarizi, S., *Storia del Novecento Italiano* (Milano: Mondadori, 2000), pp.5–52.

pressure groups formed and multiplied both for and against war.[48] Over the previous year, the mainstream political culture in Italy had become utterly intoxicated with the idea of war. A combination of the increasingly harsh treatment of Italian minorities in Austria-Hungary which stirred widespread anger, the mighty industrialists of northern Italy clamouring for war as a lifebelt amidst harsh economic currents, and the resurrection of 'Greater Italy' helped to make war seem irresistible. The interventionists, like the Devil, had all the good tunes, and by New Year's Eve 1915 seductive voices such as those of poet and literary colossus Gabriele D'Annunzio had begun to turn the pliable ears of the doubtful.[49] The irresistible impact of D'Annunzio's theatrical personality led to his words being echoed among the nationalists, above all his epic phrase *"Delenda Austria!"* ("Austria must be destroyed"), which sought to hark back to Italy's near mythological past, perfectly tailored as it was to resemble Cato the Censor's dramatic 2,000-year-old words commenting on the devastation of Carthage, *"Carthago Delenda Est"*.[50] For D'Annunzio and countless others who marched to the drums of war, Austria was Italy's Carthage and Conrad von Hotzendorf its Hannibal Barca. Socialists, liberals, reformists, royalists and democrats alike danced joyously on the way to the future slaughterhouses of Caporetto, Isonzo and the Piave.

The Italian nationalist movement had whipped the people into a bloodlust, an unstoppable frenzy of emotion which once started was impossible to stop. The socialist left attempted a final stand, desiring to prevent a war which they saw as an antithesis of Marxist ideals of brotherhood. On 1 November 1914, the Vatican joined these voices in a futile attempt to turn the masses against the coming conflagration.[51] For the Italian people though, this outpouring of national self-belief was the most say they'd had on anything for years. The triumph of Giolittism had led to a pressurized tank of human thoughts and feelings that had only become more radical with each failed piece of legislation. On 25 February 1915, after taking a principled stance against the looming bloodbath, the dogs of war finally slipped their leash. The mass politics which in the post-war period would lead to revolutions in Germany, Russia and across the myriad states of the Habsburg Empire had their model set in Italy, as the interventionists unshackled their warmongering rage onto the neutralist demonstrators. Salandra's government made sure that the police did little to restrain them, in a pattern that would continue until late spring 1915. By May of that year, the interventionist cause was unstoppable, with the Treaty of London signed on 7 May, compelling Italy to go to war. The Italians received their promise of a Greater Italy following the war, and a month later some 225,000 men and boys from Torino, Firenze, Rome, Naples and many other towns and cities the length and breadth of Italy would march into Austria-Hungary, after which there would be no turning back.

48   Lepre, A. & Petraccone, C., *Storia D'Italia Dall'Unita a Oggi*.
49   Philippe, J., *D'Annunzio* (New York: Viking Press, 1973), p.300.
50   Goldsworthy, A., *The Fall of Carthage*, p.331.
51   Pecout, G., *Il Lungo Risorgimento*, p.402.

6

The Predator: the *Regia Marina*
Understanding Italian Defence Decision-Making

The Austro-Prussian conflict of summer 1866 put a terminal point on the *Risorgimento*'s central phase. Although a desire to retake the Italianate coast of the Balkan peninsula existed on the fringe movements of the young Italian state, for the political centre Veneto had been enough. The end of an era had been signalled, and the *Risorgimento*'s myths and legends, which would be so pervasive in Italian national history, had already been written. As during the post-independence years in the United States, the age to come would be dominated by pragmatic men who, by dint of their wealth, had ample time to contribute to the cause of building the nation. Indeed, the only *Risorgimento*-related matter which slightly raised pulses among the delegates to the Torinese House of Deputies at Palazzo Carignano was the matter of Rome. The capture of Rome from French-backed Papal forces in September 1870 closed even that loophole and with the transfer of the capital to Rome in November that year, the Italian nation lost its nationalist cause, albeit temporarily. The passage into history of the first independence movement allowed two parties to dominate early Italian politics – the Historic Left and the Historic Right.[1]

The latter had its genesis within the age of liberal fanaticism that had pervaded the Torinese parliament in the immediate years prior to the unification of 1861; the former was a more recent creation, whose existence came about as an expression of discontent with the progress of Italian society post-unification. Politically, this placed their fault lines on expected places – the Historic Left agitated for the government to be more involved in infrastructure projects, whilst the Historic Right wished to tack to free markets and free trade. It was a case of Protection v. Freedom, much in line with the ideological trends of the day. Their uniquely Italian character came in their differences on foreign policy. The Historic Right represented the continuation of the *Risorgimento*. It was in the fringes of this movement that revanchist elements craving its extension to Trieste and Dalmatia lay. Within this focus on maintaining close ties

---

1   Lepre, A. & Petraccone, C., *Storia D'Italia Dall'Unita a Oggi*.

to the tenants of the independence struggle, an obsession existed with maintaining excellent relations with the French Empire, in whatever form it took. It was a preoccupation that sprung from the desire to maintain a relationship with the home of the liberal ideas which had guided the *Risorgimento*'s founding fathers in the heady days of 1848–49. These were the policies of Italian conservatism.

The Historic Left, unsurprisingly, sought to push back against the conservative positions believing that the *Risorgimento* did not need pushing ever further and that alliances were required that were not based in an imagined Napoleonic Paris bursting at the seams with militant liberalism. In this they sought to undermine the two precepts of *Risorgimento*-era foreign policy. Indeed, they wanted the new Italy to be a break from the past, desiring a clear full stop between Savoyard history and Italian history. The Historic Left's argument was that after the conquest of Rome, the pushing of the Habsburgs to the Tagliamento, the standing up to France through the humiliation of the Papal States and their enlistment of Prussian aid had dismantled the underpinnings of unification. In moving the capital to Rome, a statement of finality was made. There was nowhere where Italians lived that hadn't been incorporated into the nation, except of course for the Dalmatian coast and Istria. The Historic Left, unlike voices on the Historic Right, understood that their claims to those lands across the Adriatic were difficult to sympathize with. Even if the Historic Right's more extreme elements acted upon their Balkan desires, it would be seen as expansionism. The importance of unification as a centrifugal force thus began to slip away. In 1870's general election, a wave of young dynamic deputies, who had been children and teenagers when the *Risorgimento* had begun, came into the legislature.[2] The Historic Right's geriatric pining for untouchable lands had no purchase in their young and ambitious minds. They wished for an Italian future founded in peace, stability and national development. Calm was the watchword for these new politicians.

Sadly, nobody had informed the Giovanni Lanza government of 1869–73 of this new dynamic. The Historic Right was adamant about retaining a strong, cutting edge military which was well prepared for an expansionist campaign in Dalmatia and Istria.[3] At the same time, the government, aware of its mission to unite the Italian people within the nation as much as outside it – a goal it shared with the left – wished to construct immense rail infrastructure from north to south. It would have to maintain high defence spending and high infrastructure spending, whilst at the same time avoiding the trap of untenable debt, for its plan for massive investment in both arms and rail to succeed. However, the issue of debt had the potential to be disastrous as the Italian Kingdom simply did not have the tax base to fuel such excessive government budgets. Borrowing from investors was thus always going to be necessary, yet to acquire credit in the sums that Rome required necessitated a period of national stabilization. Creating an economy that would be attractive to investors, whilst also

---

2   Pecout, G., *Il Lungo Risorgimento*, p.226.
3   Lepre, A. & Petraccone, C., *Storia D'Italia Dall'Unita a Oggi*.

capable of high public spending was the unenviable job of Piedmont native Quintino Sella. The balancing of the budget called on the finance minister to enforce unreasonably high taxation upon the Italian people. When Sella was forced out, upon the replacement of Prime Minister Giovanni Lanza with fellow Historic Right politician Marco Minghetti in 1873, his policy would remain enforced. Although high taxation would render a surplus by the end of the Minghetti administration in 1876, its imposition had slowed the progress of private sector-led infrastructure building in the country. Politically, this was particularly damaging for the Historic Right, as their economic plan had focused on taking a private sector-led infrastructure boom, whose success would lay in the self-reinforcing element of an investment bubble. With companies put off by high regulations and taxation, progress in building a connected nation ground to a halt.

The elections of 1874 bore out the disgruntlement of the Italian electorate. They were drawn in their droves to the call of the Historic Left's message of moving infrastructure building out of private hands and into those of the government. This was particularly felt in Italy's disconnected south. Although the Historic Left had identified the incorrect cause for Italy's slowness in building infrastructure, the results spoke for themselves as 232 of 507 seats were returned for them. The Historic Right's majority was thereby slashed to just 44. The Minghetti administration danced on thin ice, as the smallest act of disunity was now liable to provoke electoral collapse. Two years later, Minghetti's teetering government fell outside of election season. Following these events, a coalition was built in the country which would provide the votes for a mandate-confirming election in October 1876. Events went as planned and a massive 400 of 504 seats would be won by the Historic Left. One hundred and twenty of these seats were won by new politicians, reinforcing the demographic shift inside the legislature throughout the 1870s. But if the new Prime Minister, Agostino Depretis, was to avoid Minghetti's fate, he would have to move rapidly. The restrictions on the economy and personal financial liberty, drafted by Minghetti and Sella, were cast away as customs tariffs and tax reforms were ushered through. Thus, the party that ideologically believed in interventionism showed little loyalty towards this guiding principle when exposed to electoral pressure. The good will bought by draining the sea of administrative bureaucracy and the slapping away of greedy government hands was entirely paid for via devouring the surplus left by Minghetti. Meanwhile, for the first years of their four-year term, the Historic Left commenced enormous projects across the maritime, rail and construction sectors.

The historic Left would be in power from 1877–91,[4] during which time two leaders came to dominate Italian politics – Depretis and Benedetto Cairoli. The enormous majority granted to them had created a party which was led by compromise, in which the moderate option trumped all others. Lamentably, this meant that nobody – not the populace nor the politicians – got what they wished for. The group that had

4   Lepre, A. & Petraccone, C., *Storia D'Italia Dall'Unita a Oggi*.

won the Historic Left the election consisted of the top portion of business owners, southern landowners who were disappointed at the results of the *Risorgimento* and northern industrialists who shared their southern counterparts' concerns. In addition, a part of the idle aristocracy of the centre and north had been seduced by the idealistic promises of the Historic Left. In short, they had won power on the backs of those able to worry about more than putting food in their mouths. Not unsurprisingly, the new regime did its best to accommodate its upper-middle and upper class constituents and focused obsessively on promoting Italian industry. Their central preoccupation lay with bringing southern Italy out of its agricultural languish and into the industrial world. To shepherd this industrial revolution across the country, Neapolitan financier Agostino Magliani was chosen. He would serve uninterrupted between 1877 and 1889, during which time industry and public works would be his mantra. His emphasis on construction brought in vast sums of investment from the United States and the British Empire, with foreign firms making fortunes betting on contracts to build the new Italy.[5] Magliani countenanced no restrictions on his spending, nor that of the private sector.

The historic and consequently collapsing cities of Rome, Firenze and Napoli received much of this money, and a speculative bubble rose from their decaying streets. The old cities were ripped out and slum clearances enacted to pave the way for the new Italy. However, an uncomfortable secret lay at the heart of these plans: they were funded by debt. By 1884, the Historic Left administration had consumed all the surplus left to them by the Minghetti premiership, and in an attempt to hide this failure Magliani submitted fudged books. When the truth was revealed during the drafting of the national budget for 1885–86, outrage erupted and a crisis in confidence emerged, bursting the construction bubble. Four years after the crisis, an economic depression set in, triggered by a mass banking crash. The next decade was worse, as the early 1890s saw an agricultural collapse produce a wave of bankruptcies and a concurrent unemployment crisis. Only the advent of Francesco Crispi's Historic Left regime of 1893–96 would see the economic situation curbed by the introduction of austerity within state expenditures. The respite wouldn't last long, and in 1896 the Historic Right returned to power under Antonio Starabba Rudini. The Rudini administration would last a mere two years, being punctuated with food riots in 1898 provoked by the Spanish-American War of the same year. By the turn of the century, the Italian state was teetering once more on an economic precipice. In 1913, another economic collapse would rock the Italian Kingdom, provoking ideological violence between right and left on a scale never before seen.[6] If the story of the Habsburg Empire from 1848–1914 was one of ethnic destabilization and the generation of friction between ruler and ruled, the Italian story was one of frequent economic collapse followed by

5   Cuccu, L., *Storia della Burocrazia Italiana*, pp.25–29.
6   Colarizi, S., *Storia del Novecento Italiano*, pp.50–55.

irresponsible splurging. It would be into this unsteady backdrop that the *Regia Marina* would undergo its formative years.

Building the *Regia Marina* – 1866-1900

Losing the Battle of Lissa was the single most important moment in the history of the *Regia Marina* that sailed to war in 1915. Indeed, without events at Lissa it is unlikely that the *Regia Marina* would have become the force that its lavish construction plans made it. It was not lost on the Italian government still in Torino that at Lissa they had lost control over the Adriatic. What had hurt more was that they had lost it to a state with no maritime tradition of note. For a nation whose perception of its own history had been front and centre of the call to unification, the Italians were acutely aware of their forebears' prowess on the seas, making the humiliating loss painful to bear. If the *Regia Marina* was to recover its honour among the Italian people, it would need patrons willing to stand up for it. The first of these defenders would be Lissa veteran Rear Admiral Augusto Riboty. In 1868 he proclaimed at Torino: "The historic mission of the Italian Navy, should be to protect the maritime interests of the nation, and to project the influence of the Italian state abroad."[7] There was in essence nothing new about this assertion, but his message was directed to the parliamentarians who had begun to question the point of the navy's existence if it could not secure supposedly easy victories. Riboty's call was that the *Regia Marina* should not be seen as having the task to win back the Adriatic from the *K.u.K. Kreigsmarine*, and as such could not be judged by that metric. Instead, its objective was to "protect the maritime interest of the nation", meaning to protect its commerce. Given Italy's shaky economic situation and reliance on imports, particularly for industrial materials, this was hardly surprising. Despite the wisdom of his words, the Italian public and the kingdom's aristocracy wanted to see a navy worthy of fighting decisive battles and winning them. Riboty was later joined by a second key defender of the *Regia Marina* in the aftermath of Lissa – Captain Carlo de Amezaga, founder of the *Rivista Marittima*. This magazine, which continues today, was from its first issue dedicated to proselytizing the cause of a large, well-armed navy. Its job was to conduct public relations for the *Regia Marina* and to win back influential and hopefully wealthy friends. To this end, the magazine's first issue led with a grand call to the people: "We [the Italian people] have the need to discover the goods that a navy can bring, we must pass laws to ensure a worthy future for this navy."

In 1873, the ailing navy was placed under Rear Admiral Riboty, acting as naval minister under the Minghetti administration. On the surface, he might have been a strange choice. Born in Nice in 1816 as a Frenchman, Riboty was admitted to the

---

7   Botti. F, *Il Pensiero Militare e Navale Italiano dalla Rivoluzione Francese alla Prima Guerra Mondiale (1789–1915), Vol. II* (Roma: Stato Maggiore dell'Esercito Ufficio Storico, 2000), p.1126.

HMS *Dreadnought* 1911. (*Encyclopaedia Britannica 1911*)

Habsburg naval yard at Pola. (Photoglob Co.)

foundational years, furnishing hundreds of officers to the service. But their preponderance in the navy's officer class concentrated power in the fleet in the hands of
northerners; southerners would barely get a look in regarding the construction of a
supposedly united Italian fleet, instead serving to make up its massed ranks of ratings.
Rear Admiral de Saint Bon's promotion was a consolidation of the rank hypocrisy
which lay at the heart of the navy's formative years. He had been present for two of
Italy's independence wars, fighting in the Adriatic during the war of 1848-49 and at
the siege of Gaeta during the subjugation of the Bourbon Kingdom of the Two Sicilies
in 1861.[11] Yet his commitment to the romantic dream of uniting north and south did
not extend into aiding Neapolitans into high office. However, aside from his perpetu-
ation of Genovese supremacy, the Saint Bon years would be beneficial and continued
to see an acceleration in the *Regia Marina*'s plans for creating a powerful fighting
fleet. Between 1873-76, he would enjoy the high defence spending that Quinitino
Sella's extortionate tax regime would allow, but instead of lavishing money on a large
unsustainable fleet, the Saint Bon years would witness a focus on quality and potency
of big ships and big guns.

The Italians have often looked towards Genova and its mercantilist people with
scorn, born of a supposed over-valuation of money. Saint Bon's behaviour would be
exemplary of this stereotype. While Rome lavished money on heavy industry – in
which shipbuilding was no exception – Saint Bon developed a scheme to deliver the
Regia Marina even greater quantities. By selling off older vessels, he sought to build
up a private fund for the navy which would enable him to bypass any restrictions that
Rome might impose. A numerically small but technologically superior fleet was his
objective. In essence, we see here the origins of the *Regia Marina*'s commitment to
Mahan's Decisive Battle Doctrine, in contrast to the Young School (see Chapter 2).
Saint Bon's sale plan called for the selling off of six cruisers, nine light units and nine
sailed vessels.[12] However, the plan was held up by the fall of Marco Minghetti, and it
wouldn't be until summer 1876 and the rise of Agostino Depretis' Historic Left party
that it would receive assent. In the three years between the proposal and its acceptance, further ships were added to the sale roster, with a final total of 33. This would
produce 66 million lira for the coffers of the *Regia Marina*. Working together with
head of naval architecture Brin, Saint Bon oversaw the commissioning of two *Duilio*
class ironclad battleships, with what was originally a third battleship being redesigned
as a new cruiser class. These three vessels were monsters of the waves, capable of transporting a whole army division and their associated equipment. With the coming of the
Historic Left regime in 1876, money poured into the *Regia Marina*, complementing
the funds Saint Bon had acquired during his sales as the government dug deep into
the surplus left by Minghetti's regime. On 8 May 1876, the rapidly constructed *Duilio*

---

11   Norwich, J., *Sicily: A Short History*, p.303.
12   Botti, F., *Il Pensiero Militare e Navale Italiano dalla Rivoluzione Francese alla Prima Guerra
      Mondiale*, pp.1112–1115.

– first of the *Duilio* class turret ironclads – was launched into service.[13] Two years later at La Spezia, its sister ship, the *Dandollo*, put to sea on the Ligurian coast.

A navy, though, is more than the vessels which it produces. Benedetto Brin, who had come to head the naval ministry in 1876 to replace Rear Admiral Saint Bon, saw this clearly. Navies have to project power, and to do so they require modern infrastructure. Brin's proposal was for the *Regia Marina* to update its infrastructure by constructing naval bases at La Spezia in Liguria, Taranto in Apulia and Venezia in Veneto.[14] In doing so, Rome would satisfy the egos of post-1866 Italy's maritime regions, whilst at the same time constructing a network of bases which would allow the *Regia Marina* to conduct operations on its eastern, western and southern seaboards. From Venezia, a fleet could maintain watch on the Adriatic and on the *Kriegsmarine*, while from La Spezia, the *Marine National* could be watched at its base in Toulon. The addition of Taranto allowed the *Regia Marina* to look south towards Africa. To achieve national unity within the *Regia Marina*, Brin concurred with his predecessor that an officer class had to be produced which was trained in a single location. The theory was sound, as for officers to produce and pass down the culture of a fleet it was their education that would have to be modified. With this objective in mind, the Bourbon naval school in Napoli and the Savoyard naval school in Liguria were amalgamated into a single academy at Livorno in 1881. During his first tenure, Brin had overseen the construction of a template for a potent and organized navy. In 1879, he would be ejected from the naval ministry to be replaced by the ministry's first Neapolitan head, the somewhat controversial figure Rear Admiral Ferdinando Acton.[15] Acton, as we will see, was a proponent of Aube's Young School and a bitter rival of the Decisive Battle Doctrine orthodoxy which had long dominated the naval ministry.

By the time Rear Admiral Acton had taken office, thanks to Brin, the *Regia Marina* had four powerful state-of-the-art turret-equipped ironclads. Yet these proud instruments of the *Regia Marina* were looked down upon with scorn by Acton as they stood in the face of his Young School convictions. He instead decided the unarmoured cruiser should be the primary battleship of the fleet, and that Italy's joining of the big ships race throughout Europe should be cancelled. Despite initial protestations, the Naval Superior Council accepted his proposals, reducing the firepower of the fleet as well as its sophistication in favour of a larger, faster but less potent fleet. The commonly cited reason for supporting this switch came from those who saw Vienna as the Italian Kingdom's most likely adversary. The lighter cruiser had a shallower draught, which allowed it greater manoeuvrability and the ability to dock in older ports. This would allow more of the fleet to use the ancient docks at Venezia, from which they could better contest the shallow, narrow stretch of water

13   Konstam, A., *European Ironclads 1860–75: The Gloire*, p.32.
14   Botti, F., *Il Pensiero Militare e Navale Italiano dalla Rivoluzione Francese alla Prima Guerra Mondiale*, pp.797–798.
15   Alberini, P. & Prosperini, F., *Uomini della Marina: 1861–1946*, p.14.

that separated the two states. These new Italian cruisers would seek to replicate the so-called 'English style', coming in at 11,000 tons and constructed in a composite manner – utilizing a wooden and metal hybrid system. The *Regia Marina*'s engineers would send their plans to English shipyards to produce them, since the Italian industrial base was not sufficient for the initial construction process. These cruisers were designed to be torpedo vessels, in line with Young School thinking. In war, they would follow Aube's and Paixhans' proscription of attacking enemy trading lanes, thus reducing enemy thalassocracy to a meaningless concept.

Under the turn to the Young School, three of these light vessels would be commissioned: the *Ruggero di Lauria*, *Francesco Morosini* and *Andria Doria*. Although they were commissioned in 1881, Italy's underdeveloped industrial base would not permit their launch until 1890.[16] Their construction would be caught up in the collapse of the Italian economy during the late 1880s and early 1890s which resulted in material shortages at Italian shipyards. This was a reflection of the poor shape of the Italian industrial base, which still fell far short of the desires of every government since the unification in 1861, all of which had been preoccupied with producing an industrial nation. The fact that Italy's southern half could not create an industrial revolution, but that the government wished for half of all naval construction to take place there, created an artificial retardation of usable maritime industrial capacity. An example of the delays can be seen in the case of the *Lepanto* and the *Italia*, *Duilio* class turret ironclads. Both vessels were completed in 1882 but were not ready for launch until 1885. This was despite the state investment in shipbuilding, focused around the Terni metal works in central Italy, as nevertheless, production of materials would remain inadequate.

In 1884, the Young School was defeated within the *Regia Marina* as Brin and his devotion to Decisive Battle Doctrine returned to occupy the office of the Naval Ministry. His second tenure would last six years and would see the Terni metal works exponentially increase in capacity, attempting to rectify its poor reputation. In 1887, Brin would ask for 30 million lira to complete his previous fleet plan, determined to push back on Acton's fleet plans. With the new budget, Brin sought to maintain the *Regia Marina*'s grasp on the maritime world's ever-changing fleet technologies. In 1888, his previous fleet plan was increased in potency, with him requesting a force of 20 second-class vessels, 30 third-class vessels and 16 dedicated transports. Twenty-six small coastal vessels were also requested by Brin. Instead of 30 million lira, this would require 85 million lira. This fleet plan and its associated budget would be in action until the dawn of the 20th century. Although Brin had vehemently opposed the Young School, which was visible through his actions, he recognized the benefits to maintaining a strong torpedo fleet, as evidenced through his retention of a large fast-boat component in his 1888 projections for the *Regia*

16   Botti, F., *Il Pensiero Militare e Navale Italiano dalla Rivoluzione Francese alla Prima Guerra Mondiale*, pp.999–1069.

Marina's future force composition. During this second phase of Brinite construction, in contrast to the original English-built designs, all ship constructions would take place in Italian shipyards. This development of a large fast-boat component occurred at the exact same time that it would within the Habsburg navy. The torpedo fleet, though, continued to have significant involvement from English and German yards. Out of 91 torpedo vessels produced during Brin's second tenure of 1884–91, 66 would be built by Italian firms. By 1895, the country's maritime industrial capacity had become sophisticated enough to support its significant size. Alongside the Terni metal works, the renowned English artillery maker Armstrong had established a factory in Pozzuoli, Venezia had its own torpedo manufactory, Napoli had given birth to the Guppy Mechanical Works and Genova had seen the launch of the Ansaldo Mechanical Works.[17] As the *Regia Marina* steamed into the 1900s, Italy's naval industry sailed with it.

Brin's second tenure would also see the completion of his aforementioned overhaul of the navy's infrastructure. The unified naval academy at Livorno was considered impressive, with excellent training standards. The bases at La Spezia, Taranto and Venezia had been complemented by further naval bases at La Maddalena in northern Sardinia, Gaeta in Lazio and Messina in north-eastern Sicily. The economic hardships that would be inflicted on Italy in the 1880s would brush past the country's shipbuilding trade, which unlike other sectors of the economy, was one that Rome was content to spend lavishly on. The Regia Marina would emerge into the 20th century as one of the world's most powerful on paper, and a credible threat to the Anglo-French thalassocratic control over the Mediterranean. Nevertheless, the immunity of the *Regia Marina* would not last, as the banking collapse of 1893 and food shortages of 1898 burned through the economy. But although naval cuts resulted, improvements in the running of the navy continued, even if its project to contest the existing powers in the Mediterranean would have to be put on hold. On 23 November 1889, the Ministry of the *Marina* was reorganized under Brin's second tenure to include the Naval Cabinet, Naval Staff Office, Naval Engineering High Command, Hydrographic Service, Maritime Health Service, Office for Naval Engineering and Financial Office.[18] In addition, four directorates came into existence: the Directorate for Naval Construction, Directorate for the Artillery, Armaments Directorate and Directorate for the Merchant Marine. From 1866 until 1900, the *Regia Marina* had sprung forward, using its surprising defeat at Lissa as a chance for serious introspection as to what went wrong. The result was a powerful navy, addicted to the Decisive Battle Doctrine yet willing to be flexible with its strategic planning.

---

17   Botti, F., *Il Pensiero Militare e Navale Italiano dalla Rivoluzione Francese alla Prima Guerra Mondiale*, pp.884–885.
18   Botti, F., *Il Pensiero Militare e Navale (1789–1915), Vol. II, Tomo II* (Roma: Ufficio Storico dello State Maggiore dell'Esercito, 2010), pp.812–814.

A Contest Approaches – Preparing the *Regia Marina* for War, 1900-15

The late 19th century had seen Italian foreign policy switch under the Historic Left from the *Risorgimento*-era fascination with liberal France to an alignment with first Prussia and then, after 1871, Germany (see Chapter 5). For the majority of the post-Lissa era, Rome's target for maritime competition had been the French Third Republic, whose frustrations of its designs on Tunisia in 1888 had provoked a rupture between the two states. The break in relations had been on the cards since Italy annexed Rome in 1871,[19] using a distracted France to march into the city. The entrance of the Italian Kingdom into the Pan-Germanic bloc known as the Triple Alliance in 1881 put Franco-Italian relations firmly on ice. Since 1886, the *K.u.K. Kriegsmarine* and the *Regia Marina* had been cooperating in operations regarding the Eastern Mediterranean. That year, the two forces had been part of a British-led task force to Greece to deter a Greco-Turkish war. Their operations, consisting of blockades, were positive experiences for the two parties and allowed the *Regia Marina* to enter into good relations with the Royal Navy. On 12 February 1887, London concluded an agreement with the Italian government to peacefully govern the Mediterranean.[20] At the end of that year, a formal agreement to defend the seas of the Ottoman Empire was concluded between the Habsburg, Italian and British diplomatic corps. The Historic Left administration of Francesco Crispi, attempted to use these agreements as a basis for further maritime cooperation with the *K.u.K. Kriegsmarine*. In 1888, overtures were made to Vienna at the Barcelona World Fair with the aim of gathering allies to deter French aggression towards Italy. Rome's diplomatic efforts towards Vienna were in vain though, with nobody in the Austrian military decision-making sector envisioning launching a war against the French Republic's *Marine Nationale*. In 1892, another round of entice-ments were embarked upon with King Umberto I visiting Berlin to lobby for both a Triple Alliance naval agreement and the execution of joint manoeuvres. However, after witnessing uninspiring naval exercises near Venezia, Admiral Alfred von Tirpitz and Kaiser Wilhelm turned down the proposal.[21]

The objective to push Vienna into making commitments to Rome over a potential anti-French partnership regarding the Adriatic and Western Mediterranean received a body blow in 1900 with the assassination of King Umberto,[22] a man who had been wholly sympathetic to the Habsburg Empire. The ascension to the Roman throne of his anti-Habsburg son, King Victor Emmanuel III, in the same year, provoked the *K.u.K. Kriegsmarine* to bolster its preparations for conflict. The first indications of its increasingly insecure stance in regards to a coming contest with the *Regia Marina* over commanding the Adriatic came immediately after the coronation, with

19   Taylor, A.J.P., *The Struggle for Mastery in Europe*, p.209.
20   James, L., *The Rise & Fall of The British Empire* (London: Abacus Publishing, 1998).
21   Sondhaus, L., *The Naval Policy of Austria-Hungary, 1867–1918*.
22   Lepre, A. & Petraccone, C., *Storia D'Italia Dall'Unita a Oggi*.

The SMS *Viribus Unitis*. (Editions d'Art Co.)

The SMS *Tegetthoff*. (Richard Elles Photographs)

Austrian premier Ernest von Koerber hurrying the construction of the Prague to Trieste rail line.[23] In December that year, a concerned Berlin forced through a Triple Alliance naval convention, in the face of increasing positive contacts between Paris and Moscow. The naval agreement concluded at the convention saw the Kingdom of Italy granted *de jure* thalassocracy over the Western Mediterranean, but much to Italy's chagrin, the *K.u.K. Kriegsmarine* would take possession of the Adriatic, declining the *Regia Marina* its chance to win back its prestige against the Habsburg navy in a revenge battle to rival Lissa. As Franco-Italian relations warmed with the *Regia Marina*'s visit to Toulon in 1901, a process of target-switching was underway, and in 1902 the Habsburg Empire's *K.u.K. Kriegsmarine* would become the *Regia Marina*'s main target.

The rationale for Italy's drifting into the Franco-Russian camp can be found in Chapter 5, yet it is sufficient to say that Rome had never wished to enter into any state of tension with the British Empire. In 1904, the British Empire signed the *Entente Cordiale* with France, bringing it into the Russo-French sphere and out of its hitherto neutral position.[24] The Italian government would never countenance a move against London, so the Italian commitment to the Triple Alliance faded. Two years before their official change in position, the *Regia Marina* possessed 16 pre-dreadnought battleships, seven armoured cruisers and 27 unarmoured fast cruisers.[25] Eleven destroyers were incorporated into the fleet, as were 145 low-tonnage torpedo boats. All Italian pre-dreadnought classes were larger, faster and possessed of superior firepower to anything the *K.u.K. Kriegsmarine* held in its shipyards. Yet the *Regia Marina* still had glaring internal problems, even after its golden age of construction. The foremost issue was one of confusion; by the first decade of the 20th century, it had still not resolved its Young School v. Decisive Battle Doctrine dilemma. Nor had it found a role for the destroyer. The Italian naval industry had maintained its inefficient reputation, and due to a scandal relating to the Terni shipyards in 1906, the produce from its slipways had started to be viewed with suspicion. The sordid details of the Terni scandal consisted of allegations that its material products were substandard, but that their inadequate nature had been covered up by Naval Minister Admiral Giovanni Bettolo during his tenure in office from 1899–1900. This was made all the worse when it was revealed in the 1906 Franchetti inquiry that the state had paid far above the necessary price,[26] under the assumption that the product was of better quality than it was. The difference was pocketed by Bettolo. Foreign companies collaborating with Terni then paid over the odds for their products, based on their confidence in a company used by the *Regia Marina*. The affair seriously damaged the credibility of the Italian maritime industry.

23   Taylor, A.J.P., *The Habsburg Monarchy*, p.213.
24   Taylor, A.J.P., *The Struggle for Mastery in Europe*, p.415.
25   Botti, F., *Il Pensiero Militare e Navale (1789–1915)*, pp.868–893.
26   Lepre, A. & Petraccone, C., *Storia D'Italia Dall'Unita a Oggi*.

Nevertheless, corruption, poor materials and theoretical confusion were swept away with the successful launch of the Regia Marina's first dreadnought, the *Dante Alighieri*, an event undertaken in reaction to both the unveiling of HMS *Dreadnought* and the construction of the *K.u.K. Kreigsmarine*'s debut dreadnought, SMS *Viribus Unitis* in 1908.[27] With the *Regia Marina* now focused on preparing for war against the *K.u.K. Kriegsmarine*, and Vienna being fully aware of that fact, the Adriatic Dreadnought Race of 1909–13 began in earnest. Just as Sir John Fisher had predicted (see Chapter 2), the unveiling of a dreadnought by one side of a naval rivalry immediately made the dreadnought-less fleet obsolete. Everywhere this naval building contest occurred, from Northern Europe to Latin America, a costly and resource-draining race commenced. In the summer of 1910, the *Regia Marina* was allowed to lay down three more dreadnoughts, increasing the gap between the two states' naval capacities. The simple construction of these vessels – *Giulio Cesare*, *Leonardo da Vinci* and *Conte di Cavour* – was enough to instigate further panic in Vienna. By March 1912, the *K.u.K. Kriegsmarine*'s SMS *Viribus Unitis* had joined the fleet, to be followed by SMS *Prinz Eugen* and SMS *Tegetthoff* a year later. In doing so, the *K.u.K. Kriegsmarine* would beat the *Regia Marina* to the punch in the evolving dreadnought contest, with the Italian navy not receiving their first complete dreadnought, the *Dante Alighieri*, until January 1913. Positive Triple Alliance-Italian diplomatic developments in 1911, though, looked as if they would render the naval competition between Vienna and Rome a pointless waste of time and money, as warming relations with the Habsburg Empire provoked the *Regia Marina* to return its gaze west to the *Marine Nationale*.

The return of Francophobia to the halls of power in Rome had occurred due to the Italian invasion and conquest of Libya from the Ottoman Empire in 1911. The French Third Republic had been unwelcoming of the event, seeing the move as a potential threat to French plans for dominating North Africa.[28] The Italian Kingdom's good relations with France had always been predicated on its desire for good will with London. With the British Empire occupied with the build-up of the *Kaiserliche Marine* (German Navy)[29] – whose constitution was clearly aimed at contesting the North Sea – it had no time to maintain a presence in the Mediterranean. With the Royal Navy elsewhere, the *Regia Marina* was free to strategize against the *Marine Nationale*. By late 1912, Rome had contacted Berlin, whose armies underwrote the power of the Triple Alliance. Generals Helmut von Moltke and Alberto Pollio, standing in positions as chiefs of staff for their respective nations, then began to share war plans for a general conflict with France.[30] The Italian vision foresaw that in case of war, the French Third Republic would seek to reinforce its military position within metropolitan France by moving its African armies into southern France. These forces, both

27   Kramli, M., *Austro-Hungarian Battleships and Battleship Designs: 1904–1914* (Szeged: Belvedere Meridionale, 2021).
28   Fenby, J., *The History of Modern France*, p.233.
29   James, L., *The Rise & Fall of The British Empire*.
30   Botti, F., *Il Pensiero Militare e Navale (1789–1915)*, pp.886–887.

generals anticipated, would seek to unify the African and continental French armies in France proper to repel Germany's massed divisions. The *Regia Marina* would seek to prevent this by commanding the Mediterranean, using torpedo boats to attack French troop convoys, whilst attempting to draw the *Marine Nationale* out to fight a decisive battle in open water.

To facilitate the coordination of a Triple Alliance naval strategy, the new year would see the opening up of the Triple Alliance Naval Convention of 1913.[31] However, mutual suspicion between the *K.u.K. Kriegsmarine* and the *Regia Marina* slowed progress on a joint naval strategy considerably. Since 1904, both navies had been in hot competition, and although the Italians were the warmer party diplomatically, the frosty reception they received from Vienna continued unabated. At the end of March 1913, the *Marine Nationale* visited the Royal Navy's base at Valletta in Malta to demonstrate a united naval front. Their aspiration was to deter any Triple Alliance action in the Mediterranean, for in combination the Royal Navy and the *Marine Nationale* were unstoppable. The fear provoked by the unification of these forces provoked a hurried scramble back to the previously cooling negotiation table for Vienna and Rome. Both the *K.u.K. Kriegsmarine* and the *Regia Marina* had new representatives by this time – Admiral Anton Haus and Admiral Paolo di Revel respectively. On the face of it, Admiral di Revel was an odd choice to head up the *Regia Marina*'s delegation to the Triple Alliance Naval Convention, as his adherence to the Young School, and his own conceptualization of guerrilla warfare at sea, had put him at odds with the power of the Decisive Battle Doctrine dominant in the *Regia Marina*'s theorizing. But his ability to think outside of the box and his possession of a remarkable *aide-de-camp*, Captain Angelo Ugo Conz, former head of Naval Intelligence – combined to make him an excellent negotiator.

Although a joint strategic convention was agreed upon on 9 May 1913, the Austro-Hungarians would continue to refuse to share codes with the *Regia Marina*, having determined to keep them from their old nemesis. The objective of the *Regia Marina* at the conference was more insidious: they wished to acquire the title of supreme commander for all Mediterranean operations, thereby making the *K.u.K. Kreigsmarine* the subordinate party. On 23 June, the parties agreed that in the event of war they would meet up at Messina's deep harbour, from where they could wreak havoc on French convoys.[32] It was a plan which was well at home with di Revel's theoretical loyalties to the Young School. However, the two sides still had profound suspicions. In the autumn of 1913, the Habsburg naval attaché in Rome, Prince Johannes von und zu Liechtenstein, was denied an invitation to watch *Regia Marina* gunnery exercises. All this coordination though was for nothing in the end but when war came in 1915, it would be (see Chapter 5), for in August 1914 the Kingdom of Italy refused to join the war. The rather contradictory figure of Admiral di Revel would come to head

31   Sondhaus, L., *The Naval Policy of Austria-Hungary, 1867–1918*.
32   Sondhaus, L. *The Naval Policy of Austria-Hungary, 1867–1918*.

the *Regia Marina* into conflict, alongside Duca Luigi Amadeo di Savoia serving as Commander in Chief of the Italian fleet. Thirteen days before Italy joined the war on the side of the Allies in May 1915, the *Regia Marina* held its first naval convention with the *Marine Nationale* in Paris.[33] The results granted the *Regia Marina* command of the First Allied Fleet stationed at Brindisi. At the time of the Italian Kingdom's declaration of war on 23 May 1915, the *Regia Marina* would go into battle on the seas with an active fleet 137 vessels strong, composed of 17 battleships, 10 armoured cruisers, seven fast cruisers, four older auxiliary cruisers, 33 destroyers, 48 torpedo boats and 18 submarines. With this fleet, the *Regia Marina* entered the war with the overriding objective to establish thalassocracy over the Adriatic.

33   Botti, F., *Il Pensiero Militare e Navale (1789–1915)*.

7

The Prey
The *K.u.K. Kreigsmarine*
Understanding Habsburg Political Decision Making, 1866-1914

Defeat in the Inter-German conflict of 1866 between the Habsburg monarchy, the Kingdom of Prussia and the Kingdom of Italy reopened the racial question which had dogged the Habsburg Empire since 1848. The issue at hand centred on discovering by what source the Habsburg dynasty claimed to have the right to rule Hungarians, Italians, Slovenes, Croats, Serbs (to a limited degree) and Poles. The traditional answer had been that the imperial family had inherited, by the sanctioned European norms of the pre-Napoleonic age, the lands which those nationalities called home. When they had acquired Galicia, Hungary and Dalmatia, the Austrians had never cared about the beliefs of the indigenous peoples of those lands in relation to their right to be on those lands. For the longest period of time, these peoples had little to say, even on their own account, as to the rights of the Habsburg line to rule over them instead of ethnic self-determination. The maintenance of a feudal society had ensured that the people had remained tied to the land, so it mattered little if the land changed hands. As long as those who directly assumed power over the massed peasantry (the aristocracy) spoke the same language, had the same customs and confessed the same faith, friction was minimal. Loyalty to an extra-national emperor mattered little. When the French Revolution of 1789 transformed the world, that consensus was ripped apart. In the world that emerged after the Napoleonic Wars, the people were paramount, the conflict having awakened their political consciousness. It was a process which went hand-in-hand with the late 18th-century pan-European mobilizations of young fighting men from across Europe into the maelstrom of revolution and counter-revolution. As the Italian people discovered, to the Habsburg Empire's detriment, in a world without the all-encompassing power of the Church and in an industrializing society where the people were being released from chains to both lord and land, the concept of popular nationalism made more sense than loyalty to old realities.

The formation of national feeling within the hearts of the empire's vast array of ethnic groups was not an equal process. The Slovenes, for example, would scarcely have a separate identity even by 1918. But three groups had always possessed a feeling of 'otherness' that the Habsburg dynasty had never managed to quell. These peoples – the Italians, the Magyars and the Czechs – had required little encouragement to, at least mentally, issue a challenge to the rightfulness of Habsburg rule. Indeed, it was this overwhelming sentiment that they did not belong and did not share the royal family's destiny that motivated the Italian populace in its entirety to coalesce around nationalism and rip themselves free from the Austrian yoke in 1848. For the majority of the 19th century, it was thought among statesmen loyal to the ruling Habsburg family that nationalism might be the solution to its own cursed creation. The Magyars and Czechs may have bristled against imperial control, but they feared the 'other' equally as much. In fact the sole reason why the empire lasted beyond the great uprisings of 1848 (where the Habsburg monarchy very nearly came to a premature demise) had been because they were able to exploit inter-ethnic hatred to demonstrate to the state's constituent peoples the result of a weakened royal line. Specifically, Czech, Magyar, Slav and German all mutually threatened each other, and if the power of the Habsburg Empire was lessened in any way, then perpetual ethnic conflict would emerge. While their nationalist leaders still pursued the desire for independence, particularly among the aforementioned Czechs and Magyars, post-1848 they were all acutely aware that freedom would mean armed contest with their new neighbours. Thus, an obsession with inter-racial competition would develop in every area within the confines of the Habsburg state. What these politicians would increasingly want was concessions to allow them to gain the upper hand on their racial rivals within the Habsburg imperium.

Before proceeding to examine the mechanism of the empire's infantilized legislature and its effect on shaping the *K.u.K. Kreigsmarine*, a note should be made on the role of ethnic Germans. What we might today call 'Austrians' had never had any identity other than that of Germans. They spoke German, they looked 'German' for the most part and they indulged in much the same traditions. Their cultures differed in some superficial respects, but beneath the surface – and particularly to another ethnic group – they appeared identical to their imperial German brothers to the north-west. The only difference between what the Allies would in November 1918 term German-Austrians and the imperial Germans was their choice of master. Even their homeland, the former Duchy of Austria, should have been incorporated into a vast German Empire stretching into both Poland and Central Europe. However, at the same time they did not all identify with the ruling family. German nationalists agitated for unification with the German Empire, not for their own state, whilst German liberals decried the lack of progress made on regulating the empire according to the dreaded confines of a 'constitution'. As much as their national consciousness could be understood, their desires were wholly oriented towards either Berlin or a democratic but imperial Vienna. Never was there any question that they might be their own people, distinct from the royal family but equally distant from their German brothers. It was a thought process not dissimilar to that which rendered Kaiser Franz Josef I and his inadequate successor, Karl, so detached from the reality of the eponymous state after 1848. In the case of the royal family, they could not fathom the concept of nationalism. Mentally, they could not accept the new world that had been created by Napoleon and Robespierre; that nationalism – both liberal and not-so-liberal – was the pre-eminent force of the mid- to late 19th century.

The fossilized thinking of the Habsburg dynasty delayed the constitution of anything that might have been called a parliament. That was until the empire's Prime Minister, Count Ricardo Belcredi, pointed out that if the state's ethnic groups' mutual suspicions could be fostered in a safe environment, then they could be manipulated in an easier fashion. By creating a parliament, then filling it with delegates from all ethnic groups enjoying an equal share of legislative power under an equal set of rules, backroom deals, 'understandings' and favoured nationalities were ejected as governing tools. All would now stand under the same roof. When Belcredi stepped down in 1867, he was succeeded by Friedrich Ferdinand von Beust, whose beliefs turned to heading off the national issue – particularly profound among the Magyars – via granting special measures to Budapest.[1] Von Beust proposed that Budapest should become a wholly devolved portion of the empire, only responsible to Vienna on issues of defence, foreign policy and finance. On 7 February 1867, the separation of Hungary from the rest of the Habsburg Empire was executed as the *Ausgleich*. This measure permanently granted the lands of St Stephen autonomy to decide policies on all domestic issues. Although it had been undertaken to aid nationalist pressure, the act re-established the unique nature of the Magyars within the empire. The plan to create a legislature in which all ethnic groups were on the same level and carried the same weight would be concluded by von Beust in his short tenure. Yet without the Magyars being included in that parliament, and given their status as a wholly separate entity, the plan tacitly promoted the Magyars to a parity position with the Austro-Germans, whilst at the same time demoting all the other races of the empire. When the *Reichsrat* came into existence as a real parliament (it had existed in name since 1861),[2] the Magyars had no part of it. Its so-called governance only stretched to Cisleithania – all non-Magyar portions of the empire. The body was not a simple decision-making system though, as the parliament's members simply elected men within their number to the Delegations, a body charged with policy-making on defence matters comprising members of the Habsburg and Magyar parliaments. Only when one was chosen to form part of these bodies did the parliamentarian in question have any role aside from nodding one's head. Although it proceeded without the Magyars, the other races of the empire were kept in check by the presence of their dreaded neighbours. Aside from the liberal movement which had adherents from across society, the parties were broadly ethnic and thoroughly nationalist in outlook. Because of the overriding priority granted by these groups to race, they all voted together, and division was not tolerated. Their goals were absolutist – freedom and independence – which in turn bred absolutist methods.

1   Taylor, A.J.P., *The Habsburg Monarchy*, pp.144–145.
2   Taylor, A.J.P., *The Habsburg Monarchy*, p.146.

The result of the balance of power between the races outside of the state's Hungarian portion was that no legislation could be passed if the legislators were asked to vote on mere consciousness. Aside from the liberals, all nationalist parties would vote for their own interest and against the interest of the others. Deadlock was then constant, aside from in the Delegations. This political system was that which came to shape Habsburg naval policy throughout the 19th century and the first years of the 20th century. For roughly the first decade of its existence (1861-73), the system was tempered by the presence of the liberal movement. This party frequently played kingmaker among a *Reichsrat* built to ferment permanent disagreement. In doing so, they allowed for some kind of legitimate resistance to the policy preferred by Vienna, as although the legislature's constitution forced compliance with the Kaiser, the body was permitted to delay legislation through debate. The liberals forced these parliamentary discussions to occur, and if not for their influence the nationalist parties would have consistently agreed to legislation posed by the government. Indeed, government decisions were the only ones which all nationalities routinely favoured. This was because their origins were in the Hofburg – the principal Habsburg imperial palace in Vienna – and not in Zagreb, Prague or Budapest. As long as all agreed with official imperial policy, then the balance of the races was maintained through the mailed fist of Habsburg power. During the liberal period, however, their complete support was never guaranteed. In 1873, however, the Vienna stock exchange crashed and the politicians of the *Reichsrat* and the people themselves put the blame at the door of the liberal movement. The emphasis in the *Reichsrat* on the utility of *laissez-faire* economics, and their prominence in the empire's economic circles, rendered them easy targets when the search for a scapegoat began. But because this occurred in the Habsburg Empire, an inevitable racial dimension existed. In this case, the liberal movement had always drawn its support from Austrian-Germans and from the Czechs. Only these two groups had a *petite bourgeoise* and an industrial class who would be remotely interested in the tenets of liberalism over nationalism. The Magyars, 'little Slavs', Czech nationalists and German nationalists believed a Czech and German liberal conspiracy to be to blame. As such, support for their cause vanished almost overnight, leaving the *Reichsrat* in the hands of the nationalists alone.

When Eduard Taaffe came to power in 1879 as Minister-President (essentially a Prime Minister),[3] he sought to exploit this new reality. What might be called the Taaffe Doctrine consisted of maintaining the racial deadlock in the *Reichsrat* and using that as an 'iron ring' to produce permanent support for the government (due to the perception of the royal line as a neutral non-racial party.). If the *Reichsrat* ever had the temerity to attempt a resistance to legislation, as had not been uncommon during the liberal movement's presence in the chamber, then the monarchy could threaten to impose universal suffrage. If that ever occurred, all members of the *Reichsrat* knew imperial collapse would soon follow, in the wake of which would surely come ethnic

3   Taylor, A.J.P., *The Habsburg Monarchy*, p.169.

The Habsburg port of Trieste. (Fratelli Treves Editori)

Social Democrats. These forces consisted of imperial loyalists whose demands were economic rather than racial, to the extent that all they cared about was securing good deals for the working classes. This meant securing jobs, and that required debates on government spending. In the face of their mass appeal, the *Reichsrat*'s nationalist elements began to lose influence. An optimistic man might think the empire had just been saved by absolutism's traditional enemy – the socialist movement. But war has a habit of turning past certainties on their heads, and as we shall see in later chapters, its advent provoked a return to nationalism and the end of everything Habsburg. It was into this maelstrom of racial politics and ethnic tension that the *K.u.K. Kreigsmarine* of the First World War was shaped.

Climbing the Ladder – The Political-Naval Matrix, 1848-1912

The *K.u.K. Kreigsmarine* of 1914 had been born in 1848. Prior to that date, the imperial navy was a mere extension of the Venetian armada which had existed prior to the dissolution of the old Venetian Republic in 1797. Before the incorporation of the Most Serene Republic, the Habsburgs had been represented on the waves by a token force based in Trieste; a force which had only existed since the reign of Kaiser Josef II (1765–90) and was a simple offshoot of the empire's brown water force which existed to patrol the Danube.[7] As such, it had no maritime tradition of any importance, so when the Venetians were incorporated into the empire permanently in

---

7   Wilson, P., *The Holy Roman Empire*, p.751.

1815[8] it stood to reason that their fleet should continue to exist, except now the republican fleet would be in service to the Habsburg dynasty. Venetian fleets had a racially stratified existence equal to that of any arm of the Habsburg state. Within the closed confines of its decks, the Venetian fleet was comprised of Croats and Italians. Croats served below deck, whilst Italians served above decks, confined to the officer classes. When the Habsburgs took possession of Venice's naval tradition for themselves, they inherited this racial make-up. In 1848, the comfortable compromise that the Habsburgs had established with their Italian subjects in Venezia was permanently ruptured. That year, nationalist uprisings rocked the Italian peninsula, and among the worst of these were those that occurred along Venice's canal systems. The twin revolutionaries, Manin and Tommaseo, declared an independent republic based in Venice – the *Repubblica di San Marco*.[9] In one fell swoop, these revolutionaries stripped the Habsburg Empire of its naval capabilities, as Venice had been its main port. Trieste at the time paled in significance in both size and prestige. Although the little republic would last but a year – Venezia was returned to Habsburg control in spring 1849 –, the damage to the reputation of the Italians as loyal subjects was profound. A process of de-Italianization swept through the navy post-1849, and from that point onward Italians were forbidden from joining the navy's officer corps.[10]

The process of removing the Italians from their positions of power within the navy continued in 1866 through the loss of Veneto to the Italian Kingdom. Without Venezia, the Habsburg navy was forced to base itself in Pola on the Istrian peninsula, scattering its bases down the Dalmatian coastline. This coastal area was entirely inhabited by small fishing villages and larger ports such as Dubrovnik (then Ragusa), housing 400,000 Serbs and Croats, who in turn were governed by 15,000 Italians.[11] The latter were living as middle- to upper-class overlords in sea view villas, considered by Vienna to be little more than proxy rulers. This ethnic distribution along the empire's only coastal territory allowed the *K.u.K. Kreigsmarine* to maintain its traditional racially based enlistment policies, handed down by the navy's Venetian forebears, although in a break with the past, Dalmatian Italians who joined the navy were never allowed past the NCO ranks after 1848. In this way, the old Venetian ways were retained well past 1866 and into the 20th century. Unfortunately, hard data on this topic only goes back as far as 1887, when records showed that of all ratings 33.4 percent were Italians.[12] The next date for which we have figures is 1896 and shows a decline to 27 percent of ratings, a trend which would suggest that Italian representation prior to 1887 was far higher than was recorded then. Croats also sustained their

8   Galibert, L., *Histoire de la République de Venise*, p.562.
9   Zamoyski, A., *Phantom Terror: The Threat of Revolution and the Repression of Liberty, 1789–1848* (Glasgow: William Collins, 2015), pp.479–499.
10 Sondhaus, L., *The Naval Policy of Austria-Hungary, 1867–1918*.
11 Tanner, M., *Croatia: A History from the Middle Ages to the Present Day*, pp.23–27.
12 Sondhaus, L., *The Naval Policy of Austria-Hungary, 1867–1918*.

Venetian-era disproportionate presence in the *K.u.K. Kreigsmarine*, never dropping below 46.5 percent of naval manpower during the same nine-year period. Despite their numbers, the days of an Italian-directed Habsburg navy were at an end. And while the cramped decks of the Habsburg navy's warships might have danced to the tunes of Italian sea shanties and the dulcet tones of the Croat tamburica, its captains' cabins were an exclusively German affair.

The *K.u.K. Kreigsmarine*'s officer class, like in all other navies, determined the direction of the fleet, its command culture and its purpose, all of which were completely Austrian-German in their outlook. This is backed up by hard data from 1896, when the officer corps was reported as being 55 percent German. The Habsburg military would stand by the royal dynasty until the very end, and in the autumn of 1918 it would be the officers of the fleet and army who would negotiate with the Allies when all others had fled their responsibilities. Like the army, the *K.u.K. Kreigsmarine*'s officer class had been largely insulated from the rise of nationalism in the empire, even if their ratings eventually succumbed to its influence (see Chapter 9). What amounted to a vaccination was their system of advancement, which in an absolute monarchy without any signs of liberalization was entirely based on royal patronage. It was not just the prospects of promotion which relied on this system, but the furtherance of the naval cause itself. In 1866, it looked as if the *K.u.K. Kreigsmarine* of 1914–18 might fail to materialize at all. The Battle of Lissa may have been a spectacular affair (see Chapter 2) which had delivered the Habsburg Empire one of its only victories in the ill-fated Brothers War of 1866, but Kaiser Franz Josef I was not possessed of sea-legs. Like many in the Hofburg, he failed to understand the importance of the navy within the grand strategic thinking of any power that wished to be taken seriously. The Habsburg Empire simply did not think that way. To battle for influence within a patronage system is one thing; to do so when the prospective patron has never shown an iota of interest in the concept at hand is quite another. In light of this situation, in September 1866, a little over two months since Lissa, the Habsburg battlefleet was disbanded. Consequently, the navy was reduced to a paper-only existence. The manner in which this was resolved is instructive as to how the late Habsburg political system operated in regards to institutional challenges.

In 1866, the *K.u.K. Kreigsmarine* triumphed over a numerically and technologically superior *Regia Marina* at Lissa. For the multi-ethnic people of the empire, the heroic ramming of the *Re di Italia* by Admiral Wilhelm von Tegetthoff's SMS *Erzherzog Ferdinand Max* served as the propagandistic centrepiece of the maritime contest. The epic imagery conjured up by the act propelled von Tegetthoff to fame among the nobility.[13] His celebrity appeal was unrivalled at the time, the adulation of his person doing a great deal to heal the Habsburgs' wounded ego in the wake of Koniggratz. It also served to distract the Austrian-German elites, many of whom embraced German nationalism, from the traumatic truth that they had slaughtered

13   Sondhaus. L, *The Naval Policy of Austria-Hungary, 1867–1918*.

their brother Germans. Lissa was a victory against the despised Italians, a people who had done much to accelerate the empire's downfall. The Habsburg state's Teutonic aristocracy would be forever grateful for that mercy, and as a consequence von Tegetthoff's celebrity endured until the empire's end. When Kaiser Franz Josef I dismissed his beloved fleet, his fame alone was responsible for saving it. The Kaiser's mother, Princess Sophie (from the Wittelsbach dynasty, rulers of Bavaria since the 11th century), put pressure on her son as to why the navy had been humiliated in such a manner. What saved the navy, though, was von Tegetthoff himself, whose towering reputation led to him being granted a most peculiar task of immense importance. On 19 June 1867, over 6,000 miles from his birthplace at the Schonbrunn Palace, Emperor Maximilian I of Mexico – the younger brother of Kaiser Franz Josef I – was executed on a windswept hill in central Mexico.[14] The event brought much anguish to the Kaiser, as well as to their mother in Vienna, to whom the bullet-ridden body of one of the sons of Europe's most illustrious noble house had to be returned home. The thought of his corpse laying for eternity in colonial soil was too much to bear; it must be brought back at any cost. The task, one which was highly personal and carried profound weight, could only be handed to someone whom the dynasty could trust. Trading off his colossal fame, Wilhelm von Tegetthoff was the first thought in every nobleman's mind. In undertaking this macabre task, the admiral formed a tight personal bond with the Habsburg dynasty which would permit him to bypass every hurdle that the state would otherwise have thrown at him. After the operation had concluded successfully, the favours came flooding in thick and fast. The next year, von Tegetthoff was restored to the position as *Marinekommandant*, and that year's naval budget was passed without a single obstruction, an event wholly due to the favourable light in which the Kaiser now saw the admiral. It was in this manner that business would be undertaken throughout the decades leading up to the First World War. The empire's governing structures were as personal and dynastic as they had been a century beforehand. The fate of the navy would hereafter ebb and flow parallel to the degree of amicability between Kaiser and *Marinekommandant*.

After spectacularly manoeuvring the navy back into existence, the 'Tegetthoff years' of 1868-71 would ultimately prove a time of drastic change for the *K.u.K. Kreigsmarine*. During his three-year tenure, he could not achieve the establishment of a marine minister nor true administrative independence. He did, however, save the navy once again; just as before, it would be his personal connection with the dynasty which proved decisive. Early in the first year of his tenure, the dominant idea in imperial defence circles was to reduce the *K.u.K. Kreigsmarine* to a simple patrol force. The heavy lifting of coastal defence against the *Regia Marina* was to be handled by static naval fortifications. To fend off the imposition of this policy, von Tegetthoff utilized his relations with Archduke Albrecht, Commander-in-Chief of the *Landstreitkräfte* (Habsburg army). As a result, the navy avoided this terrible fate. With his relationship

---

14   Detroyat, L., *L'Intervention Francaise au Mexique* (Paris: Amyot Editeur, 1868), pp.219–285.

in funding had allowed the *K.u.K. Kreigsmarine* to swell in numbers so that it now threatened even the British Empire's Royal Navy. Montecuccoli's downfall was close to hand though, as under his premiership he began to borrow unauthorized sums of money to be used to fuel naval expansion. Imperial banks, private investors, private bankers and industrialists forked out these monies in 1910 and 1911, but in 1912 the Landerbank began demanding the money back – money that the navy couldn't afford to pay. Montecuccoli's previous good relations with the Kaiser fell to pieces, and in the summer of 1912 he was asked to retire. His successor was Anton Haus, the man who would lead the *K.u.K. Kreigsmarine* into the First World War. By the time Haus entered Pola's foreboding landscape, the *K.u.K Kreigsmarine* had climbed from the lowly position of a neglected relative of the army to the forefront of imperial decision-making. But what about the evolution of the navy's fighting capabilities?

Reform of Mind and Body – Shipbuilding and Tactics, 1866-1914

The fortunes of the physical force that the *K.u.K. Kreigsmarine* was able to bring to the fore, as we have seen, depended entirely on the favour with which its head was held. Although the Battle of Lissa had provided the navy with the gift of having fought one of the three decisive sea battles of the century, their achievement of victory there had sealed the fleet's temporary demise. The institution would technically still exist, but Kaiser Franz Josef I was determined that the ships and its infrastructure were not needed after Lissa. His logic, although not impeccable, was less contentious than one might imagine. His prime rationale rested with the truth that Lissa had secured Habsburg control over the Adriatic. For the *Regia Marina* to attempt to retake the Adriatic would require a *casus belli*. The Treaty of Prague had granted the Italian Kingdom Veneto in 1866,[20] so Vienna could assume that Italy's natural composition had been achieved. Without a reason for war, the Habsburg Empire could count the sea as part of its vast fiefdom. According to this thinking, the Italians were no longer the *de facto* enemy of the Habsburg state; that honour went to the Prussians, and to fight Prussia, no seagoing fleet was necessary. The Habsburg navy thus only need exist on paper. For the officers and sailors who stayed with the mothballed navy during the period immediately prior to Tegetthoff's rise in dynastic favour in the summer of 1867, it was a frustrating time. The *Regia Marina* was frantically building new vessels (see Chapter 6) in a bid to prepare itself for a time when it could once more challenge the *K.u.K. Kriegsmarine* for the Adriatic, evidence that Torino did not agree with the Kaiser's naïve theories. Max von Sterneck would comment at that time that if Tegetthoff benefitted from British-built vessels like the *Affondatore*, then "such a force would be frightful ... our navy now has poor ships".

---

20   Taylor, A.J.P., *The Struggle for Mastery in Europe*.

Despite official unwillingness to maintain a fleet which barely existed as a tradition within the state superstructure, a second problem lay beneath the royal family's lofty disinterest in maritime affairs. It was an issue it shared with the Italian state it sought to rival – an inadequate industrial base – and it could not be solved with inter-aristo-cratic diplomacy. The Habsburg Empire was a rural society. Had it not been, and had it experienced the Industrial Revolution as early as Britain – or for that matter France – its ancient system of government would not have survived. Much like the American South of the same era, failure to develop industry had kept cities and the educated classes small. One of the many detrimental effects of such a conservative outlook was the inability to field a proper industrial navy in a manner which did not force the state to rely on foreign material providers. In 1866, the only domestic factories capable of producing naval guns were House Waldstein's Skoda works in the Bohemian city of Pilsen.[21] Even these works only dated back to 1859, with a workforce yet to break a thousand strong. Their shipyards were equally poorly prepared. When Venezia was lost to the Italians, a good portion of the Habsburg navy's engineering staff was lost, alongside the empire's largest and oldest shipyards. After 1866, the Habsburgs had been forced to relocate their naval manufacturing to Trieste, where the San Rocco Yard and *Tonello Navale Adriatico* picked up the work which formerlly belonged to the newly liberated Venetians. Meanwhile, the *Regia Marina* had fixed their issues with Italy's industrial inadequacy by using London's forges. This solution was not avail-able to the Habsburg monarchy, who deemed imports too expensive an option for an endeavour they were only tangentially interested in pursuing.

The emergence of von Tegetthoff as among the Kaiser's favourites in 1867 gave the navy a chance to attempt to make requests that were previously impossible. Among these was one to reconfigure the navy's force plan. The result was Tegetthoff's shipbuilding programme of 1868, which envisioned an armoured battlefleet of 15 ironclads and an unarmoured force of fast ships comprising frigates, corvettes and gunboats.[22] The total number of vessels within the force would be calculated at 34. The ironclads would form the fist of the *K.u.K. Kriegsmarine*, wheeled out to under-take decisive battles and presumably to challenge the *Regia Marina*'s growing naval power across Adriatic. The unarmoured fast fleet would be charged with ceremo-nial duties, naval diplomacy, special operations, the execution of anti-smuggling customs operations and to facilitate maritime policing. To fund the reformation of the Habsburg fleet, a budget of 25 million gulden would be required. The ironclad fleet was partially underway prior to the passing of the budget, with the *Kaiser* to be transformed into an ironclad at Pola's naval shipyard. Seven other ironclads already existed, and now the navy was no longer mothballed their purpose could be real-ized. This brought the total up to eight ironclads ready for duty. The construction of new ironclads would be the most burdensome part of the new battlefleet plan.

21   Konstam, A., *European Ironclads 1860–75: The Gloire*, p.16.
22   Sondhaus, L., *The Naval Policy of Austria-Hungary, 1867–1918*.

The 1869 budget, however, granted Tegetthoff only 8.8 million gulden to be used for the fabrication of just two ironclads. To placate the army, these would be called *Albrecht* and *Custoza* after the commander of the Habsburg army and the battle of 1866 respectively. Although Tegetthoff's relations were good with the imperial court, there could be no escaping the finances involved in building a large and technologically powerful fleet. Lamentably, economic constraints could not be surmounted by performing charades at Habsburg dinner parties.

The budget for 1870 would reflect another small increase in the monies afforded to the K.u.K. Kreigsmarine (9.8 million gulden[23]), despite opposition within the Delegations, further reflecting their irrelevance in the face of dynastic support for the naval effort. The new budget renewed the amount of the previous year, with an additional million advanced to Tegetthoff's administration with a view to continuing the naval construction programme underway at Trieste. At that time, SMS *Albrecht*, SMS *Custoza* and SMS *Kaiser* dwindled in the dry docks of the aforementioned Trieste yards. Although the money flowing into the fleet had been exponentially rising, the fermenting of the nascent industries of the Habsburg Empire into manufacturing goliaths could not be achieved through force of state capital. The required industries were simply not present within the empire's borders. Only the British Empire could supply what the Habsburgs desired; ironclads were not yet 20 years old, and as such only the premier industrial nation in the world could manage their ever-advancing production needs. For these vessels to be completed, materials paid for at a premium from Great Britain were necessary. Soaring costs, shipping delays and supply chain issues would be the result for the Habsburg Empire, not to mention dependence for its defence products not simply from a foreign power, but from the world's premier power. As the Tegetthoff years melted away into the reign of Admiral von Pock from 1871–84, the acceptance of increasing budgets and construction programmes fell away alongside the termination of Tegetthoff's alliance with the House of Habsburg.

The von Pock years combined with advancements in naval technology to produce a perfect storm for a renewed decline of the physical fleet (see Chapter 2). The technical problems the *K.u.K. Kriegsmarine* began to run into from the 1870s until the 1910s related to maintaining their vessels – particularly those being built to the ever-changing standards of the day. Among these evolving components, armour, gun placement and propulsion ranked as the more expensive technologies to remain in advance of. After Lissa, the importance of the ram was believed to have been of optimum significance for the age of naval tactics to come. By 1875, however, the development of the gun turret[24] threw that hypothesis out of the water, whilst at the same time torpedoes were being eyed by creative minds who sought to use them to guarantee the victory of offensive power over the ironclad's ground-breaking defences. During the same period, gunnery – in particular those whose providence could be traced to the Krupp

23   Sondhaus, L., *The Naval Policy of Austria-Hungary, 1867–1918*.
24   Konstam, A., *European Ironclads 1860–75: The Gloire*, p.10.

firm – advanced the potency of projectile weapons. These factors conspired to render obsolete important parts of the battlefleet that von Tegetthoff had envisioned in 1868. One victim of these phenomena was the ironclad SMS *Tegetthoff*; it began sea trials in October 1881, but by its launch its casemate turrets – impressive in 1870 – were considered utterly outdated.[25] The rate of technological redundancy was astounding, as was the consequent level of wasted expenditure. As naval architects attempted to cope with the tide of exponentially increasing financial burdens on their shipyards, a far less costly concept was being trialled at Pola. This idea related to the construction of a class of vessel which combined the rapidity of torpedo boats and the versatility of turret ships. A warship that was a cross between an armoured cruiser and a composite (wood and steel) ship, weighing 850–1,000 tons, was the result.[26] The fleet classified these new warships as 'destroyers'. It was an impressive feat for a Habsburg naval establishment so stuck in the past.

At the dawn of 1880, the *Regia Marina* received its most sophisticated ironclad yet – the *Duilio* class namesake vessel *Duilio*.[27] Fear of the challenge to Habsburg thalassocracy over the Adriatic represented by the vessel's launch spurred Kaiser Franz Josef I into action, whether or not the man who headed his navy was in favour. In July, the Kaiser's committee on how to meet the challenge decided upon the unveiling of a shipbuilding programme to meet that envisioned by Italy's Benedetto Brin. In detail, this would provide the *K.u.K. Kreigsmarine* with 16 state-of-the-art ironclads and 10 rapid cruisers. To do this, the navy would need to be provided with six new armoured warships to complement those already under construction. The realities of finances and industrial capacity forced the *K.u.K. Kreigsmarine* to confront stringent compromises, should they wish to gain parity with the *Regia Marina*. The starkness of the situation forced the imperial navy's planners to question their loyalty to Decisive Battle Doctrine (see Chapter 2). In 1880, the committee meeting to decide the fate of the navy during the von Pock years played witness to the first glimpses of resistance to Decisive Battle Doctrine on the part of two of those in attendance: Archduke Albrecht and Rear Admiral Max von Sterneck. During a lull in conversation, these men introduced Young School thinking into the *K.u.K. Kreigsmarine*'s decision-making processes for the first time. Von Sterneck's proposal was for von Pock not to lobby for an expensive programme to produce already obsolete vessels, but to produce cruisers and torpedo vessels. This lighter and more agile fleet would be composed of 16 fast and deadly but cheap ships, where losses would be easily replaceable without bankrupting the empire. Von Sterneck advocated for this hypothetical fleet to be used not to confront the *Regia Marina* in battle, but to cut off Italy's access to Africa and the Levant and to strangle its economy by targeting its expansive maritime trade.

25   Konstam, A., *British Ironclads 1860–75: HMS Warrior*, pp.16–21.
26   Sondhaus, L., *The Naval Policy of Austria-Hungary, 1867–1918*.
27   Botti, F., *Il Pensiero Militare e Navale Italiano dalla Rivoluzione Francese alla Prima Guerra Mondiale*, pp.750–762.

However, if the debut of the Young School was to be effective, a member of the Habsburg dynasty had to be co-opted. At the time of the committee, Archduke Albrecht had already come to the same conclusion as von Sterneck, believing that any battle over the Adriatic should be done in a defensive manner. The Habsburg thalassocracy over the sea should not be contested, and instead a 'little war' in which the Italians would wreck their fleet on Habsburg coastal fortifications should be undertaken. The Habsburgs' ironclad fleet, in his conceptualization, should not be scrapped, but certainly not extended. He impressed this attitude on the other naval officers at the committee of 1880. The passing of the Young School past the barrier of the *K.u.K. Kreigsmarine*'s internal philosophy was thus complete and made clear in 1881's fleet plan, in which von Pock cut his ironclad orders significantly. The focus shifted instead onto cruisers and torpedo boats, eight of the latter being produced at 400,000 gulden each, whilst three obsolete steamers were to be converted to light cruisers at 600,000 gulden each. In May that year, the *Reichsrat* approved the fleet plan, reflecting the endorsement it had received from the royal family. By 1882, exercises focusing on proving the ability of torpedo boats to render decisive results in battle were undertaken. The next year, ironclads were added to these exercises to produce a standard operating formula for mixed ironclad/torpedo boat tactics. The resulting battle system consisted of employing ironclad vessels to lay down smoke screens which the torpedo boats would exploit, rapidly manoeuvring into range. When close enough, the torpedo boats would fire from within the smoke, obscuring the view of the oncoming torpedo and rendering the target unable to escape. It should be noted that these expansive exercises confirmed the redundancy of ironclads configured for ship-to-ship combat, further enhancing the case for scrapping Tegetthoff's plans for a naval iron fist.

Despite his role in promoting the Young School at the highest level, Admiral von Sterneck's dedication to the idea did not survive his ascension to head of the navy wholly intact. From the commencement of his tenure in November 1883, the *K.u.K. Kreigsmarine* would begin construction on the largest pair of battleships the force had ever seen. In 1884, the first of these vessels, the 6,900-ton SMS *Kronprinz Rudolf*, was laid down at Pola naval arsenal; contemporaneously, its sister ship, the 5,100-ton SMS *Kronprinzessin Stephanie*, was laid down at Trieste's naval shipyards. These vessels would be in service by 1890 and carried the largest armaments in the history of the *K.u.K. Kreigsmarine* in the form of three 30.5cm Krupp guns for the *Rudolf* and two for the *Stephanie*, contained within rotating turrets on the vessels' decks.[28] These would be the Habsburg navy's first pre-dreadnought battleships. Yet von Sterneck's Young School zeal had not dampened, and by 1891 he had commissioned 53 further torpedo boats into the fleet, weighing between 55 and 78 tons each. Six of the *K.u.K. Kreigsmarine*'s unique destroyers were also produced under the name *Torpedofahrzeuge* and were intended to fit comfortably into the new Young School focus of the fleet. The light cruiser component of the navy was also augmented during his tenure, with two

28   Sondhaus, L., *The Naval Policy of Austria-Hungary, 1867–1918*.

formerly British light cruisers – the *Leopard* and *Panther* – obtained from Newcastle in 1885. These English warships were then copied and produced as the *Tiger*. These light cruisers were built for speed and came in at just 1,500 tons each. The budget of 1887, with its 13.2 million gulden allotment, had the specification that the majority be spent on destroyers and torpedo boats. Battleships were not to be bought or built.

The Young School amid Habsburg ranks would not survive the death of Admiral von Sterneck in 1897, as the arrival of von Spaun would see a return to Decisive Battle Doctrine with proposals for a nine-strong battleship fleet. During his tenure, destroyers and torpedo boats would be put on hold, and all focus would be placed upon producing the steel leviathans of the dawning century. The turn away from Archduke Albrecht's Young School was facilitated in the main by the subconscious embrace on the part of the Kaiser's heir, Archduke Franz Ferdinand, of the Decisive Battle Doctrine. On a visit to Pola in the spring of 1898, the would-be Kaiser concluded that the fleet needed battleships. He stated that the *K.u.K. Kreigsmarine* had to "acquire several large battleships, of at least 8–10,000 tonnes ... and more good and fast cruisers". Subsequent to this, von Spaun would submit his fleet plan for 1899–1908, envisioning the production of 12 battleships, 12 cruisers, 12 destroyers, 72 torpedo boats and six monitor vessels for a brown water fleet.[29] The latter component would be used to patrol the Danube, which in the event of war with the Russian Tsardom could be of as yet indeterminable use. However, the *Reichsrat* was not in a position to be able to forward him the immense 20.5 million kronen budget required to commission all his vessels in short order. They were prepared instead to grant him the funds for one battleship at a time, and for 1899 to provide him with a budget of 16.8 million kronen, a sum later pumped up to 17.8 million kronen to cover the additional costs of cruiser construction. One of the more welcome aspects of the departure from the Young School would come in the form of its relation to the nation's industrial base. In 1900 – von Spaun's third year in office – 90 percent of naval expenditure for construction and maintenance was now spent within the empire's borders. The focus on fostering the Habsburg Empire's domestic industry had been part of his plan from the first instance, attempting to endear the *Reichsrat*'s nationalist parties to the navy through promising them a slice of the construction pie. Fostering the dominion's industries allowed the acceleration of shipbuilding programmes, and between 1899 and 1904 the navy laid down six battleships. The start of the Montecuccoli years from 1904–12 saw him inherit this modern, Decisive Battle School-led navy, whose potency was every bit the match of the *Regia Marina* in open battle. During the year of his entry into the position, Montecuccoli published his own battlefleet plan. The revision called for 13 battleships, 12 cruisers, 18 destroyers and 82 torpedo boats. Six novel submarines were also requested. The launching of HMS *Dreadnought* in February 1906 convinced Montecuccoli and the *K.u.K. Kreigsmarine* that their 14,500-ton proposed battleships were sufficient, and that competing with the *Dreadnought* would be folly.

---

29   Sondhaus, L., *The Naval Policy of Austria-Hungary, 1867–1918*.

In November 1906, this judgement was reversed, and the budget was extended to provide the starting costs for a new class of super-potent 14,500-ton battleships, of which Montecuccoli wanted three. These would be classified as the Radetzky-class battleship.[30]

The commissioning of these sub-dreadnoughts proved the *K.u.K Kreigsmarine*'s commitment to its rediscovered dedication to Decisive Battle Doctrine. The Radetzky-class carried 12in. guns, alongside a powerful secondary gun battery consisting of eight 9.4in. guns. Their speed matched HMS *Dreadnought*, coming in at 20.5 knots.[31] Their construction took place wholly within the confines of the empire. Skoda built their guns; their armour originated from the Witkowitz Mines & Ironworks firm in Moravia and boilers were built under licence from Yarrow of London in Trieste. The project came together at the naval yards in that city, where the *Stabilimento Tecnico Triestino* forged them together. The first vessel of this type was laid down in 1907 and completed the following year, to be christened as the SMS *Erzherzog Franz Ferdinand*. Its sister vessel, the SMS *Radetzky*, was launched in 1910 alongside the SMS *Zrinyi*. To account for their production, naval budgeting skyrocketed to 73.4 million kronen in 1908. Torpedo boat production, as predicted by the shift back to Decisive Battle Doctrine, slackened, and only 12 of the 110-ton vessels were constructed by the end of the century's first decade. The crowning glory of the Montecuccoli years would come in 1908 with the construction of the *K.u.K. Kreigsmarine*'s very own dreadnought, SMS *Viribus Unitis*, the first of the Tegetthoff class. It would serve as a stark temple to the Austro-Hungarian belief in Decisive Battle Doctrine and serve to stamp the Habsburg Empire's claim to thalassocracy over the Adriatic with terrifying aplomb. The releasing of the *Tegetthoff* class ships onto the high seas sent dockyards the length and breadth of Italy into a vigorous display of frantic energy. By March 1911, the dreadnought programme was officially announced, and on 5 December 1912, the *K.u.K. Kriegsmarine* joined the navies of the world as a potent force with the launch of the SMS *Viribus Unitis*.[32] The years of toil were at an end and the empire could sail into the First World War ready to defend its title as master of the Adriatic.

30   Kramli, M., *Austro-Hungarian Battleships and Battleship Designs: 1904-1914*.
31   Roberts, J., *The Battleship Dreadnought*, p.16.
32   Kramli, M., *Austro-Hungarian Battleships and Battleship Designs: 1904-1914*.

8

The Genesis of the MAS Boats: Fasana, 1916

The MAS forces which the Italian state created by the dawn of the First World War, like all rapid-acting torpedo boat units, were generated by those who adhered to the Young School ideas of the late 19th century. In the Italian case, this force was pioneered by the charismatic Torinese career naval officer Paolo Thaon di Revel. Born in 1859, the future fleet admiral took command of the *Regia Marina*'s machine school in Venezia in 1905, beginning a long association with the city.[1] It was a city whose shallow waters allowed him to be present for the first experiments with the *Regia Marina*'s nascent MAS force, an experience which would do much to secure his revulsion in the face of the contemporary triumph of Mahan's Decisive Battle Doctrine. During his tenure there, the Italian navy undertook a series of experiments with a new line of speedboats, contracted by the Italian government, with the idea of producing a unit capable of patrolling the Venetian coast.[2] The littoral zone around Venice was dotted with hundreds of small islands, tiny inlets and gaping river mouths. During countless conflicts over the centuries, this difficult maritime geography had made invading the Most Serene Republic of Venice a task so dangerous that even their most daring foes had feared the obstacles lurking in its murky waterways. During Venice's golden age, the keels of enemy galleys had time and again been churned up by rocks, invisible sandbanks and grasping wetlands. For the Italian Kingdom that had come to possess these territories in 1866, the dangers were not lessened, and neither were those presented by the Habsburg monarchy. Thus, the Veneto coastal plain required policing by a government unacquainted with it, lest the *K.u.K. Kreigsmarine* should worm its way into city's perimeter.

The environment in which this coastal security unit was supposed to operate determined the tools which this task would require. In this case, that tool would be a vessel whose required specifications were that it be fast, well-armed and able to operate both on sea and riverway. In essence, there was a requirement for the machine to

---

1   Alberini, P. & Prosperini, F., *Uomini della Marina: 1861–1946*, p.513.
2   Botti, F., *Il Pensiero Militare e Navale (1789–1915)*, pp.868–874.

Admiral Paolo Thaon di Revel.
(Italian Navy Archives)

The MAS homeport at Venezia. (Photochrom Prints Collection, Library of Congress)

The Preserved MAS 96. (Vittoriale degli Italiani Estate)

be equally useable by either a brown water or a blue water navy. In addition, it must be able to operate in Venezia's tight canal systems and dock in the shallow naval infrastructure which these housed. These demands called for a synthesis between a sea-going and river-going vessel. However, an obstacle to achieving this would be the sheer harshness of the Upper Adriatic's seascape, stretching on the Italian side from the Venetian coastline in the north-east 134 miles south to Ancona.[3] Across from Ancona lays Zadar, set among Dalmatian cliffs which run continuously up to Fiume (modern Rijeka) and into the Istrian peninsula (for a full description, see Chapter 1). In the winter and autumn, this enclosed sea becomes subject to the brutality of the deadly 'bora' wind, a weather phenomenon inducing random gusts of freezing air onto anyone unfortunate enough to become caught up in its blast. Even the littoral geography bordering these waters is an unforgiving one, replete with enclosed rock formations which whip the calm seas found on the open waves into frenzied whirlpools.

The design concept lay dormant for six years in filing cabinets in the offices of the *Regia Marina*'s technical department in Venezia. Only when di Revel returned to

3   Ivetic, E, *Storia dell'Adriatico*, pp.1–4.

War in the Corridors – Jutland, di Revel and Decisive Battle Doctrine

When war was declared between Italy and the Habsburg Empire in the spring of 1915 (Rome's war with the German Empire wouldn't begin until 28 August 1916),[13] it had been done so with the express intention of expelling the last vestiges of Habsburg domination over Italians. Its rationale was entirely linked to a visceral will to liberate all Italians everywhere from foreign rule, and to establish Rome's dominion over anywhere with even the most tangential link to Italy. In this mode of thinking, no claim was stronger than that of Dalmatia and Istria (see Chapter 5 for an in-depth explanation). Through laying claim to the western Balkan shoreline, Italy also believed it had inherited a god-given right to rule the Adriatic Sea. The Battle of Lissa did little to weaken those beliefs, except that after Lissa, to obtain the maritime domination Italy sought, a tooth-and-nail fight would have to be undertaken with the *K.u.K. Kreigsmarine*. Yet although that battle was the *Regia Marina*'s *raison d'être* during the First World War, its actions within that theatre were wholly framed by the Italio-Habsburg terrestrial conflict on the kingdom's eastern frontiers. There, at the River Isonzo, the legendary struggle of modern Italy was written. In Italian historical culture, this struggle's significance is equal to that of Verdun or the Somme and is perceived – in contrast to the Second World War – as a people's struggle.[14] It is viewed as a justified fight against the archenemy in order to preserve Italy's core lands and expand the wars of Italian independence past the Julian Alps to free the Italians still trapped in the Habsburg Empire proper. But although in spring 1915 Rome was full of bloodcurdling desire for its ancestral lands across the sea, the war fervour aimed at the Habsburg Empire was nothing in comparison to the Italiophobia which gripped Habsburg citizens in Vienna upon the Italian declaration of war on 23 May 1915.[15]

The Habsburg monarchy had been waiting for an opportunity to destroy the Italian Kingdom since its formation in 1861. The House of Savoy had effectively stripped the Habsburgs of their relevance in the west and had rendered them wholly dependent on their power in the east. This had been an event which had done much to pave the way for the First World War, predicated as it was by a forced confrontation with Russia over the fate of Serbia, a state whose ambitions mirrored those once seen among the zealous adherents of Italian nationalism over 50 years beforehand. Among those who shared the view that the woes of the Habsburg state lay entirely at the door of the Savoyard kings of Italy, none was more prominent than *Feldmarschall* Franz Conrad von Hotzendorf. Unfortunately for Rome, this name belonged to one of Vienna's most prominent warlords, the commander-in-chief of the Austro-Hungarian military, a

13   Thompson, M., *The White War: Life and Death on the Italian Front, 1915–1919* (London: Faber & Faber, 2008), pp.35–39.
14   Colarizi, S., *Storia del Novecento Italiano*. pp.69–82.
15   Herwig, H., *The First World War: Germany and Austria-Hungary, 1914–1918*, pp.149–154.

position Hotzendorf would hold until 1917.[16] To the chagrin of the German Empire, Hotzendorf resolved to punish the Italians, even if it meant losing to the Russian Tsardom. His strategy for tackling the Italian nemesis involved attacking from Trentino high in the Dolomites, before sweeping into the Po basin and cutting the kingdom off from Veneto. Habsburg forces from beyond the Isonzo would come west from Central Europe and punch through to Venice, seizing the city. With that, north-east Italy would be returned to Habsburg control in any post-war settlement, and the dynasty's credibility in the West would be restored. On 15 May 1915, Austro-Hungarian forces prematurely flooded into north-eastern Italy, and in the wake of a ferocious artillery bombardment a general offensive was mounted, ending with imperial forces taking 20km of Italian soil. Yet by the end of the month, the advance had stalled as Habsburg logistics failed and their supply lines came under immense pressure. Exhausted by the rapid movements of spring, a pattern of static fighting would set in across the River Isonzo until 1917.

On 23 June 1915, 18 Italian divisions fought against eight Austro-Hungarian divisions as the Italian Second and Third Armies pushed against Habsburg positions on the Isonzo. It was the first of 12 battles which would see the frontier continually pushed and pulled until it finally broke at Caporetto. On 25 March 1916, the Habsburgs attempted an attack from a different direction; instead of the well-trodden paths of the Isonzo, Hotzendorf planned to put into action his scheme to cross Trentino and into the Po Valley. However, the Habsburgs had failed to take note of the climactic conditions and the area's difficult geography. Consequently, they became stuck among the peaks, and although they did succeed temporarily, by June that year they had been stopped before they broke into Emilia-Romagna and could threaten Padua.[17] On both the Trentino and Isonzo fronts, the two sides increasingly sunk into a costly stalemate. Out on the waves of the Adriatic though, the opposite could not have been more true. Here, in contrast to this environment of stalling offensives and resolute rearguards, a rapid and brutal naval campaign centred on the high seas of the Upper Adriatic.

A month after the Italian spring declaration of war against their historical enemy, the *K.u.K. Kreigsmarine* began its Adriatic campaign, an epic effort which would last until the final days of November 1918 but which would go without a single decisive battle. The latter fact would cause much disconcertion as to the point of the Italian naval arm. The maritime portion of the Austro-Italian contest opened up as it meant to go on, with the *K.u.K. Kreigsmarine* unleashing a devastating series of coastal bombardments in early summer 1915.[18] Their targets, as would be the case throughout the war, were the Italian Army's positions along the Isonzo. The *K.u.K. Kreigsmarine* thus began acting as artillery support for Hotzendorf's interminable

16   Watson, A., *Rings of Steel: Germany and Austria-Hungary at War, 1914–1918* (London: Penguin Publishing, 2014), pp.300–301.
17   Herwig, H., *The First World War: Germany and Austria-Hungary, 1914-1918*, pp.336–351.
18   Sondhaus, L., *The Great War at Sea: A Naval History of the First World War* (Cambridge: Cambridge University Press, 2014), p.164.

series of assaults on the Italian border. On the surface it may seem strange that a navy so dedicated to the Decisive Battle Doctrine of the previous century might relegate its forces to the meagre status of mobile maritime artillery. Yet these minor acts fell within *Marinekommandant* – Admiral Anton Haus' strategy to preserve the *K.u.K. Kreigsmarine*'s dreadnought fleet.[19] His fear was not entirely unfounded, for the Habsburg Empire was not in a position to easily replace its losses. As seen in the previous chapter, the Austrian imperium was on the edge of an ethnic collapse, its industrial power marred by a quota system and hampered by a requirement to appease lesser industries in Hungary. In short, it was not a society capable of recovering from devastating naval defeats. But in avoiding battle, Anton Haus realized the fears elucidated by France's *Amiral* Aube during his tenure as head of the *Marine Nationale* from 1886-87,[20] namely that battleships (his logic easily extended to dreadnoughts) would come to a point where their firepower, armour and expense would lead to international parity. The result of any clash between them could thus only ever be inconclusive, as their weapons and armour were equal. Once this happened, it was argued, no advantage could be attained on either side, and if just one dreadnought sank, its immense cost would render it irreplaceable. It followed, therefore, that the Habsburg fleet would switch to prioritizing submarine warfare to maintain its power on the seas, in lieu of sallying forth with their exposed dreadnoughts. This forced the *K.u.K. Kreigsmarine* to start thinking along Young School lines, with a developing objective to prey on enemy commerce so as to deny the *Regia Marina* thalassocracy in the Adriatic.

The *Regia Marina*'s leadership became aware that this would be the character of the Adriatic campaign on 7 July 1915, when on a glorious summer's day the 9,800-ton *Pisa* class cruiser *Amalfi* was torpedoed and sunk by *K.u.K. Kriegsmarine* submarine *U26*.[21] The proximity of the attack, a mere 20 miles from Venezia, instilled fear and awe in equal measure among the Italian navy's decision-makers. At the top of this contemporary decision-making tree were Admiral Paolo Thaon di Revel and his direct superior, Duca Luigi Amadeo di Savoia. Their relationship was not a happy one, and as with all organizations, trouble at the top often spells trouble for the structure as a whole. The situation was not aided by the pre-war decision to site the *Regia Marina*'s primary base in Taranto, some 700 miles from the Gulf of Venice[22] where the campaign was unfolding in earnest. The southern sector of the Adriatic was largely quiet, and as so often in military affairs, pre-war conflict preparation had been wholly incorrect in its geographic dimensions. But the main bone of contention between the Italian navy's two leading officers was not the command structure's poorly located headquarters,

19   Sondhaus, L., *The Naval Policy of Austria-Hungary, 1867-1918*.
20   Fontin, P., *Guerre et Marine : Un Essai sur L'Unite de la Defense Nationale* (Paris: Berger-Levrault Éditeurs, 1906), p.129.
21   Sondhaus, L., *The Naval Policy of Austria-Hungary, 1867-1918*.
22   O'Hara, V., Dickson, D. *et al.*, *To Crown the Waves: The Great Navies of the First World War* (Annapolis: Naval Institute Press, 2013), pp.188–190.

but in their contrasting approach to naval warfare. Like many in Europe's aristocratic classes on both land and sea, Duca Luigi Amadeo di Savoia sought glory and
the pursuit of history-making battles, confrontations in which his name could be
echoed down the centuries and be the subject of marvellous paintings, as had been
the case with Tegetthoff after the Battle of Lissa. To this end, he had been wholly
consumed by the promises of Decisive Battle Doctrine, whereas, as we have seen, di
Revel had always been of the opposite view. The two positions were utterly irreconcilable. Meanwhile, the war in the Upper Adriatic had become an intense battle of
submarines, torpedo boats and destroyers. It was active and hectic. The Veneto front
line was vulnerable to coastal bombardment and amphibious incursions. As a result,
di Revel saw Veneto as Italy's greatest point of weakness and where the *Regia Marina*
would be of most use, serving to deter Habsburg raiding fleets. He saw the young
duke's desire to remain in Taranto along with the *Regia Marina*'s First Fleet for what
it was – vanity.

The desire for the *Regia Marina*'s commander-in-chief, Duca Luigi Amadeo di
Savoia, to force a battle in the Adriatic led to the aimless wandering of Italian naval
forces up and down the seaway. Without taking measures to allow for the danger of
Habsburg submarines, this decision was disastrous; by the autumn, the Italians had
lost two armoured cruisers, one destroyer, three torpedo boats and four submarines,
as well as two airships. The unabated shelling of towns along the front line by the
immense power of the Austro-Hungarian fleet's naval artillery had caused political
chaos in Rome, and the cost of the war soared. The lack of leadership in Taranto
contributed a good deal to producing this apocalyptic state of affairs. As the Italian
Army held back the Habsburg hordes in bitterly cold snow and sleet, the *Regia Marina*
was increasingly perceived as an institution which had failed to defend the nation. On
27 September 1915, the destruction via sabotage of the 13,400-ton pre-dreadnought
Benedetto Brin crowned the navy's slow decline. Someone had to take the blame for
their poor performance, and unshielded by aristocratic privilege, that man would
be *Ammiraglio* di Revel, who found himself exiled to Venezia to become the Upper
Adriatic's operational commander.[23] The hapless duke would remain untouched in his
command position, and under his watch he would get two chances to engineer the
decisive battle he so craved.

On 29 December 1915, the *K.u.K. Kreigsmarine* sallied forth from their main base
at Pola on a routine harassment operation of Italian forces in Albania.[24] The force in
question consisted of the 3,500-ton *Novara* class scout cruiser SMS *Helgoland* of 1911
vintage, accompanied by five 880-tonne 1911-built *Tatra* class destroyers. At Durazzo
(modern Durres in Albania), this light raiding force came into contact with a *Regia
Marina* minefield off the Dalmatian settlement's port. The sea mines tore apart the
destroyers SMS *Lika* and *Triglav*, the noise of which alerted the *Regia Marina* to the

23   Alberini, P. & Prosperini, F., *Uomini della Marina: 1861–1946*, p.514.
24   Sondhaus, L., The *Great War at Sea*, p.178.

attack. Before long, a superior Italian force backed by elements from the Royal Navy's Mediterranean fleet and the *Marine Nationale* arrived to give chase. As the remaining four ships of the Habsburg force steamed for the imperial port at Kotor, the joint Allied fleet gave pursuit. During the race to safety, the *K.u.K. Kreigsmarine* lost a further destroyer, SMS *Tatra* (later towed to safety), and as the 29th merged into the dawn of the 30th, the Habsburg fleet had been forced to retreat. During the winter of that year, Britain's Royal Navy decided to close the Straits of Otranto with an enormous blockade. The Admiralty's objective was to trap the *K.u.K. Kreigsmarine* inside the confines of the Adriatic, removing its ability to venture across the Mediterranean, ensuring Allied control of the vast sea until the end of the war. In doing so, the Royal Navy, provided the objective of all Habsburg naval activities throughout the conflict – the breaching of the Otranto blockade and the breaking of the fleet into the Mediterranean theatre. Indeed, on 22 December 1916, the Adriatic would witness the largest nautical confrontation yet – the first attempt to breach the Otranto blockade..[25]

On a freezing winter's night, Captain Notowtny led the 400-ton *Scharfschutze Huszar* class destroyer alongside three of its sister vessels in a night-time raid against the blockade line. The Otranto barrier comprised an immense net designed to tie up propellers, trapping vessels inside. Underneath the net was positioned a plethora of mines of varying types to finish off disabled vessels. On either end of the massive fortification system was positioned a fleet of auxiliary steamers designed to maintain the defensive system. Termed 'drifters', these vessels were slow and near obsolescence, so they became the favoured targets of light Austro-Hungarian vessels. On that bora-filled December, night their preferential status remained at the forefront of the captains' minds. When Captain Notowtny sighted them, the *Huszar* class destroyer's 7cm/45L Skoda naval guns poured devastating fire on the decrepit drifters, sinking two Royal Navy vessels in the act. Once again, Habsburg actions caused a general alert among Allied warships in the area, provoking the arrival of a combined fleet. This force consisted of *Marine Nationale* destroyers, local *Regia Marina* destroyers of the 672-ton *Indomito* class and an immense Royal Navy light cruiser constructed in 1909, HMS *Gloucester*. As in the Battle of Durazzo described above, the *K.u.K. Kreigsmarine* had no choice but to flee, fighting a ferocious rearguard which damaged two French destroyers,[26] likely 809-ton *Bouclier* class vessels. It was becoming increasingly clear, even to the stubborn aristocrats at Taranto, that a decisive Austro-Italian battle of the scale of Lissa would be impossible to force. The most they could expect would be continual small actions, mainly prosecuted by destroyers against enemy vessels equal or lesser in size. Even if they had managed to produce a dreadnought-on-dreadnought battle for the ages, it is likely its conclusion would have been equally disappointing. It was a lesson which had been learned in the spring of that year off a seemingly insignificant Danish peninsula known as Jutland.

25   Sondhaus, L., *The Naval Policy of Austria-Hungary, 1867–1918*.
26   Sondhaus, L., *The Naval Policy of Austria-Hungary, 1867–1918*.

The Battle of Jutland would be the First World War's largest surface vessel confrontation. Its breadth was staggering, a total of 250 warships engaging with each other across miles of open sea.[27] The battle's objective had been to break the Royal Navy's blockade of the German Empire and to permit the German High Seas Fleet to operate in the North Sea, thereby threatening British access to its enormous globe-spanning commercial empire. If successful, the Germans could have taken the British Empire out of the war. When the much-desired battle took place, the losses were heavier on the Royal Navy's side than that of the Germans, but not decisively so. The ships involved were equally matched, but the dreadnought fleets of either side did not see the light of day. Instead, the battle was fought by pre-dreadnought battleships, light cruisers, armoured cruisers and destroyers. The fact that the Royal Navy had been able to maintain its blockade of the North Sea without either dreadnought fleet being present dented the idea that battles could only be won by the latest giant battleships. What had seemed to be the apex of Decisive Battle Doctrine thinking – the Dreadnought class – now looked to be a wasteful expense of the highest order. As the institutional power of the doctrine's adherents waned after Jutland, waves were being made in Venezia towards a different way of waging war at sea.

The Debut of the MAS – the Fazana Channel Raid of November 1916

When *Ammiraglio* Paolo Thaon di Revel was sent into exile to Venezia from Taranto and cast out from the company of Duca Luigi Amadeo di Savoia, it had initially been a severe blow to his prestige. However, his dismissal allowed him to take charge of a port whose military component had been tied up with the production of torpedo boats and the housing of the *Regia Marina*'s rapid reaction forces.[28] Given the presence of the *K.u.K. Kreigsmarine*'s main base of operations at Pola, directly opposite Venezia across the Adriatic, the combat experienced there was more frequent, albeit on a smaller scale. Two main threats operated in the Upper Adriatic zone which had become di Revel's sole preserve by the beginning of 1916 – submarines and torpedo boats, both emanating from Pola. Three years beforehand, when di Revel had previously been stationed in Venezia, he had conducted experiments into naval aviation. In 1913, he had even managed to produce a report looking into the matter and their efficacy at surveillance against these types of targets in the future. Thanks to his interest, by June 1914 a force of prototype aircraft carriers had been created for use with seaplanes. These vessels had been created out of the pre-dreadnoughts *Vittorio*, *Emanuele* and *Roma*, operating alongside the armoured cruisers *San Giorgio* and *San Marco*.[29] They carried New York-built model F Curtiss flying boats, which at the time

27   Macintyre, D., *Jutland* (New York: Norton & Company, 1958).
28   O'Hara, V., Dickson, D. *et al.*, *To Crown the Waves*, pp.182–185.
29   O'Hara, V., Dickson, D. *et al.*, *To Crown the Waves*, p.204.

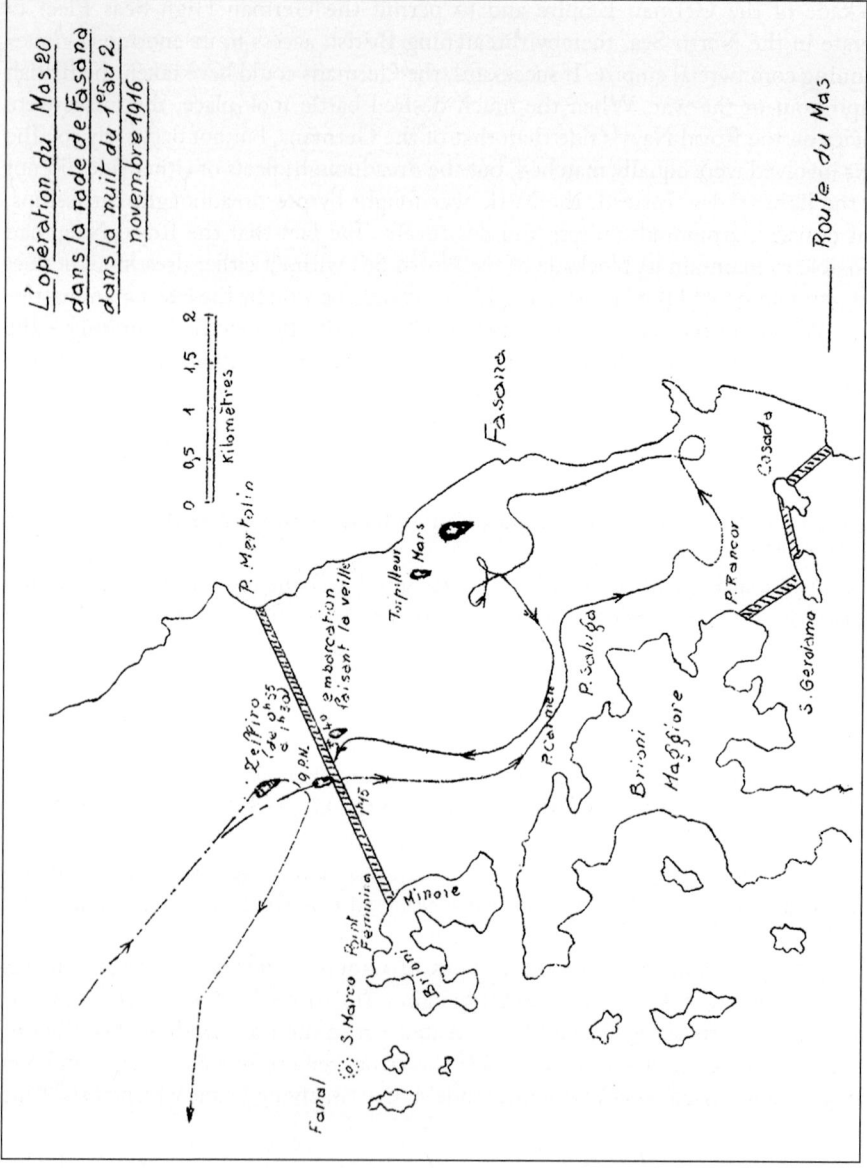

Fasana Channel raid (1).

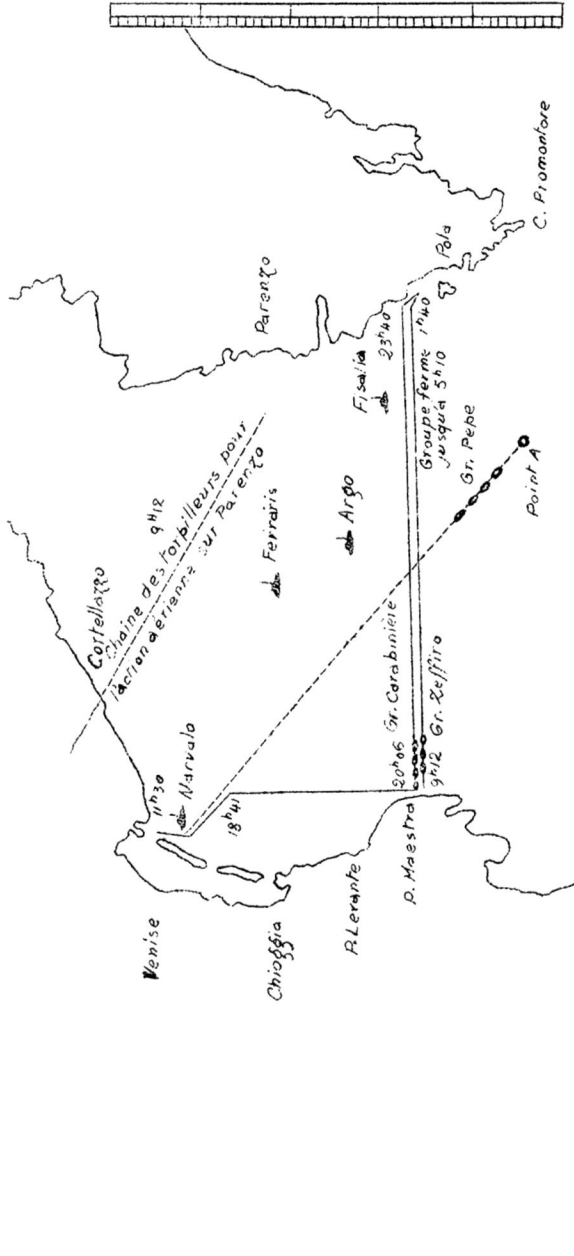

L'opération du Mas 20 dans le Canal de Fasana dans la nuit du 1er au 2 novembre 1916

Routes du groupe "Zeffiro" g P.N. 'Mas 20'.

Positions de différents groupes d'appui à 9h12 du 2 nov.

Parcours de différents groupes.

Fasana Channel raid (2).

were cutting edge machines, having only come onto the market in 1912. With their lengthy five-hour endurance and 4,500ft service ceiling, they were tailor-made to perform the role of maritime reconnaissance aircraft. Yet when di Revel was moved to Venezia, they had only been assigned anti-submarine warfare roles. Di Revel had other ideas about their utility, and on 28 October 1916 he tasked the *Regia Marina*'s naval aviation element to carry out reconnaissance over the Bay of Fazana,[30] which he suspected of harbouring a monster 10,500-ton Erzherzog Karl-class battleship – an excellent prey, if the reports were true.

Feedback from naval aviation was positive, and also succeeded in identifying a scout cruiser of an unknown class in the shallow Dalmatian port. The purpose of the aerial reconnaissance was to give di Revel the green light for the first operation of the Italian navy's MAS special forces squadrons. He had long been a believer in Aube's Young School and had furthered the theory with his own conceptualization of irregular warfare upon the waves. In his eyes, the transplantation into maritime combat of the idea of guerrilla warfare was possible. Instead of being waged by highly trained terrestrial commandos and zealous bands of resistance fighters, however, the naval variant of guerrilla warfare would be fought by torpedo boats, aviation and the exploits of daring sabotage divers. Until di Revel's relocation to Venezia, this had been a mere pipe dream, but upon his transfer he had made the acquaintance of Pignati Morano, the commander of the Venetian torpedo boat flotilla. Morano greeted di Revel's thoughts with ecstatic curiosity and became an easy convert to his version of nautical irregular warfare. The two men had initially disagreed as to where this prospective form of naval warfare should be tested. The admiral-in-exile repeatedly lobbied for Pola to be the proving ground for his unorthodox ideas. Morano's counter-suggestion was that the first MAS operation should take place instead at Fazana, where reportedly the *K.u.K. Kreigsmarine* docked its battleships. It is more than likely that Morano's interjection saved the MAS forces from a quick and ignominious end within Pola's labyrinthine defensive systems.

Fazana Bay, 5km north of Pola, is home to a large Italianate town whose Roman ruins were only discovered at the beginning of the 20th century.[31] From the bay's picturesque fishing villages, one can look out to the immense Isle of Brioni, which is actually divided into 14 different land masses spread across 8km, dotted with the small stone houses of centuries of continuous settlement.[32] Before war ravaged the Balkans, Fazana was a settlement that had been considered spectacularly beautiful. Like most places up and down the western Balkan coast, the main trade at the time was that of the fisherman or the farmer. Indeed, such was the reliance upon this work for the sustenance of the community that the people who lived there held annual festivals in honour of the sardine. At the advent of war, this resplendent town had

30   Kern, I., *Actions des MAS Italiens en Adriatique*, p.322.
31   Rottauscher, M., *With Tegetthoff at Lissa*.
32   Tanner, M., *Croatia: A History from the Middle Ages to the Present Day*, pp.2–10.

been subjected to the cruel imposition of wartime architecture; in this case the positioning of a minefield composed of 1,450 mines, combined with a series of sunken obstacles topped off by a large net, in the waters between Fazana Bay and the Isle of Brioni.[33] This vast underwater barrier was kept in place by two metal barrels which were positioned at its two extremities. Additionally, war had seen the building of fortresses on Mali Brijun and Veli Brijun, situated on the archipelago facing the Italianate settlement. There was also a lighthouse on the east-facing side of the island chain,[34] which every night cast a glow over the bay's defences. In addition, drifters were positioned on the periphery of the bay's defencesr to maintain a security cordon in the event of intruders.

For their debut operation to succeed, preparation would be key for the MAS vessels. For this purpose, a replica barrier was set up in the Venetian Gulf. During their initial training, the immediate issue the Italian mariners discovered was that the MAS boats were not sufficiently optimized for stealth. Their petrol engines were simply too noisy. This led to the fitting of electric motors onto the boats, completing their evolution which had begun in 1906. During the same exercises, it was also revealed that the torpedoes primed for use with the MAS boats had propellers which gave off too much noise; these were subsequently muffled. To penetrate the defences, the lead vessel – MAS 9 – was fitted with two 1,900kg lead cylinders which would be used to brush aside the obstacles hidden in the channel. The vessel's shallow draught would prevent it coming into contact with the mines positioned below the surface. Once the technical preparations had been made, all that remained was to pick a date for the operation. After the *Regia Marina*'s aviation wing's positive reconnaissance report of 28 October 1916, the date was set for the night of 1 November, to take advantage of a holiday day in the Habsburg Empire. Striking at this time would ensure lower levels of defensive surveillance.

Lead the attack would be Captain Costanzo Ciano, a Sicilian of dedicated focus and possessor of a deep sense of responsibility. According to the Italian poet Gabriele D'Annunzio, Ciano was an individual whose shoulders "could carry any weight of duty or command".[35] He was daring when needs be yet considered and collected when required; the very image of the disciplined yet risk-loving commando. At 5:30 p.m. on the night of 1 November, with a force of torpedo boats and destroyers in support, Ciano's MAS 20 was dragged into position. After he detached his vessel from its tow, the unit embarked on its first mission. They believed their target, was an Erzherzog Karl-class battleship. Had this been the case, they would have been up against a 10,500-ton pre-dreadnought of fearsome prowess, complete with a 740-strong crew and 28 shell-firing guns, four of them being the remarkably potent 24cm Skoda L40/K97 main guns. Such a vessel might have even survived the MAS boats' torpedoes,

33   Kern, I., *Actions des MAS Italiens en Adriatique*, pp.22–23.
34   Tanner, M., *Croatia: A History from the Middle Ages to the Present Day*, p.318.
35   D'Annunzio, G., *La Beffa di Buccari* (Milano: I Fratelli Traves, 1918), p.28.

equipped as they were with 7.3cm of Witkowitz Mines & Ironworks-fitted steel plate anti-torpedo bulkheads along their bottom.[36] If the Italians had managed to sink an armoured beast on this scale, the story would have been as legendary as their later exploits. As they began to cut through the defensive network intended to keep them at bay, they could see the actual vessels that stood before them. As MAS 20 made its way through the debris lurking beneath the water's surface, it switched to its electric engines at 1:00 a.m. to remain undetected in pitched darkness. But instead of arriving to deal with their expected worthy foe, they were faced with an obsolete ironclad – the SMS *Mars*.[37] The aged vessel was of only 7,400 tonnes and posed no credible danger to the *Regia Marina*, nor the Italian war effort in general. However, beggars cannot be choosers, and MAS 20 pressed on undeterred.

Ciano steered close into the bay, until they were nose-to-nose with the *Mars*, at which point they launched their torpedoes at the ancient vessel. Unfortunately, MAS 20's torpedo percussion cap failed and its munition failed to penetrate the vessel's armour, leaving it relatively unharmed. The torpedo merely bumped into the *Mars* and detonated outside. This led the ship's crew to frantically radio to the bay's authorities, but due to a misunderstanding it was believed that the attack had come from the air. At dawn the next day, it became obvious that some other force had been in operation, but the MAS had long gone in search of a better target. The operation came to a close at 03:40 a.m., Ciano's vessels speeding out of the bay to avoid the attention of the area's awakened authorities. Their departure was by the same route that they had entered through the bay's torpedo nets. Although they had not achieved the destruction of their objective, they had established that nowhere was safe from the *Regia Marina* in the Adriatic. Furthermore, their action earned the *Regia Marina* some prestige at a point where it was at a considerably low ebb with regard to the army, a body with which it would have to frequently fight for funding allocation throughout the war. In this respect, the operation was of immense political importance in securing much-needed esteem for the navy. More importantly for the MAS units, the operation served as ample proof of the concept for Paolo Thaon di Revel's future vision for Italy's naval special forces.

36   Kramli, M., *Austro-Hungarian Battleships and Battleship Designs, 1904-1914.*
37   Kern, I., *Actions des MAS Italiens en Adriatique*, p.23.

9

The Triumph of the MAS Fleet

On 18 August 1917, the *Regio Esercito* (Royal Italian Army) launched the 11th and last prior to the Caporetto rout the following autumn, major offensive operation on the Isonzo Front.[1] It was the latest in an apparently endless series of attacks and counter-attacks along that frontier, which had become part and parcel of the war's Italian campaign. But although the Habsburgs had successfully repelled Italian forces time and again, their manpower was dwindling. Each battle gradually contributed to an exponentially declining number of troops on the battlefield for the Austro-Hungarians. The Italians, defending home soil, did not have that problem and were capable of bringing up constant reserves of men without cessation. The Habsburgs were forced to conscript from an empire which was rapidly collapsing into ethnic chaos. The result was that their manpower demands were harder to meet, a fact not improved by Vienna's enormous commitment to the Eastern Front in aid of the war effort against the Tsar. The reality – unfortunately lost on Vienna – was that in order to win the war, the Russians had to be knocked out of the game, which meant the conflict in the East deserved far more resources than a campaign fought for petty dynastic revenge. Indeed, the Italian obsession at the Hofburg palace would continue even upon the ascent of Kaiser Karl I in the wake of his grand uncle's death in November 1916.[2] During a sweltering meeting amid the high summer of 1917, the new monarch would lecture Kaiser Wilhelm II on the axiomatic nature of Italy within Austro-Hungarian foreign and defence policy. Thankfully for the German war planners, they did not have long left to listen to the Habsburg's banal justifications, as the campaign's end point came ever closer. Vienna had at last understood that the constant attrition had to be stopped and a decisive land battle had to be won.

During the late summer of 1917, German and Austro-Hungarian generals consulted in preparation for a joint operation of colossal magnitude. It would mark the first occasion in which the German Empire was seen to join with their fellow Teutons in

---

1   Herwig. H., *The First World War: Germany and Austria-Hungary, 1914–1918*, pp.336–351.
2   Taylor, A.J.P., *The Habsburg Monarchy*, p.259.

the Italian conflict following Berlin's declaration of war against Italy on 28 August 1916. Up until now, their cooperation had been purely material, usually in the form of submarine sorties into the Adriatic. German cooperation in an operation across the Isonzo would mark their entrance in earnest on the Italian Front, a theatre of the war which it had heavily lobbied against. Yet the Germans knew that if they didn't intervene, the Habsburgs would throw themselves fruitlessly against Italy's resolute mountain frontiers. In the process, the empire would be drained of much-needed munitions, men and treasure. On 29 August, *Landstreitkräfte* commander General Alfred von Waldstatten, on behalf of Austro-Hungarian Chief of the General Staff Arthur Arz von Straussenburg, visited generals Hindenburg and Ludendorff to seek German assent for a joint operation on the Isonzo.[3] Despite the innate understanding that if the Habsburg armies did not break through into Italy they would be quite happy to waste away their resources until their use to the Central Powers was totally dissipated, the German warlords were hesitant to offer their approval. They feared that if the Habsburgs broke into the Po Valley and secured it all the way from Venezia to Torino, then it was likely they would negotiate a separate peace. Berlin's assumptions would have almost certainly been correct, for if Vienna could once again ascertain a voice in Western Europe through conquering north-east Italy, then its concern with the Balkans would be greatly reduced. However, the German reservations turned out not to be too deeply held, and German forces under General Otto von Below were duly committed to the Italian Front.

From 20 September 1917, logistics trains began to run across the Austro-German frontier and up to the border with the Italian Kingdom. The effort, consisting of 2,400 military trains composed of 100,000 wagons and taking up 33 percent of Habsburg railroad capacity, shunted men and munitions to the Alpine front lines.[4] On 24 October, von Below's Fourteenth Army – composed of hardened veterans from both the Eastern and Western Fronts – unleashed ferocious gas attacks, in the face of which the Italians were helpless; their respiratory equipment was not modern enough to handle the chemicals being fired at them. This was followed by unrelenting German pressure from General Krauss' pan-German army on the Tagliamento River, the defence of which broke on 2 November. Two days later, the Italian armies, which had so stoically faced wave after wave of Austro-Hungarian infantry, collapsed after a mere 10 days of German pressure. On 10 November, Generals Krauss and von Below were poised to cross the Piave River and advance into Veneto proper, thereby seeking to undo the past century of Italian reconquest.

It was not long before the oftdormant *K.u.K. Kreigsmarine* was called on to support the Germanic invasion of this waterlogged quagmire, with *Marinekommandant* Admiral Maximilian Njegovan (Admiral Anton Haus had died in February 1917) dispatching the two Trieste-built, *Monarch* class battleships SMS *Budapest* and SMS

3   Thompson, M., *The White War: Life and Death on the Italian Front*, p.311.
4   Herwig, H., *The First World War: Germany and Austria-Hungary, 1914-1918*, p.338

Wien, to the Upper Adriatic, alongside the 2,456-ton *Zenta* class scout cruiser SMS *Aspern* and its brother vessel, the 3,500-ton SMS *Admiral Spaun*.[5] However, unfortunately for both sides in the conflict, the war in Italy was to drag on further, as what looked like the end of the road for the Italians was avoided by a return to stalemate courtesy of support from the British Empire and the French Third Republic. Neither London nor Paris was prepared to let the Italian Kingdom fall, and on 5 November, a tripartite agreement was signed at Rapallo to hold an 80-mile front from Asiago in the Alps to the Venetian coast. Later that month, at Monte Grappa, pan-German armies were halted by the *Regia Esercito*. With progress halted, the Germans could no longer see the benefit to their continued participation in Italy; and when the British Army launched the Battle of Cambrai on the Western Front on 20 November,[6] German attention was diverted away from the Italian Front.

On 2 December 1917, Kaiser Karl I agreed to cease activities on the Italian Front to allow the German Empire to swing its efforts westward[7] in a bid to hold back the British advance. Nevertheless, it was not lost on the Italians that Caporetto had been a bruising defeat, as a result of which their ancient enemy had established positions a stone's throw from Venezia itself. If the Germans were successful in holding the Western Front and then pushing on to Paris, there was a good chance the Habsburgs would break through and seize Venice. For the *Regia Marina*, the hardship caused by the defeat at Caporetto was incalculable in terms of their newfound vulnerability. The Venetian naval command had contained within its influence the *Regia Marina*'s naval aviation arm, its torpedo boat fleet and many of its destroyers: all now a paltry 40 miles or from the Austro-Hungarian army's forward positions.[8]

Duca Luigi Amadeo di Savoia di Abruzzi was permanently stripped of his position as Commander-in-Chief of the fleet in February 1917,[9] as a result of the dismal performance of the *Regia Marina* during the previous year. In his place, *Ammiraglio* Paolo Thaon di Revel was recalled from Venezia and installed in Taranto, taking up his old position of Chief of Naval Staff. By the time the Italians were pushed back to the outskirts of Venezia, he had come to the opinion that it was necessary to make arrangements for a short-notice evacuation plan from the city. To ensure the continuance of his precious MAS boats, he relocated their manufacture from SVAN's Venetian boatyards to factories in La Spezia on the Ligurian coast. The leading naval construction firm given this duty was Baglietto S.p.A., a company that like that of the Camuffo family had been founded in the middle of the 19th century. Its founder was the Genovese shipbuilder Pietro Baglietto, who had operated from Varazze, a small town 20 miles from Genova, since 1854. Like its Venetian counterpart, the firm had specialized in providing sports yachts to the motorboat racing world which took off in

5   Sondhaus, L., *The Naval Policy of Austria-Hungary, 1867-1918*.
6   Watson, A., *Rings of Steel: Germany and Austria-Hungary at War*, p.518
7   Herwig, H,, *The First World War: Germany and Austria-Hungary, 1914-1918*, p.371
8   O'Hara, V., Dickson, D. et al., *To Crown the Waves*, pp.182–212.
9   Sondhaus, L., *The Naval Policy of Austria-Hungary, 1867-1918*.

University.[16] His talents were by then obvious, and he was admitted to the highly prestigious Karlsruhe Institute of Technology, a body founded by the Hohenzollern dynasty to promote the German Empire's scientific prowess. Focusing on mechanical engineering for three years led Popper to specialize in naval construction. From his graduation day until the empire's dissolution in 1918, he would be immersed wholly in the creation of a modern roster of vessels for the *K.u.K. Kreigsmarine*. Such was the breadth of his skill that he was the lead architect behind all the navy's roster of vessels during the First World War.[17]

The *Monarch* class was his first attempt at bringing the navy into the contemporary era – an attempt that was widely successful. However, it cannot be said that the *Monarch* class's impressive design was wholly down to his genius. Indeed, the class had been heavily copied from the Royal Navy's *Royal Sovereign* class battleships, the world's first true pre-dreadnought, post-ironclad vessels, which Popper had the pleasure of witnessing in their construction stage during an 1884 visit to Tyneside's Armstrong Mitchell & Company. The northern English shipbuilding firm was then contracted to produce a pair of new vessels for the Habsburg navy, which at that time did not possess the industrial base to build their own warships. By the time the *Monarch* class was being mused over in Pola's decision-making lobbies, Habsburg shipbuilding had leaped forward, so that in Austria and Bohemia at least there was a sufficient industrial base to produce the vessels almost completely indigenously. As a result, four domestic companies had a hand in the construction of the Monarch series of ships – Skoda, Witkowitz Mines & Ironworks, Krupp and *Stabilimento Tecnico Triestino*, or STT. At this point, Skoda had not yet the skill nor capacity to build naval guns under their own steam, so cooperated intimately with Germany's leading arms manufacturer, Krupp. The Moravian raw materials and metal working firm Witkowitz was backed by the Rothschild banking family and was wholly responsible for producing the vessels' armour. All components when finished were shipped to Trieste, where they were combined to form the warships. When the projects were completed, they were launched at the San Rocco shipyard near the commercial port of Muggia on the outskirts of Trieste. Both the *Wien* and *Budapest* were built employing this process and to identical specifications. Their launch, in 1895 and 1896 respectively, marked the conclusion of the Habsburg shipbuilding industry's first attempt at battleship production.

Their design called for an armament roster of four 24cm Krupp L/40 C/94 shell-firing guns as a main armament, with six 15cm Skoda L/40 shell guns as a secondary armament. The former was equipped with a horizontal breech sliding wedge loading mechanism, while the latter was loaded via a sliding block.[18] The Krupp guns could

16   Sondhaus, L., *The Naval Policy of Austria-Hungary, 1867-1918.*
17   Noppen, R., *Austro-Hungarian Battleships, 1914-1918* (New Vanguard series, 193) (Oxford: Osprey Publishing, 2012), p.5.
18   Noppen, R., *Austro-Hungarian Battleships, 1914–1918*, pp.5–8.

Captain Costanzo Ciano.
(Italian Ministry of Foreign Affairs)

Rear Admiral Luigi Rizzo in
1935. (Great War Gold Medals
Commission)

achieve a rate of fire of around three rounds per minute, over a range of 10½ miles at a speed of 690 metres per second. The 15cm Skoda guns, meanwhile, could manage four or five rounds per minute, over a range of 8½ miles. The muzzle velocity for these smaller guns was predictably higher, at 800 metres per second. For what we might today call a Close-In-Weapons-System (CIWS), these warships were equipped with 10 4.7cm Skoda L/44 cannons to be operated in conjunction with four 4.7cm Hotchkiss L/33 cannons.[19] Their role was to eliminate incoming torpedo boats, damage frigates and attack destroyers. With the advent of naval aviation during the first years of the 20th century, these cannons could also serve an anti-aircraft role. Although the Skoda cannon's rate of fire is unknown, the Hotchkiss gun fired 30 rounds per minute, reloading via a vertical breech sliding wedge. Its preferred target profile is betrayed by the armament's limited range of 3.7 miles. Due to its shorter length, the cannon's muzzle velocity was limited to 571 metres per second. However, its diminutive power was more than made up for by its rapid fire capacity. For repelling borders, a Skoda M1893 heavy machine gun was mounted on the vessel, firing 8x50mm Mannlicher rounds at a staggering 250 rounds per minute. However, there was only one of them – if the vessel had been swamped by speedboats, for example, it would likely have been helpless. To round off the *Monarch* class's impressive armament, two 45cm torpedo tubes were fitted to the vessel.

The vessel's outer protection was wholly constructed from nickel-steel plate and protected everything above the waterline. The armour was thickest across the armoured belt which traversed the length of the vessel, tapering out at either end, measuring 27cm thick at its greatest extent. The top deck was protected by 4cm of armour. The vulnerable bow had 12cm of nickel plate as protection. The remaining armour distribution was saved for the weapons housings. The vessel's six non-rotating casemates containing its Skoda 15cm secondary guns were mounted on both the starboard and port side, and each was protected by 8cm of nickel-steel plate, whilst the two primary rotating gun turrets were armoured with 25cm-thick plate. The two barbettes upon which these 24cm Krupp primary guns were mounted were also heavily armoured, with 22cm of nickel-steel plate. It should be noted that the construction did not include anti-torpedo bulkheads along the vessel's bottom; should it be hit by a torpedo, its chances of survival were low. The ship was propelled by four cylindrical boilers of unknown origin producing enough steam to power two vertical four-cylinder triple expansion engines. The mechanism powered two shaft-driven 4m propellers, producing a top speed of 17½ knots. Loaded to their maximum coal capacity of 500 tons, these ships had a range of 3,500 nautical miles, meaning they could sail from Pola at the tip of the Istrian peninsula to Dakar on the west coast of Africa without a single stop for refuelling.[20]

19   Kramli, M., *Austro-Hungarian Battleships and Battleship Designs, 1904–1914.*
20   Kramli, M., *Austro-Hungarian Battleships and Battleship Designs, 1904–1914.*

On 16 November 1917, the pair of *Monarch* class battleships bombarded *Regia Esercito* positions along the River Piave.[21] As young men from Bologna, Palermo and Rome fought side by side in rain-swept trenches attempting to hold off the advance of the grey tide of German stormtroopers, they were hit by massive 24cm 151kg high explosive shells.[22] Their impact tore apart solid positions and flesh indiscriminately. When the *Wien* and *Budapest* retired to the Gulf of Trieste, di Revel made sure to watch them carefully. During December, the vessels had received orders from Pola to bunker down in the 3-mile-long channel which separated Muggia from Trieste, tucked away in the north-western neck of Istria. Whilst docked there, the two vessels' crews – each comprising 26 officers and 397 ratings – were doubtless looking forward to wintering in the region's mild climate.[23] Despite their proximity, the histories and cultures of Muggia and Trieste could not be more different. Whilst Muggia had consolidated its Venetian ancestry and dialect, Trieste's inhabitants had long given up those Italianate trappings in favour of the customs of their long-standing Austrian masters.[24]

Sinking SMS *Wien* – the Operation of December 1917

Since becoming Chief of Naval Staff again, di Revel had been forced to take a backseat regarding the activities of his beloved MAS units. After his departure from Venezia, he had been forced to hand over the reins to the Sicilian Captain Costanzo Ciano, a man whose exploits at the Fazana channel had already earned him an impressive pedigree in the eyes of the MAS squadrons. Unfortunately, despite in-depth research, it has proved impossible to trace the decision-making chain which led to the tasking of the MAS forces with the destruction of SMS *Wien* and SMS *Budapest*. Their attacks on the Piave front, however, had certainly given impetus to discussions around the vessels' survival, and the timing of the operation – December – is unlikely to be a matter of chance. Whatever the situation, Captain Ciano's close confidant, Lieutenant Luigi Rizzo, had been given the job – either by Ciano or di Revel himself – of surveilling the Gulf of Trieste with a view to identifying and sinking the two *Monarch* class ships.[25] Rizzo's initial explorations had been promising, but upon his return Ciano still had several concerns about such a mission. Firstly, he believed that the sentries at the port of Muggia – home of the San Rocco shipyard and an incredibly important naval asset for the Habsburgs – would likely be particularly vigilant. These sentries, he argued, would be stationed on the jetties leading into the harbour, giving them excellent views of the channel's entrance. Secondly, when the attackers were discovered, the sentries

21 Sondhaus, L., *The Naval Policy of Austria-Hungary, 1867–1918*.
22 Herwig, H., *The First World War: Germany and Austria-Hungary, 1914–1918*, pp.366–372.
23 Noppen, R., *Austro-Hungarian Battleships, 1914–1918*, p.6.
24 Tanner, M., *Croatia: A History from the Middle Ages to the Present Day*, p.110.
25 Kern, I., *Actions des MAS Italiens en Adriatique*, p.9.

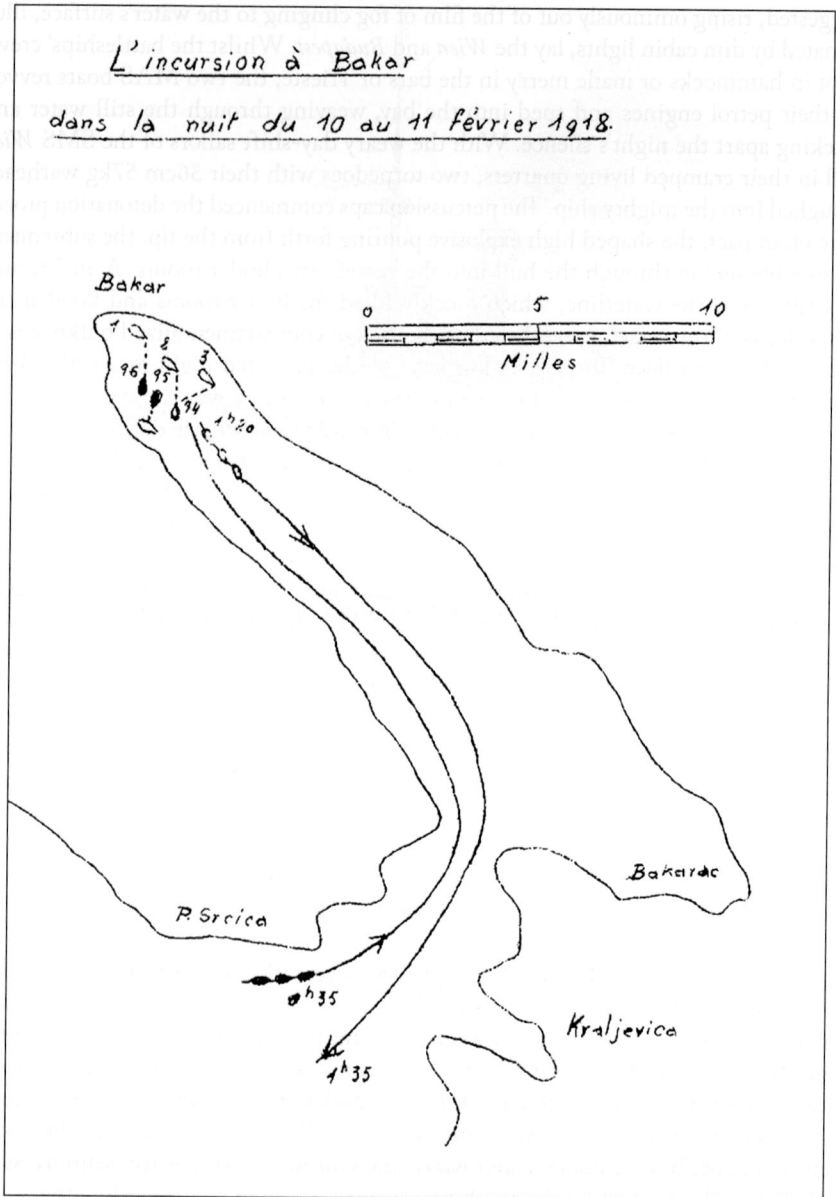

L'incursion à Bakar

dans la nuit du 10 au 11 février 1918.

The incusion into Bakar on the night of the 10th to 11th of February 1918, with an accompanying scale in miles. The circular symbols represent MAS boats, whilst the lines flowing from them, represent both their exit and entry route, respectively. Map taken from Kern, I. Actions des MAS Italiens en Adriatique Pendant la Grande Guerre et Reactions des Autrichiens (Paris: Ecole de Guerre Navale, 1935).

When the photograph of these three unlikely bedfellows was taken, they had scarcely completed an operation. Indeed, D'Annunzio's weary expression denotes a man recovering from exhausting exertion. Their mission had begun the previous morning, at 10:45 a.m. on 10 February 1918. Under Ciano's leadership, three vessels – MAS 94, MAS 95 and MAS 96 – had meandered down the treacherous channels which formed outer Venezia's geography. Their destination was the isle of Urinj, some 40 miles west of Pola. Unusually for the Adriatic winter, the water was still, the atmosphere dense with impenetrable fog. As their synchronized watches hit 10:20 p.m., the captains found themselves positioned at the mouth of the River Fianona, a small waterway leading into Istria from its eastern side. At this juncture, the destroyers that had towed them across the Adriatic released their charges. From eastern Istria, the MAS boats faced a rapid 15-minute journey to the cove that housed the Croat port of Bakar. Paolo Thaon di Revel, the head of the Italian navy, had chosen the site in advance, noting its proximity to the vast *K.u.K. Kreigsmarine* complex at Rijeka, behind only Pola or Trieste in its importance. A demonstration of force so deep into Habsburg waters, while inflicting tremendous morale damage on the Austro-Hungarian fleet, would also serve to replenish Italy's dwindling war enthusiasm, an emotional reserve which had been in terminal decline since the heavy defeats of autumn 1917. It had been with the objective of restoring the emotional resilience of the Italian people that Gabriele D'Annunzio had been invited to take part; an odd decision on the face of it. Yet it had been D'Annunzio who, in the later words of Benito Mussolini, had done more than any other to force the Italian state into the 1914–18 war.[33] His ability to whip up frenzied crowds was a remarkable skill, one he would use constantly when addressing the nation's tired sailors, airmen and soldiers. To the rankers of the country's armed forces, he was a near mythical figure,[34] whilst to those above him, his particular talent lay in embarrassingly lurid hagiographies whose lines would appear in his wartime writings. Indeed, as Ciano and Rizzo began to start up MAS 96's stuttering petrol engine, D'Annunzio busied his landlubber's hands with writing lavish tributes to his marine protectors.

As the MAS boats commenced their voyage to Bakar from the mouth of the Fianona River, a navigational challenge of the highest order awaited. Luckily, Ciano was more than up to the task. Born in Liguria, his life had largely been lived upon the seas, even his shoreside existence having been smothered by his native land's profound cultural affinity with the sea. In combination with Rizzo, his daring Sicilian colleague and destroyer of the SMS *Wien*, the exceedingly competent duo possessed an unbreakable will and undying determination. In a predictably vain move, D'Annunzio would claim in his later retelling to have been a part of this skilled relationship, when in reality he was a mere day-tripper. Once MAS 96's petrol engine fired its cylinders and the screw propulsion system began to turn, their vessel darted off on its hunt. For D'Annunzio,

33   Colarizi, S., *Storia del Novecento Italiano*, p.74.
34   Philippe, J., *D'Annunzio*.

the journey from the river mouth to the Gulf of Rijeka must have been one of futurist ecstasy. Their maximum speed evened out at 17 knots, just short of that produced by the 1903 Monaco Regatta winner.[35] However, it would not be long before Ciano and Rizzo were forced to cut short the poet's love affair with speed. At 12:35 a.m., they arrived in Bakar Bay, and under the cover of a black, smog-filled night the two captains switched from petrol propulsion to electric. As they neared the harbour, their hitherto seamless movement through calm waters came under the fierce influence of the region's currents, but thanks to the skill of their pilots, the three-vessel commando force navigated successfully through the bay's dangerously narrow entryway under silent electronic propulsion. Due to the guile of their crews and the MAS boats' sleek nature, their movements went undetected by the guards of the immense guns of the Kraljevica battery to the squadron's immediate right.[36]

As they crept into position within the bay, Ciano and Rizzo perfectly understood their opportunity, despite the heavy fog and dark night that engulfed all in the bay's restricted confines. At 01:20 a.m., the squadron opened fire on three enemy steam-ships. Weaving among the tall masts of the settlement's fishing vessels, the MAS boats jumped from position to position, firing as they went. Six torpedoes were loosed in total, but only one detonated. With the swinging of lanterns and the Germanic cries of whom they assumed were sentries breaking the calm in the bay, Rizzo and Ciano immediately comprehended the danger they were in. Fifteen minutes after launching their attack, they beat a hasty retreat, disappearing into the night at an incredible speed of 22 knots. Despite their inability to sink any of the vessels at anchor in the bay, the attack's purpose was realized the moment D'Annunzio committed the operation to memory. Within a year, his dramatic retelling would be diffused across the whole of Italy, greatly enhancing morale and providing new hope to the Italians. The legend of their hunt, the subsequent chase and the near-erotic feelings of exhila-ration which D'Annunzio committed to paper were, however, fabrications. Not that the world would find out until the war's close.

The rather mundane truth was that their escape from the operation had been so easy because their entry into the bay had gone unnoticed. Unknown to the Italians, from 1 February until the 10th, the *K.u.K. Kreigsmarine* had been immersed in an interne-cine conflict of mutinous violence between the fleet's officers and sailors. Lashed by spitting rain and the soaking force of the tides, the navy's blue-and-white-uniformed ratings had exchanged fire with the Habsburgs' white-clad soldiery for nine days.[37] So busy were they with their own mutineers that the ruptures that MAS 96 inflicted during its nocturnal antics were not noticed until the following morning. Only when an undetonated torpedo was discovered were the harbour authorities even aware of the raid. The noises that had convinced Ciano and Rizzo to escape so rapidly had not

35   Desmond, K., *The Guinness Book of Motorboating*, p.38.
36   Kern, I., *Actions des MAS Italiens en Adriatique*, p.35.
37   Sondhaus, L., *The Naval Policy of Austria-Hungary, 1867-1918*.

been provided by patrol vessels hunting them down, but by night-time fishermen, a peacetime practice that bizarrely had continued to be permitted by the shoreside commander after the outbreak of war with Italy in 1915.[38] Yet the attackers cared little whether the reality matched the fantasy, as both Ciano and Rizzo would emerge from the operation with increased prestige. For di Revel, the MAS boats had once again been vindicated.

For the Austro-Hungarians, the operation would be the last to occur under the tenure of Admiral Maximilian Njegovan, a man whose talents had not stretched to original thinking and who had kept to Anton Haus' obsessive focus on preservation of naval assets. As a result, Habsburg naval activity had been consistently restricted to light operations, mainly focused on the Upper Adriatic. With his retirement as a result of the Kotor mutiny on 1 March 1918 came the ascension of a young, ambitious and determined Hungarian captain, Miklos Horthy, and with it a change in strategic direction that would see the K.u.K. Kreigsmarine attempt to break the Otranto barrier for the first time since 1916. It would be an attempt which would end in utter failure, due once again to the decisive actions of di Revel's MAS commandos.

38   Kern, I., *Actions des MAS Italiens en Adriatique*, p.85.

10

The Death of the *Szent Istvan*

For the German Empire and the Habsburg monarchy, 1918 would be a year of final chances. In the Adriatic, the pressure throughout the year came from the ever-nearing collapse of the Habsburg state. The death of Franz Josef on 21 November 1916 had kick-started the process of imperial disintegration which had been temporarily halted by the advent of war. For the conflict's first two years, it had seemed that the war might have cured the nationalist sentiment within the multi-ethnic polity by exacting a consolidating force on the state's disparate territories. However, the second half of the First World War had led to the Austro-Hungarians having to be rescued by their German allies on every front.[1] The consequence was a reduction of the state to a mere satellite of Berlin, dependent on Germany for both its economic well-being and the preservation of its territorial integrity at any future negotiated peace. The obvious failure to succeed by arms severely weakened the Habsburg state's ability to wield internal coercive power against its constituent peoples. As nationalism rose, Vienna's legitimacy to rule had come to rest on its military power, which by now was propped up only by Berlin. At this point, it was Berlin and not Vienna that directed Habsburg policies both internally and externally. As a result, from 1917 onwards, the German Empire would come to be seen as the future arbiter of inter-ethnic relations in any peace with the Allies. The Habsburg Empire would have no choice to comply with any document produced by German and Allied hands. This explicitly threatened Bohemia, whose dominant Czech and Slovak population had always housed significant numbers of Bohemian Germans. The Czechs feared that the Germans would use their presence as a pretext to involve themselves in Bohemia, to their great detriment. Threatened with this future, Czech – and to a lesser extent Slovak – nationalism soared in popularity, creating intense friction between Vienna and Prague throughout 1918. This contest would later result in industrial action, rallies and disruption across the overwhelmingly Bohemian Habsburg industrial sector.

---

1   Taylor, A.J.P., *The Habsburg Monarchy*, pp.250–272.

The Habsburg Empire's Balkan territories, particularly Dalmatia, witnessed similar pressure from nationalist movements as 1918 dawned. Their gripe, in contrast with the Czechs, was that the Italians and not the Germans would become the judging power in any Allied resolution concerning the division of the Balkan. If that occurred, hopes of breaking free from the Magyar government – which had claimed Dalmatia since the 12th century (see Chapter I) – or from the Habsburg state, whose control over part of Dalmatia had been established in 1797, would come to naught. In order to head off this possibility, the Slovene, Croat and Serb intellectuals in the Habsburg Empire began to agitate seriously for the creation of Yugoslavia (see Chapter 10) to defend them from Italian arbitration.[2] All subject peoples were pressing to switch their futures away from the teetering empire. By the time the Treaty of Brest-Litovsk was signed on 3 March 1918,[3] ending the war on the Eastern Front, the empire's internal authority had collapsed to the extent that open racially based anarchy was observable throughout the dynasty's lands. Bands thousands strong – composed of violent, hungry and desperate deserters – roamed the countryside. As ethnic strife, internal insecurity and disintegrating armies spread throughout the empire, productivity ground to a halt, inflation increased and the state currency became meaningless.

On 3 September 1918, the United States recognized the legitimacy of the state of Czechoslovakia,[4] and with it the transfer – in American eyes – of both the Pilsen-based Skoda Works and Witkowitz Mines & Ironworks in Moravia outside of the Habsburg Empire. The following month, as Field Marshal Douglas Haig's British armies – alongside both American and French forces – pushed their exhausted German adversaries to breaking point, the Habsburg dynasty entered into freefall.[5] On 29 October, sensing the imminent defeat of both Berlin and Vienna, and aware of the certainty of a victorious Italy's demands *vis-à-vis* Dalmatia, the southern Slavs consolidated into the new state of Yugoslavia. The next day, the *Reichsrat* proclaimed the state of German-Austria, uniting the German-speaking lands of the Empire into Austria. By the beginning of November, the only remaining vestige of an empire which had dominated Central Europe for over four centuries was its armed forces. On 3 November, that too was cast away as the Habsburg army formally signed an armistice with the Italian Kingdom. From the Adriatic shore to the banks of the Piave, the war thereby came to an end.

It was into this final landslide year of internal chaos and dissolution that the *K.u.K. Kreigsmarine*, the *Regia Marina*'s number-one enemy, sailed when the sun rose on 1 January 1918. And it was not long before the ethnic fires that burned in the empire's inland vastness reached its ports. Disgruntled officers began to complain that the naval high command in Pola had seemingly given up, and that the southern Slavs had

2   Tanner, M., *Croatia: A History from the Middle Ages to the Present Day*, pp.114–117.
3   Stone, N., *The Eastern Front 1914–1917*, pp.182–183.
4   Taylor, A.J.P., *The Habsburg Monarchy*, pp.264–267.
5   Herwig, H., *The First World War: Germany and Austria-Hungary, 1914–1918*, pp.392–416.

already begun preparations for a new world upon the war's end, an event not lost on the thousands of navy ratings drawn from the Dalmatian coast's picturesque fishing villages. At Pola, Anton Haus' policy, continued by Maximilian Njegovan, of battle-ship preservation had led to bored multi-ethnic crews killing their long idle hours with discussions, reading and ingestion of news from across the Habsburg Empire. A general sense of resentment and apathy set in among the sailors, and according to future admiral-in-chief and later inter-war regent of Hungary Miklos Horthy, "the battlefleet was not in good form, for three years their crews had been inactive".[6] This breakdown in military order was witnessed by the concerned Hungarian upon his first day aboard his new ship, SMS *Prinz Eugen*. The over thousand-strong crew of this 1912-built dreadnought frequently refused to eat their meals, in defiance of a navy whose mission they no longer believed in. At night, anti-Habsburg slogans would be hollered from vessel to vessel, whilst the state's response was to reduce their food rations – a foolish act made unavoidable by the deep economic hardship into which the state was plummeting.

By the close of January, the Dalmatian coast had exploded into ethnic tensions and strikes by nationalist workers. On 14 January, a factory belonging to German weapons firm Daimler was attacked by protestors, and days later the *K.u.K. Kreigsmarine*'s main shipyard – *Stabilimento Tecnico Triestino*'s San Rocco Yard – at Muggia was shut down by rioters. On 22 January, all industrial activity in Bohemia, the empire's only indus-trially developed region, came to a halt as Czech nationalists shut down operations. At its Pilsen site, for example, the Austro-Hungarian navy's preferred armaments builder, Skoda, was besieged by 30,000 striking workers.[7] The next day, the protests spread to Pola itself, with Italians standing alongside Croats and Slovenes demanding the formation of Yugoslavia. In reaction, the Habsburg military's law enforcement arm was dispatched to Pola to restore order,[8] something they did successfully by the 28th, whereupon work resumed. Further south, however, an event was underway which had profound implications for the direction of the navy in its last year, a direc-tion which would deliver two of the Habsburg fleet's most irreplaceable assets into the hands of the dreaded MAS squadrons. The *K.u.K. Kreigsmarine*'s base at Kotor lay in Montenegro, over 300 miles south of Pola,[9] and had been a highly active zone throughout the conflict. Like Venezia for the *Regia Marina*, Kotor had been the home of the *K.u.K. Kreigsmarine*'s rapid reaction elements. The Light Cruiser Flotilla, First Torpedo Flotilla and Fifth Battle Division were all based there. In sharp contrast to the predominant boredom at Pola, this port had been rendered persistently abuzz with ship-related industrial activity. For four years, its maintenance crews had been worked

6   Sondhaus. L, *The Naval Policy of Austria-Hungary, 1867–1918: Navalism Industrial Development and the Politics of Dualism* (West Lafayette: Purdue University Press, 1994)
7   Sondhaus, L., *The Naval Policy of Austria-Hungary, 1867–1918*.
8   Taylor, A.J.P., *The Habsburg Monarchy*, pp.250–272.
9   O'Hara, V, Dickson, D. et al., *To Crown the Waves*, p.16.

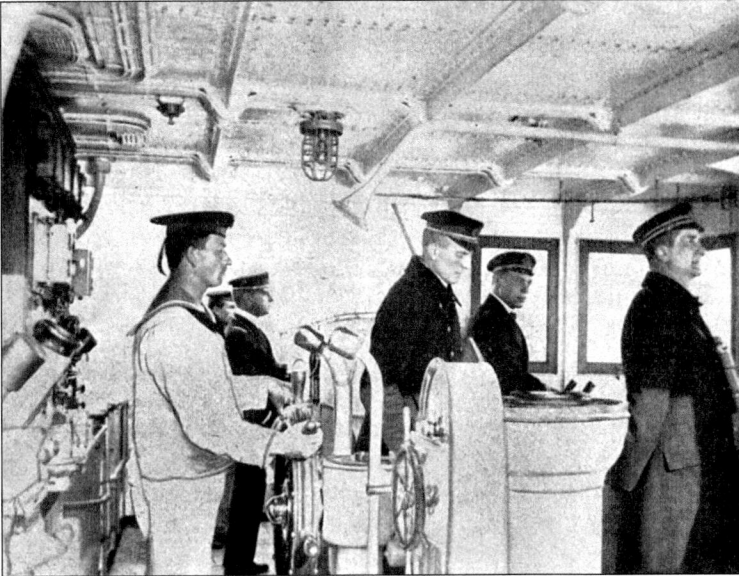

Admiral Miklos Horthy, final C-in-C of the Habsburg fleet. (Magyar Adria Association)

to physical exhaustion, its vessels were working to their mechanical limits and on the face of it, the workforce was much more stable.

When this stability broke down, the point of friction lay not originally with politics, but with the manner by which Rear Admiral Hansa, the base's tyrannical commanding officer, had deliberately intensified poor relations between sailors and officers. Hansa had engendered a situation whereby the officer class lived high on their own wealth, whilst the ratings consistently found their living conditions in decline. Officers were also engaged in a black market trade for clothing, at a time when the ratings couldn't afford new clothes or were told they were unavailable. The dire state of the Habsburg economy at the time reduced every provision to the bare minimum, except for officers, who continued to sit on surplus stock. Officers frequently rubbed their privileges in the noses of their underlings, taking seaplanes to brothels and forcing ratings to wash their pet dogs, whilst refusing to grant them soap for their own use. On 1 February, the ship's crews had reached breaking point, and at around noon, Croat rating Jerko Sizgoric shot Captain Egon Zipperer von Arbach in the head, triggering a general mutiny. To cries of *Hurra-Rufe!* (a popular nationalist incantation of the time), the port's officers were barricaded inside their rooms, and by 2:30 p.m. the red flag of mutiny flew above all vessels in the port. That evening, Rear Admiral Hansa was given a list of demands, the mutineers' requests providing an interesting insight into what was at the forefront of the sailors' minds at this point. Their demands included full political independence for the people, a declaration of support for the Russian Revolution, a call for demobilization and a begging lamentation for the end of the war.

This all pointed to an exhausted, war-weary staff who were well aware of the well-trodden road of imperial collapse that the Habsburg monarchy was walking down.

Fortunately for the dynasty, the Austro-Hungarian military was the only component of the state which was still capable of performing its duty. By day three of the Kotor mutiny, the *K.u.K. Kreigsmarine* had restored control over the site, bringing in soldiers from the surrounding area and their own heavy artillery. Seven days later, Jerko Sizgoric was shot by firing squad, bringing the sorry episode to a swift end.[10] Nevertheless, the events there forced Kaiser Karl I to rethink his attitude towards the navy. Vienna was concerned about what had transpired at Kotor within a usually steadfast organization and sent Archduke Karl Stefan to investigate and present a report to the Kaiser. The identified causes related particularly to the age and attitude of the officers presiding over the base. This reinforced a view in the young Kaiser's mind that had been gestating for several years, namely that the *K.u.K. Kreigsmarine* must have its command structure divided. Karl I felt that the administration and operations sections had to be held by different people, and that those people had to be younger, not just high-ranking officers well past retirement age, who gained lofty posts simply to put them out to pasture. On 27 February, determined to be perceived to have done something to remedy the situation, Karl I sacked Maximilian Njegovan. His replacement would be the rather surprising choice of Captain Miklos Horthy, at that point a simple dreadnought captain. Horthy's claim to fame had been a failed ramming attack he had conducted on the 'Town' class British light cruiser HMS *Dartmouth* during a savage battle off Durazzo in May 1917.[11] Although brave, such an action could hardly be cited as an example of his suitability for high office. The rather bizarre decision was due entirely to the young Kaiser's insistence that the navy needed younger, dynamic commanders.

Upon his promotion, but unbeknownst to Horthy, he would become the last *Marinekommandant* of the Habsburg navy. The quite predictable reaction to his appointment was a series of mass sackings, an event owing almost wholly to the *K.u.K. Kreigsmarine*'s rule that officers could not serve under those junior to him. However, it is hard to imagine that disgruntlement with the promotion of one so young did not also play a part. Horthy himself was as shocked as anyone at the enormity of the promotion but found it an irresistible opportunity to better his status in life. Despite his youth, in many ways he perfect fitted the new Kaiser's demand for a young and aggressive command structure to replace the slow 'dinosaurs' who had dominated the navy throughout its existence. As a sweetener for the promotion, Admiral Horthy was granted *carte blanche* to mould the *K.u.K. Kreigsmarine* any way he wanted. In the weeks succeeding his assumption of power, he would reward Kaiser Karl I for putting his faith in the Magyar seaman. The greatest issue which confronted Horthy upon his entrance into the navy's decision-making strata was the coal situation. As

10   Sondhaus, L., *The Naval Policy of Austria-Hungary, 1867–1918.*
11   Sondhaus, L., The *Great War at Sea*, p.310.

things stood on the cusp of spring 1918, the navy had a mere 95,000 tons of fuel left to maintain vessels which consumed 1,000 tons of coal per hour. As further unwelcome discoveries were made by the energetic Hungarian, it became clear that hesitancy was the least of the *K.u.K. Kreigsmarine*'s problems. Anton Haus and his Croatian successor's policy of fighting a destroyer-based conflict without using dreadnoughts seemed to have paid off, and by 1918 it was hard to argue that Habsburg small vessels did not dominate the Adriatic's trade lanes. The previous year, a total of 960,000 tons of supplies had been shipped over the old Venetian Republic route from Rijeka down to Durazzo, and from there into Albania, to support Central Powers forces in the Balkans. This had been carried out in an uninterrupted manner, with only three steamers lost to enemy action since the start of 1917.[12]

For Horthy, like many of the admirals in European navies throughout the conflict, a small-action war was not ideal. But in the claustrophobic confines of the Adriatic, with the entrance into the Mediterranean blocked at Otranto, minor battles were all that could be fought. The *Regia Marina*, afterall, was as adverse to producing a decisive battle on the waves as Anton Haus had been, particularly since the promotion of Young School protégé *Ammiraglio* di Revel in early 1917. The Habsburg naval staff had realized, through Horthy's mouthpiece, that if they wanted a 'real' battle they would have to lead the fleet triumphantly into the Mediterranean. Only there could they find the contest they so desperately sought against the Royal Navy and the *Marine Nationale*, two forces which had been spoiling for a fight in southern waters since 1914. To exit into the Mediterranean would require the breaking of the Otranto barrier. A victory there would set the tone for the remainder of the year on the waves, and likely place the *K.u.K. Kreigsmarine* in a better place in relation to the army when post-war decisions were carried out regarding Habsburg defence policies. His logic was sound, except that to blow through the barrier and then confront the world's foremost naval power in a pitched battle would require – for the first time – the mobilization of the Habsburgs' slumbering dreadnought fleet. Without that force, the Allies' First Mediterranean Fleet – based in southern Italy and composed of French, Italian and British ships – would tear them to shreds. But the Austro-Hungarian navy had a long way to go if it was to be ready for such a challenging confrontation.

To ready the much-neglected main fleet for battle, Horthy sold the navy's obsolete vessels to reduce the fleet's logistic weight. Then, in spring 1918, he launched a series of large-scale maritime exercises aimed at improving gunnery and fire control. He also did much to rein-in the mutinous environment which had washed over the navy from 1917. Horthy was able to recognize that apathy and political radicalism existed hand-in-hand with the war-weariness which the navy as a whole experienced, factors he identified as leading to behaviours which undermined the navy's unity of purpose. Without that, it would be difficult to get men to put themselves at risk, for ideas they no longer believed in and for a state which was

12   Sondhaus, L., *The Naval Policy of Austria-Hungary, 1867–1918*.

obviously collapsing. During Horthy's tenure, the torpedo boat 80-T attempted to launch a mutiny at Pola, but his response was swift, with the culprits' immediate execution in front of the present vessel's crew. Subsequent discipline improved markedly. With the navy put in its place under a single ruthless head, and their warfighting muscles given renewed vigour by persistent exercise, Horthy's *K.u.K. Kreigsmarine* was soon ready to seek its 20th-century Lissa. Only the matter of climate held back the multi-ethnic fleet, as atrocious weather in the Upper Adriatic persisted until May or June annually.[13] Until that time, manoeuvres, gunnery practice and low-intensity raiding on the Italian coast were carried out to facilitate crew intimacy with combat procedures and weaponry on board vessels which had been at rest for two years. As the weather cleared at last in early June, Admiral Horthy encountered his much-coveted operational window. On the morning of the 11th, Horthy sent the navy's four *Tegetthoff* class dreadnoughts – SMS *Viribus Unitis*, SMS *Tegetthoff*, SMS *Prinz Eugen* and SMS *Szent Istvan* – from Pola to Kotor, whereupon they would be joined by a further three *Erzherzog* class 10,472-ton battleships and Habsburg light cruisers.[14] Their first objective was to unite and then to destroy the Royal Navy's aviation station at Otranto, before attacking the barrier itself. At that point, he gambled on the Allies steaming to meet his force and that in the resulting decisive battle the Habsburgs would make their entrance into the Mediterranean theatre.

Admiral Horthy Must be Stopped – the Targets

On 31 May, *Ammiraglio* di Revel pursued his government in order to get the green light for a strike on the Habsburg dreadnought fleet. He was aware that it was scheduled to leave Pola in days, yet he knew nothing about where it was heading or why. His guess was that they were going to attempt to break through the Otranto barrier, but he did not know at what time specifically or where the ships would be at the time they sought to conduct the advance south. The seeking of permission for an operation which would have no plan, other than for the MAS units to be sent to a general area where they would await their pray, was a risky proposition. That the plan worked at all was down almost wholly to Captain Luigi Rizzo, whose experienced eyes and gut feeling led him to follow a smoke trail which he had assumed was left by torpedo boats. If he had been less curious, he might have given up the chase there and then, but on the day his tracing of the smoke plumes proved vital to locating the enemy dreadnoughts. Yet when di Revel asked Rome for permission, all was still up in the air as regards how events would transpire. All that he knew for certain was that any sinking of the Austro-Hungarian navy's irreplaceable dreadnoughts

13   Ivetic, E., *Storia dell'Adriatico*, pp.1–30.
14   Kern, I., *Actions des MAS Italiens en Adriatique*, pp.43–44.

Viribus Unitis class vessel. (Harry Heusser Paintings)

– made particularly precious due to the Habsburg Empire's disintegrating Czech industrial base – would be catastrophic. The dire domestic situation made any vessel sunk utterly irreplaceable, and when any armed forces get to the point where they are unable to replenish their numbers, the conflict is already lost. Given the context, it must be wondered whether Admiral Horthy may have been better listening to his erstwhile predecessors as to the *K.u.K. Kreigsmarine*'s wartime strategy. If the MAS boats managed to strike, and strike well, then the Habsburg fleet would come under monumental political pressure to withdraw its forces back to safe ports. In doing so, Horthy's attempt to force the Strait of Otranto and produce a decisive battle there would be dashed, and with it the last chance for the *K.u.K. Kreigsmarine* to be remembered as anything other than an auxiliary to the overbearing Habsburg army. Its ships would be held up in port, and all the Italians would need to do would be to wait until the war came to a close. In essence, the consequences of taking out just one of the hulking dreadnoughts would bring Italy closer to maritime victory than it had been in years.

The target to which di Revel had been particularly attracted was the SMS *Szent Istvan*. Unknown to di Revel, the *Szent Istvan* was a ship of particular importance politically to the *K.u.K. Kreigsmarine*, a value that in the disastrous climate of the late Habsburg Empire was not to be underestimated. For the *Szent Istvan*

Vice Admiral Ziegler, head of the MTK shipyards, criticized the lack of action on the class's inadequate torpedo defence in a 30 November 1909 report. His dossier claimed that the hull structure had been weakened by the attempt to place massive 30.5cm guns on the deck whilst still rigidly sticking to the 20,000-ton weight limit. In doing so, the *Tegetthoff* class's builders had been forced to strip armour from the torpedo defence layer at the vessel's base. Ziegler advocated instead to follow Tirpitz's advice that the 30.5cm guns were too large and the torpedo protection too weak. His preferred alteration for weight redistribution would see the main guns reduced in size and the introduction of 50mm torpedo bulkheads protecting compartments 2.4–2.8m tall and 1.2m across. That would be an improvement but was still well short of the 4m across design favoured by the *Kaiserliche Marine*. It was something the Habsburg navy would pay for dearly.

The first vessel in the Tegetthoff family – SMS *Viribus Unitis* – set the template for the rest of the class. In general, the vessels were built to a weight specification of 21,595 tons, along a length, width and height distribution of 152.2m x 27.3m x 8.9m, with a crew of 1,098 men divided into 38 officers and just over 1,000 ratings. As per the design process, the construction was carried out at Trieste using a wholly indigenous roster of contractors and sub-contractors. Krupp's assistance for the ship's metal supply continued unabated.[19] The resulting warship bristled with weaponry, possessing a total of 42 guns: 12 30.5cm horizontal sliding-breech block loaded Skoda primary L/45 guns, a further 12 15cm horizontally loaded Skoda L/50 K10 secondary guns and 18 CIWS 7cm horizontally loaded Skoda L/50 K10 quick-fire guns.[20] Two machine guns for anti-boarding and anti-torpedo boat usage were also fitted to the vessel in the form of 8mm Schwarzlose guns. Four 53cm Whitehead torpedoes were also fitted on the ship. This enormous floating weapons platform was armoured at its thickest in an armoured belt stretching from stern to bow formed of 28cm of cemented steel. This class of warships was the first to be armoured entirely above the waterline. The ship's thinnest armoured portion was found in the machine room's ceiling armour, with 3cm of cemented steel. All four of the Tegetthoff juggernauts would be propelled by 12 boilers powering four German-American AEG-Curtis steam engines, connected to two 4m propellers. This locomotive assembly produced 27,000hp, allowing a top speed of 20 knots and a range of 4,800 miles on one 2,000-ton load of fuel. Geographically, this would allow transportation, without fuelling, from Pola in Istria to Rostock in Germany. In wartime, this would permit them to travel across the whole of the First World War's maritime battlespace, without halting once to take on fuel.

Four of these dreadnoughts that were planned during the pre-war period were duly made.[21] But one, that vessel which di Revel sought to target, was somewhat different

19   Kramli, M., *Austro-Hungarian Battleships and Battleship Designs, 1904-1914.*
20   Noppen, R., *Austro-Hungarian Battleships, 1914-1918*, pp.21–28.
21   Sondhaus, L., *The Naval Policy of Austria-Hungary, 1867-1918.*

to the others. When the prospect of exterminating all four of the Habsburg Empire's dreadnoughts came up, di Revel's sights were set only on the SMS *Szent Istvan*. His mind was made up late on 7 June 1918, and he would only give the order to proceed on the 9th. When he did so, it is unlikely that he quite understood the importance of the *Szent Istvan* to the internal strife unfolding in the crumbling empire. In 1903, the Magyar government had signed an agreement with the *K.u.K. Landstreitkräfte* regarding industrial orders. A year later, an identical deal was signed with the *K.u.K. Kreigsmarine*. The details of both inter-governmental contracts deemed that 34.4 percent of products used by the Habsburg armed forces were to come from the lands of the Magyars. This was part of the obsession with providing concessions to national groups in order to secure their compliance in the *Reichsrat* (see Chapter 6). However, the Hungarian politicians negotiating the industrial pacts understood that their industrial base – by far the empire's weakest – was incapable of producing what the *K.u.K. Kreigsmarine* in particular needed. For a modern navy required modern manu-facturers, not to mention the colossal amount of raw materials – dug from the ground by hand and machine – demanded by the forges of the shipyards. Consequently, compensation deals were introduced by which when the navy needed ships which the Magyars couldn't build – but which the Czechs and Austrians could – they had to contract for other things from the Hungarian state. For example, Magyar industry could not produce large-calibre ships' guns, but it could manufacture rifles. Therefore, when their naval guns were turned down, the Habsburg army would have to buy enough rifles to equal the price they would have paid for naval artillery. In essence, it was a system designed to prevent the 'servant races' (composed basically of all the empire's Slavs) from benefiting from their more developed industries, particularly in the case of the Czechs, whose territory housed both Skoda and the Witkowitz Mines & Ironworks.

The shipbuilding boom that occurred at the end of the 19th century, extensively documented throughout this book, provoked much paranoia from Budapest. The Magyars saw that the navy, with its vast industrial requirements, had the potential to entirely freeze out the Hungarian economy. Their power was entirely tied to the land's agricultural output,[22] something which could sway the army with its massed illiterate manpower but which had little influence on the navy. At the same time, naval budgets were consistently rising, and as Budapest controlled the empire's most fertile region it was the leading producer of non-artificial economic activity in the empire. For a state that was still largely agricultural rather than industrial, this meant its nobles were the country's richest. The new navy would require to be at least half-funded by the Magyars,[23] yet their economy was not going to benefit from the construc-tion of the new fleet. Their enemies in Bohemia, in contrast, would pay little but gain much. To rectify the situation and to make sure the Czechs did not acquire too

22   Taylor, A.J.P., *The Habsburg Monarchy*, pp.30–33.
23   Sondhaus, L., *The Naval Policy of Austria-Hungary, 1867–1918*.

much force within the Habsburg naval–industrial matrix, the Hungarians stipulated that they should be granted 50 percent of all shell production in return for support in the *Reichsrat*.[24]. A secret quota – whose details are still not fully known – was also acquired for destroyer and torpedo-boat manufacturing.

When the treaty between the Habsburg state and the Magyar government was concluded on the distribution of naval construction, the Hungarians had a single firm which could build ships. The monopoly of this company owed a great deal to the reality of Hungarian geography. Since the 12th century, the Magyar people had dominated the Croats who lived in the Dalmatian peninsula (see Chapter 1). This thin slice of land, which formed the western Balkan coastline, was filled with Italianate cities whose populations were overwhelmingly Croat, often labouring under the direction of highly exploitative Italian bosses. Yet outside of the cities, the Croats – under Magyar direction – had exerted control over their fiefs. The limited areas of Hungarian coastal settlement there meant that their lands in the empire had little maritime skill to offer. As a consequence, small-scale boat building – from whose yards shipbuilders poached many of their craftsmen – never took off in a serious manner.[25] This left the Hungarian part of the empire with a dearth of naval expertise. In 1896, an inexperienced collection of Magyar shipyards was formed into a single conglomerate – *Danubius-Schoenichen-Hartmann Egyesult Hajo-Es Gepgyar Rt* (or simply put, Danubius). In 1905, they built their first yard at Rijeka on the same stretch of coast as the Whitehead Torpedo Factory (see Chapter 4).[26] On the surface this seemed to be an independent company, undertaking a service to the state. Lurking just beneath though, as with everything related to the empire, the racial priorities of the Magyar nation bubbled violently.

The company had not come together naturally. Danubius had been formed through the Machiavellian hands of Hungary's leading bank, the *Magyar Altalanos Hitelbank* (Magyar General Credit Bank), in conjunction with the Budapest government. In fact, the Magyar state would do everything it could to fast-track the shipyard's capacity to build warships. The government's eyes were on creating space for a Hungarian yard that could construct its own battleships, rather than the inglorious task of producing small-tonnage destroyers and patrol boats. To forge a dreadnought of their own would mark their arrival as a serious player in the large warship construction industry, and in so doing steal some of the limelight from the Czechs and maintain competitivity with their Slavic rivals. On 23 August 1905, the bank used its contacts in Budapest to arrange the purchase of 10,000 square metres of land beside the former Howaldt shipyard,[27] which Danubius had bought at the beginning of the year. The land purchase was free, and thanks to the company director's close relationship with

24   Kramli, M., *Austro-Hungarian Battleships and Battleship Designs, 1904–1914*.
25   Molnar, M., *A Concise History of Hungary*, pp.87–201.
26   Ballantyne, I., *The Deadly Trade: The Complete History of Submarine Warfare*, pp.53–55.
27   Kramli, M., *Austro-Hungarian Battleships and Battleship Designs, 1904–1914*.

Magyar politicians, any infrastructure they needed was quickly provided. By 1907, the acquisition of Howaldt and the adjoining land had allowed the Danubius shipyard to construct an impressively large site located not far from Rijeka, home to the *K.u.K. Kreigsmarine*'s naval school and its torpedo instruction arm. However, the Habsburg navy's German elite failed to see the Hungarian bid for naval participation as anything more than an act of cynical ethnic politics. In spring 1909, these beliefs were proved to be correct when, after a visit to the site, a Captain Hermann Marchetti summed it up as "unsatisfactory". Not long after his arrival at the site, discussions in Vienna began as to who was to be contracted to build the *Tegetthoff* class's fourth ship.

Aware that their performance had not been satisfactory but desiring wholeheartedly to capture a piece of the dreadnought boom, Budapest poured money into Danubius' Rijeka-based yard. In 1911, Danubius took over the Ganz & Co. Machine Factory in Budapest, and once combined with the shipyard at Rijeka the company came to be the Magyars' largest industrial complex. The country's marine industrial base then received its last addition before the war, in spring 1912, with an enormous battle-ship slipway. This allowed the firm to finally conceive of building vessels larger than a destroyer. Yet the fact it received the contract to build the forth *Tegetthoff* class dreadnought owed nothing to its alleged quality. Instead, it was owed entirely to the empire's ethnic politics. When it was suggested that the class be given a fourth addi-tion, the money demanded of the Magyars was considered extortionate. A budget of over 300 million kronen could only come if they were appeased, and the Magyar price was that they be allowed to have a dreadnought of their own. In an ephemeral way, it was perceived among Hungarian nationalists that this vessel would give them the foundations of an independent Magyar navy once the empire no longer existed. On 6 March 1911, Danubius got their wish, the *K.u.K. Kreigsmarine* formally asking them to build a battleship on the STT's plans. On 20 April, a contract between the navy and Danubius was signed to the tune of 60.6 million kronen, with a deadline for completion of 10 July 1914.

The construction of the *Szent Istvan* would be a difficult affair. The principle bone of contention lay with Budapest's desire to have everything built in a non-industrial Hungary. On 18 May 1911, overtures were made to British armaments giant Vickers, Sons & Maxim to build a factory in Hungary[28] that would employ Magyar workers and deliver projects for Budapest. Concerned at the thought of growing the Magyar industrial base, the virulently anti-Hungarian Archduke Franz Ferdinand vetoed the project. This forced them to instead deal with Krupp from 1912, but that arrange-ment quickly fell through and Skoda was brought in to pick up the pieces. This delivered contracts into the hands of their industrial competition within the empire – the Czechs. Obviously, this was unacceptable, and a compromise emerged with the formation of the *Magyar Agyugyar*, a joint Czech–Magyar enterprise founded in April 1913, aimed at producing the armaments they had as yet failed to procure. As with all

---

28   Kramli, M., *Austro-Hungarian Battleships and Battleship Designs, 1904–1914.*

things surrounding the construction of the SMS *Szent Istvan*, Budapest was heavily involved, with the *Magyar Agyugyar* company's main shareholder being the Hungarian government, with shares worth seven million kronen, to Skoda's six million. These multiple complications were presenting continual delays, and the vessel's construction did not even begin until 29 January 1912. A year later, only 60 percent of the vessel had been finished, and from this dismal performance the *Baleitung Bergudi* – the body set up to observe Danubius – proposed a new deadline of 20 January 1915, six months past their original termination date of 10 July 1914.

The process of naming the colossal warship was also mired in issues. The Magyar government had expressed its wish as far back as 1911 that one of the *K.u.K. Kreigsmarine*'s dreadnoughts be named after a Hungarian. In the dying decades of the Habsburg dynasty, this had been a terrifying prospect. Unity was key to preserving the empire, whose unravelling had already begun, and by 1911 the process of Hungary's departure was well underway beneath the surface. The national heroes of the Magyar people were all connected with the struggles between Hungarian and Austrian. Any legendary Magyar person deemed suitable for the vessel's name would almost certainly have shed German blood or to have established themselves as a defender of the Hungarian people. Any glorification of this ethnic identity would be taken as an inspiration to secessionist tendencies, something the imperial family was keen to avoid fostering. The Hungarians' first suggestion was Hunyadi, an ode to Janos Hunyadi, medieval Hungary's chief defender against the Ottoman menace,[29] a legend in his own right whose veneration among Hungarian nationalists was marked. Unsurprisingly, this name was struck down by Archduke Franz Ferdinand, whose will ran undiminished throughout the military. He wished the Magyars to come up with something which echoed the strength of the dual monarchy, yet all their ideas came packaged with a similar tinge of nationalist sentiment. The suggestion of Matyas Corvinus, for example, harked back to the equally mythical figure of Matthew Corvinus, a former Hungarian king who in the 15th century had battled the first Habsburg emperor, Kaiser Frederick III (1452–93).[30] Obviously, this was also unsuitable to the Archduke. The tone-deaf Habsburg heir instead suggested the name of 18th-century Austrian general Ernst Delon Freiherr von Laudon, but Admiral Anton Haus pointed out that the Magyars would not accept this. The first Hungarian dreadnought ever built had to have a Hungarian name. Eventually, they settled on Szent Istvan, the events of whose reign were so long ago – 1000–1038[31] – that even Magyar nationalists would find it hard to find relevance in his name. The Magyar state's first wholly indigenous vessel would finally be launched on 17 January 1914, to be sailed under the name SMS *Szent Istvan*. The events of 1918 would make sure it was also Hungary's last.

29   Molnar, M., *A Concise History of Hungary*, pp.66–72.
30   Wilson, P., *The Holy Roman Empire*, pp.211–212.
31   Molnar, M., *A Concise History of Hungary*, pp.20–26.

Sinking of the SMS *Szent Istvan*

On 8 June 1918, at around 10:30 p.m., SMS *Viribus Unitis*, as Admiral Miklos Horthy's flagship, left the intimate confines of Fazana Bay, alongside its fellow dreadnought SMS *Prinz Eugen*.[32] Their destination was Tajer, a small island some 100 miles south of Rijeka. Their movements were protected by a bodyguard of five torpedo boats, in reality an anti-MAS security cordon, designed to deter hit-and-run raids. As the sun rose over the still, glistening waters of the Adriatic on the morning of the 9th, the crews of the fleet's two leading dreadnoughts woke up at their destination. But there was no time for the sleepy ratings to gather their bearings, and as the day broke upon near-transparent littoral waters, the *Viribus Unitis* and *Prinz Eugen* started up their engines once more. Thick plumes of black coal-fired smoke penetrated the fine clear sea air of the Dalmatian coast, and in their bustling deckhouses the twin captains plotted their route south to Slano,[33] a small fishing village which even today is home to no more than 579 souls. On their approach, the young ratings of these dreadnoughts must have been staggered by the locale's isolated beauty, particularly with the sublime summer weather. Yet as gorgeous as it was, the settlement was still 50 miles south of the port of Kotor, far inside the shadows of Montenegro's dominating Black Mountain. At 10:40 p.m. on 9 June, whilst the ships' crews whiled away the night with games of cards under feeble ship lights, the SMS *Tegetthoff* and SMS *Szent Istvan* also began their journey to Tajer, first stop on the way to Kotor.

If all had gone to plan, they would have arrived at Tajer at 4:30 a.m.,[34] just early enough to see the first hint of the coming dawn. But it was not to be. For the *Tegetthoff* and *Szent Istvan*,

Captains Costanzo Ciano and Luigi Rizzo, standing with Gabrielle D'Annunzio at Buccari. (Open source)

---

32   Sondhaus, L., *The Naval Policy of Austria-Hungary, 1867–1918*.
33   Sondhaus, L., *The Great War at Sea*, p.365.
34   Kern, I., *Actions des MAS Italiens en Adriatique*, p.46.

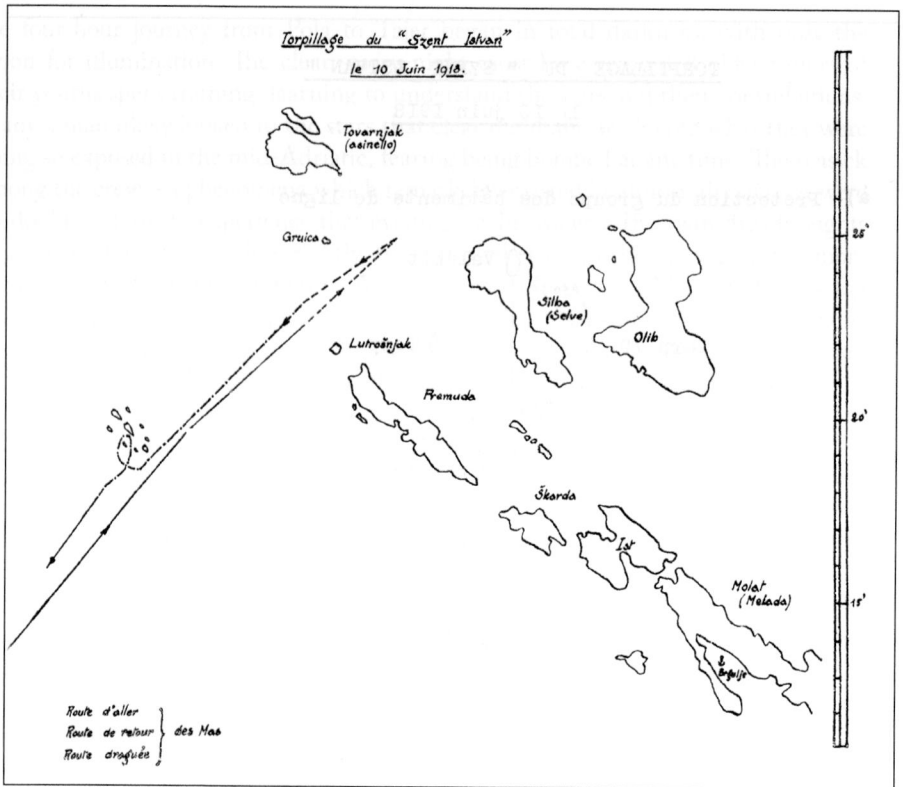

Torpillage du "Szent Istvan"
le 10 Juin 1918.

Tovarnjak
(asinello)

Gruica

Silba
(Selve)

Olib

Lutroïnjak

Premuda

Škarda

Molat
(Melada)

Route d'aller
Route de retour des Mas
Route draguée

This map represents, an operational overview of the attack on the SMS Szent Istvan. Pictured is the island chain which framed the attack. The lines show the both the attack route and retreat route. Map taken from Kern, I. Actions des MAS Italiens en Adriatique Pendant la Grande Guerre et Reactions des Autrichiens (Paris: Ecole de Guerre Navale, 1935).

preventing the vessel's demise. The energy unleashed from the torpedo's tip erupted in a shaped explosion, expanding in a triangular manner without anything to disperse it. The lack of torpedo bulkheads allowed the shockwave to rip through the ship's armour. Both torpedoes struck the twin boiler rooms, where despite the efforts of the vessel's engineers, four boilers were immediately out of operation. The remaining two were incapable of keeping the ship righted, and it began taking on water rapidly. The order to abandon ship was quickly given.

Sixty million Kronen, two years of work, an endless list of delays, a whole warship built to appease the Magyars and an operation to generate the campaign's first decisive battle – all went to the deep as the SMS *Szent Istvan* capsized at 6:05 a.m., with the loss of 89 of its crew. As it did so, Horthy's dreams came crashing down, as did those of an independent and well-armed Hungarian navy after the Habsburg Empire's now unavoidable collapse. The *Tegetthoff*, sailing alongside, believed that the *Szent Istvan* had been hit by a submarine-launched torpedo and immediately began

Contemporary artist's impression of the sinking of SMS *Szent István*. (Open Source)

L'affût des Mas et des Torpilleurs
près de l'île Premuda dans la
nuit du 9 au 10 juin 1918.
comme il aurait dû être effectué d'après l'ordre reçu.
En réalité les Mas étaient à leur retour en retard de plus de 30ᵐ
+ : point où fut torpillé le "Szent Istvan" à 3ʰ30.

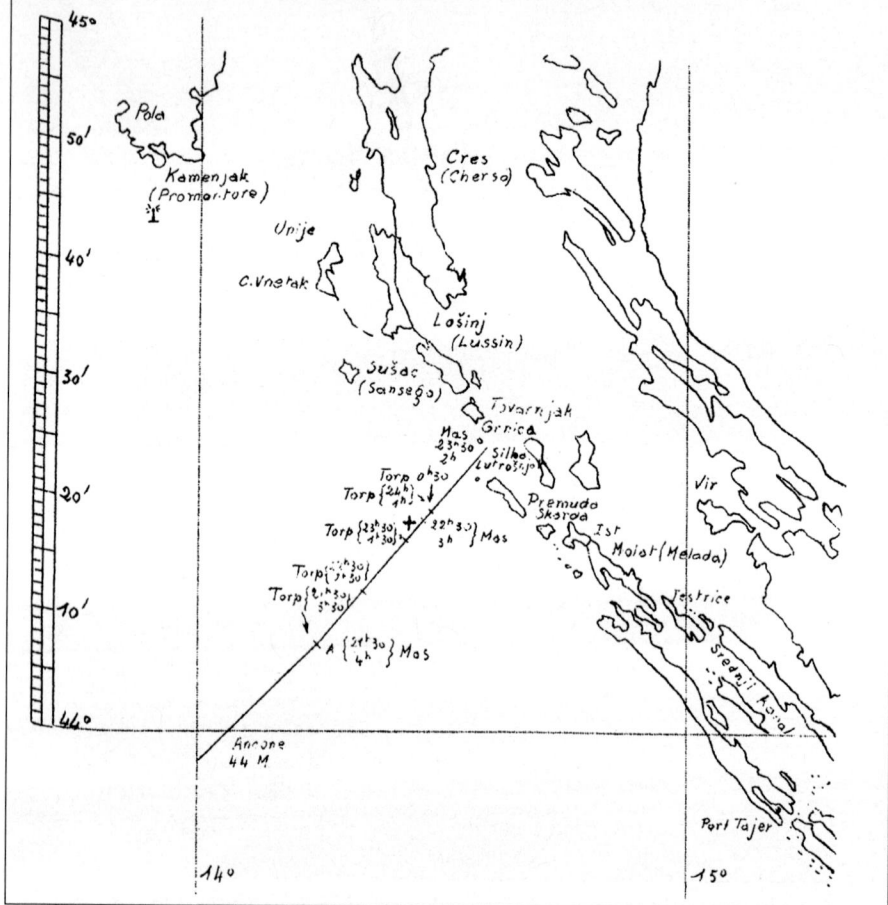

45°

50′

Pola

Kamenjak
(Promontore)

Cres
(Cherso)

Unije

C. Vnetak

Lošinj
(Lussin)

40′

Sušac
(Sansego)

30′

Tovarnjak
Grnica

Mas
23ʰ30
2ʰ

Silba
Lutroshp

Torp 0ʰ30

Torp {23ʰ / 1ʰ}

20′

Torp {23ʰ30 / 1ʰ30}   + 22ʰ30 / 3ʰ } Mas

Premuda
Skroda

Vir

Ist
Molat (Melada)

Torp {1ʰ30 / 3ʰ}

Torp {1ʰ30 / 3ʰ30}

10′

Ostrice

A {21ʰ30 / 4ʰ} Mas

Srednji Kanal

44°

Ancona
44 M

Port Tajer

14°   15°

This map represents the operation to sink the Szent Istvan on a strategic level. The line is the same line of attack shown on the second image. But it includes the position of the Szent Istavan upon its death. Represented by a cross. The caption reads: 'the route of the MAS and torpedo vessels close to the isle of Premuda on the night of the 9th to 10th of June 1918. As had been ordered' The caption also notes that these actions were completed, thirty minutes later than they should have been. Map taken from Kern, I. Actions des MAS Italiens en Adriatique Pendant la Grande Guerre et Reactions des Autrichiens (Paris: Ecole de Guerre Navale, 1935).

Sinking of the SMS *Szent Istvan*. (Bundesarchiv, Bild 134-C1133 / CC-BY-SA 3.0)

counter-measures. But these manoeuvres took the captain out of communication with the stricken *Szent Istvan*, making an aid operation almost impossible. During the confusion, MAS 15 and MAS 21 began to make their escape back to Ancona, where *Ammiraglio* di Revel was waiting for them with open arms.[37] Yet moments after Ciano believed they had reached safety, he was abruptly proven incorrect as gunfire poured into MAS 15 from a pursuing Austro-Hungarian torpedo boat. Rizzo reacted with his characteristic stoicism as he dropped grenades into the water behind them. The chase ended as quickly as it began as the grenades detonated at the exact right moment, just as the chasing torpedo boat passed above them. The Habsburg boat was ripped in two, with both its crew dying in the act. Once again, an MAS squadron had appeared out of nowhere, executed an action dolling out immense damage and then disappeared into the night. There was not even a whisper as to where they had escaped. With the tragic loss of the SMS *Szent Istvan*, the Hungarian nation mourned inconsolably and Miklos Horthy was forced to come to terms with the reality that the war was over for the *K.u.K. Kreigsmarine*. But for the once-proud Habsburg fleet, further humiliation remained – the sinking of the SMS *Viribus Unitis* by Italian hands and the navy's final scrapping in 1919, due in no small part to the heroic actions of the MAS commandos.

37   Kern, I., *Actions des MAS Italiens en Adriatique*, p.45.

Humiliation and Armistice – the Sinking of SMS *Viribus Unitis* and the Fate of the *Regia Marina*, 1918-19

Back in the dramatic early days of the First World War, in that hopeful year of 1914, the Croats and Slovenes– the Habsburg Empire's politically weakest ethnic group – feared their ancestral lands would be sacrificed for peace.[1] The Croatian people stood to miss their first chance at forming an independent existence in a millennia. Three men were determined to face down that prospect – Ivan Mestrovic, Ante Trumbic and Frano Suplio,a sculptor, politician and journalist respectively. As early as 22 November 1914, understanding that the Habsburg Empire was doomed to fail, they founded the Yugoslav Committee to push forward southern Slav interests. Like the Italians, they had seen the Austro-Hungarian failure to subdue the mathematically weaker Serbia as a portent of the root and branch collapse of imperial power in Central Europe. Like the Czechs, Magyars and indeed Austro-Germans, the Croats realized the ethnic tensions of the empire had only been held together through a policy of fostering mutual ethnic fear, backed by a powerful military. The moment that fear of imperial authority faltered, so too would the stability of Austria-Hungary.

For the Croats though, the danger did not come from other imperial ethnic groups – save perhaps for the Magyars. Instead, it came from the Italian Kingdom, a state founded upon the principles of pushing forward the *Risorgimento* until all Italians everywhere were united into a single nation. To the extremists on the Italian far right who would push Italy into war in 1915 (see Chapter 5), the nation would only be complete once it had not just taken the peninsula, but all the extra-Italianate land which had belonged to Venezia; land within which a small Italian elite ruthlessly exploited a Croat majority in a form of governance tolerated by Vienna but despised by the Croat nationalist movement. Should the Italian Kingdom be asked by the Allies to join the war, the movement's leadership knew what price Rome would demand from London and Paris – that it be allowed to finish the unification of the Italian peoples begun in 1848. When negotiations between the Italian Kingdom and both

---

1   Tanner, M. *Croatia: A History from the Middle Ages to the Present Day*, p.120.

the Third French Republic and the British Empire commenced in spring 1915, the nascent Yugoslav leadership could not have been more correct in their assumptions. The conclusion of the discussions aimed at bringing Italy into the war on the *Entente* side came on 26 April 1915 with the signature of the Treaty of London. Contained within it, under article five, was the concession that all Croats understood was coming – that in the case of an Allied victory, Dalmatia in its entirety would be handed over to Italy. On 30 April, four days after the Treaty of London was concluded, the Yugoslav Committee issued a statement rebuking its terms: "The Yugoslavs form a single nation, alike by their identity of language, by the unanswerable laws of geography and by their national consciousness. To transfer portions of them to another alien [Italian] rule would be a flagrant violation of our ethnographical, geographical, and economic unity."

The formation of Yugoslavia to protect the Croat people from the inevitable handover of their coastline to Italy was now of imminent importance. On 20 July 1917, after a year of discussions between Serbian Prime Minister Nikola Pasic and the Yugoslav Congress in Corfu, a pact was signed. The newly created Corfu Agreement of 1917 saw both Serb and Croat politicians agree to work together to form a constitutional, democratic and parliamentary union headed by Serbia's royal family, the Karadjordjevic dynasty. At the start of 1918, the Croats and Serbs were joined by the Slovenes under their leader Anton Korosec.[2] With this addition, the Italians began to suspect that something was up. Consequently, as the war drew to its conclusion in autumn 1918, Rome began to cook up a plan to avoid having what it saw as its rightful prizes being stolen from under its nose by an 'upstart' Yugoslavia. That October, the last month of the Habsburg Empire's existence, the Italian armed forces came to understand that only a show of force would compel the Yugoslavs to seek terms with Rome. The last thing that the Italians wanted was to defeat the Habsburg Empire simply to have a new archnemesis take its place. Towards the end of October, it looked like that might indeed be the outcome of the war; a war Italy had fought so hard to win. On 30 October, the last Habsburg Kaiser, Karl I, agreed to transfer all of the *K.u.K. Kreigsmarine*'s battleships to the South Slav National Council – the successor body to the Yugoslav Committee.[3] The transfer sought to include the *K.u.K. Kreigsmarine*'s three remaining *Tegetthoff* class dreadnoughts – SMS *Prinz Eugen*, SMS *Viribus Unitis* and SMS *Tegetthoff*. If this clause of Kaiser Karl I's order was to be fulfilled, then the future Yugoslav navy would be in a position to challenge the *Regia Marina* for the Adriatic, inheriting the mission that the *K.u.K. Kreigsmarine* had held before it. That eventuality was not something Rome could allow to stand.

2   Tanner, M., *Croatia*, pp.117–119.
3   Dodson, A., *Spoils of War: The Fate of Enemy Fleets after the Two World Wars* (Barnsley: Seaforth Publishing, 2020), pp.46–47.

warship's superstructure was also too fragile for its main 30.5cm Skoda guns. When fired, these weapons caused deformations in the tower, foredeck and funnels. The vessel that took to the seas in 1914, therefore, was a lumbering mammoth. And just like that prehistoric creature, its slow nature and unwieldly structure made it exceedingly vulnerable to the *Regia Marina*'s skilled MAS predators. Had the war continued for another year, there is no doubt its enormous form would have been dragged to the depths by one of di Revel's 'Old Sea Wolves', in the speeding manner of which his MAS boats had become famed. As we shall see, those 'Old Sea Wolves' had ways of getting at their targets by 1918 that were unthinkable in 1915. The use of these nefarious methods would see the return of the combat diver after an extended sojourn of nearly three centuries.

The Operation – Raid on Pola, 1918

The handover of the Habsburg fleet to the new Yugoslav state was supposed to occur on 31 October 1918.[8] On the same day that the former imperial navy's vessels were being brought up from Kotor to Pola, a profoundly concerned Ammiraglio Paolo Thaon di Revel telegrammed the head of Venezia's naval station, under whose authority the MAS squadrons and torpedo boat fleet came. His message was therefore addressed to the individual – whose name is lost – under whose orders the MAS squadrons relied. Its contents speak for themselves: "If the actions of Costanzo Ciano and Raffaele Rossetti [the operation against SMS *Viribus Unitis*] are to be attempted, then it must be as soon as possible before the acceptance of the armistice."[9] Presumably this was because di Revel understood that the moment the armistice was signed and the war ended, the *Regia Marina* would be unable to sink the vessel without an adverse reaction. The issue with mounting the operation was that the *Viribus Unitis* was moored in Pola, which had been the *K.u.K. Kreigsmarine*'s seat of power and consequently had the most intricate defensive system in the Adriatic. There were three layers of obstructions, with torpedo nets and sea mines, as at Fazana and Trieste.[10] MAS units had learned through hard experience that it was nearly impossible for their rapid boats to infiltrate the harbour at Pola. On 15 May 1918, MAS 95, alongside a Grillo amphibious warfare craft, had attempted to land at Pola harbour, but had encountered five barriers and been caught in an intense web of mutually supporting fire which tore one of the squad's boats to pieces. Land-based and naval artillery had then shelled them, forcing the scuttling of the Grillo, whilst one of the MAS crew, Francesco Angelino, lost an arm in the attempt.[11]

8   Dodson, A., *Spoils of War: The Fate of Enemy Fleets after the Two World Wars*, pp.24–25.
9   Kern, I., *Actions des MAS Italiens en Adriatique*, p.61.
10   Kern, I., *Actions des MAS Italiens en Adriatique*, p.68.
11   Montipo, G., *La Vita di un Modenese Tra i 30 della Beffa di Buccari*.

This map represents the diving operation to destroy SMS Viribus Unitis in the port of Pola on the 1st of November 1918. Important landmarks are noted as follows: the thick black symbol represents the jetties extending from the southern headland. The other rectangular objects on the map, represent deliberate obstructions thrown up inside the harbour. The circles marked R denote Radetsky class battleships. Whilst the filled in cirlce represents teh Viribus Unitis. The black circle outside the port's defences, is the MAS unit responsible for the operation. A line extending from the MAS into the harbour shows their entry point. Map taken from Kern, I. Actions des MAS Italiens en Adriatique Pendant la Grande Guerra et Reactions des Autrichiens (Paris: Ecole de Guerre Navale, 1935).

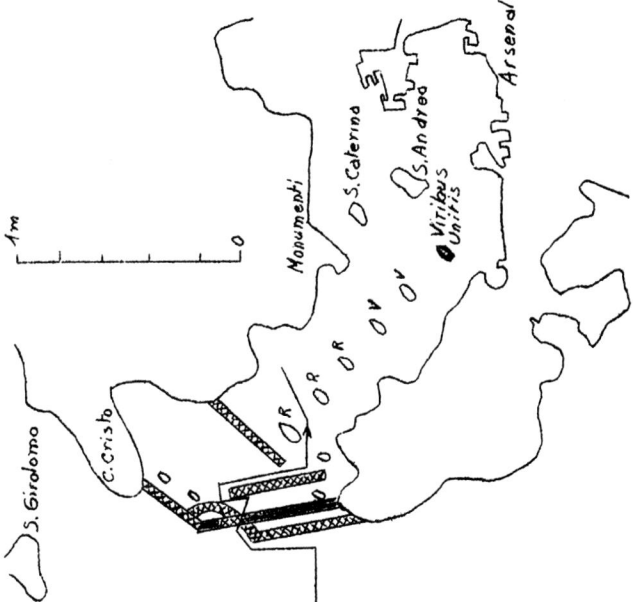

Destruction du "Viribus Unitis" dans le port de Pola
le 1er novembre 1918

P. Peneda

S. Girolamo

C. Cristo

Monumenti

S. Caterina

S. Andrea

Viribus Unitis

Arsenal

1m

0

Jetées
Obstructions
O^R Bât. du type "Radetzky"
O^V " " "Viribus Unitis"
0 Vedettes de veille
—— Route de l'appareil "Mignatta"
● Mas

The time constraints on the operation against SMS *Viribus Unitis* and its grand strategic significance for the Italian state meant that such an error couldn't be made again.
Concerned about a repeat of May's events, Captain Ciano – spurred on by di Revel
– turned to eccentric marine engineer Raffaele Rossetti. Like many sailors, Rossetti
was a Genovese native, but instead of the obvious career path of a rating he instead
chose to become an engineer. In 1904, he accomplished his dream and was admitted
to the *Regia Marina*'s naval academy at Livorno, before returning to his native Genova
to train as a marine engineer at the Superior Naval School.[12] The start of Italy's war in
spring 1915 led to his joining the Naval Technical Office in his home city. By the time
history called him to the service of Venezia's MAS units, he had crept up to the rank
of major. Since 1917, Rossetti had been working at La Spezia naval arsenal, where he
had been experimenting with the concept of a man-rideable torpedo. The objective
was to allow the MAS operatives to enhance their stealth capability by transforming
their boats from surface to sub-surface units. This would allow the MAS units to be
used in a more scalpel-like manner, rather than the shock and awe mode in which they
had been employed since 1915. The vessel he had been attempting to build was based
on of a captured German torpedo which had not detonated. A seat had been hollowed
out of the torpedo's centre, and an air motor placed inside. Two valves located near
the seat controlled the apparatus's buoyancy, allowing it to surface and then disappear
below the waves at will. The commando riding the prototype would use a variant
of diving suit somewhere between the Fleuss suit and the Davis Submerged Escape
Apparatus (see Chapter 4). The new diving apparatus consisted of a bottle-shaped
headgear connected to a standard rebreather bag, the wearer weighed down by metal
boots, akin to all diving apparatus before the Davis Submerged Escape Apparatus.
They would be the first to use diving suits for a military purpose.

In theory, the commandos could also carry containers with 200kg explosive charges.
These charges were packed into a magnetic device, which allowed them to become
attached to a target vessel's hull. The device had an integrated timer which controlled
the ignition of the fuse, which in turn would start the detonation chain. The idea
behind it was for a stealthy approach made possible by this man-useable submarine,
with the application of explosives being equally quiet. Torpedoes, although effective,
were noisy affairs, and as soon as they were launched they detonated, providing an
extremely tight window in which to escape, making any subtle operation impossible.
If the operatives could choose when the munition detonated, then they could allow
time for their escape. In addition, the invention of the rideable torpedo would permit
an escape without making a commotion through the use of powerful fast engines.
Since they would likely not be seen, they could return without the pressure of potentially being chased. Even if the charge went off before the commandos could clear the
area, the enemy would be none the wiser, as the commandos could calmly sit out the
search under the water. Rossetti named his prototype subaquatic commando taxi the

12   Alberini, P. & Prosperini, F., *Uomini della Marina: 1861–1946*, p.464.

'Mignatta'.[13] When the time came to attack the Pola harbour after such a devastating previous failure, di Revel identified the Mignatta as the perfect tool for the job. At first glance, it might seem odd that the leader of the Italian fleet, based in Ancona, might be aware of an obscure experimental craft in Venezia. However, when he had been unceremoniously dispatched to the city's lagoons in 1915, the work of the technical department based there had been of intense interest to him.[14] It had been during his exile there (until 1917) that he had first made the acquaintance of Rossetti. As the navy's minds turned to plotting the infiltration of the Adriatic's most complex port, di Revel's attentions turned once more to the Genovese engineer.

The operation had to be put into action immediately, preferably before the SMS *Viribus Unitis* had time to become considered a Yugoslav vessel. On 30 October, in preparation for the handover, all officers and ratings not of the constituent nationalities of Yugoslavia were ordered to disembark.[15] This included Magyars, Germans and Italians, all of whom were to then march into the new world which existed in the place of the Habsburg Empire. Once on land, they would have to find their way to their homes. Out of the 1,100-strong crew, some 800 were not Yugoslavs, so when they left a mere skeleton crew of 200 or so remained.[16] By the time that the Mignatta was being loaded underneath Torpedo Boat 65 at Venezia at 2:00 p.m., ready to be escorted to Pola, the *Viribus Unitis* was stranded in a political reality not of its own making. Lost and forlorn, the now exclusively Slavic crew walked down its empty corridors, musing on the rapidity with which their old certainties had been shattered. At 8:45 p.m., as the Slavic crewmen played cards under dim ship's lights and sang their sorrowful ballads, the crew of the Mignatta began to put on their diving suits. The attack team was composed of Captain Costanzo Ciano, a curious Major Rossetti, the Paduan Captain Giovanni Scapin Battista and the Roman commando Raffaele Paolucci. At 10:45 p.m., the Mignatta was released 400m from the entrance to the defences. MAS 95, which had escorted them to that point, dropped anchor to await their return.

The obstacle field was dense and took the manned torpedo two hours to cross. The weather that night was atrocious; as with all operations near the Dalmatian coast, there was impenetrable fog. However, the poor climate had its uses, the heavy rain driving the sentries off the dock's jetties and preventing them from surveying the area too closely. Now unsupported, the brave commandos drove the Mignatta forward, hugging the coast as they approached the docked *Viribus Unitis*.[17] The port's guards, whose allegiance was a confusing patchwork of ethnic loyalties, were still none the wiser when at around 4:00 a.m. the Mignatta arrived within swimming distance of the dreadnought. The ship's vastness dwarfed Major Rossetti as he swam, bomb in hand, to the vulnerable area below the vessel's waterline. The Mignatta lingered nearby as

13   Kern, I., *Actions des MAS Italiens en Adriatique*, p.54.
14   Alberini, P. & Prosperini, F., *Uomini della Marina: 1861–1946*, p.514.
15   Sondhaus, L., *The Naval Policy of Austria-Hungary, 1867–1918*.
16   Noppen, R., *Austro-Hungarian Battleships, 1914–1918*, pp.43–45.
17   Kern, I., *Actions des MAS Italiens en Adriatique*, p.56.

198 On Warmer Tides

Rossetti fixed 500kg of high explosive to the vessel's underside at 4:20 a.m. The bomb's timer was set for 5:35 a.m. – in theory giving them plenty of time to escape before the blast. Just as Rossetti began to swim back to the Mignatta, quite by chance the *Viribus Unitis'* searchlight lit up the raiders. Ciano immediatey ordered the Mignatta to dive, which it did with surprising speed, denying the enemy the opportunity to realize they were under attack. As for Rossetti, he was picked up with a crewmate (it is not recorded whether Battista or Paolucci) and hauled before the dreadnought's captain, a Croat by the name of Captain Vukovic. The two Italian officers attempted to make the captain understand that the ship had to be evacuated; otherwise he would lose all his men. Their mission was simply to ensure the destruction of the ship, not to take the lives of those on board. However, the pair knew they could not reveal how the ship would be destroyed, lest they gave away the method by which they had been inserted into Pola. Vukovic, bereft of explanations, decided to initiate a search inside the vessel for a bomb. At the same time, he raised the alarm and ordered an evacuation of the ship. It was just in time, for right on schedule at 5:35 a.m., Rossetti's device exploded, blasting through the vessel's inadequate protection under the waterline, just as had been highlighted by Grand Admiral Tirpitz, and it quickly began to sink. Confronted with the dramatic loss of his vessel, Captain Vukovic ordered his men to abandon the dock and leave the vessel to its fate. With the dreadnought's demise, the Yugoslav Navy, the would-be rival to the *Regia Marina*, experienced a harsh still-birth.

Aftermath

With what was supposed to become the Yugoslav fleet losing its only prominent vessel, the SMS *Viribus Unitis*, on 1 November 1918, the Yugoslav armed forces could no longer even hope to threaten the *Regia Marina* by steaming triumphantly up and down the Adriatic. Its army, meanwhile, had no unified form, existing in name only. Rome took advantage of this by landing Italian troops at Pola on 5 November,[18] and nine days later they took Zadar before marching on Rijeka the next day. The Italians' rationale was to head off any attempt to remove from them the spoils they had been promised by the Treaty of London. The Croatian voices supporting unification with Serbia came to realize through these actions that the Italian Kingdom was serious about its obsession with forming a Greater Italy. If the Italians had to continue the war to displace the Yugoslavs from areas they considered rightfully theirs, then that was what they would do. On 28 November, desperate for protection from the Italians, the Croats accepted Serbian Prime Minister Pasic's terms, and Prince Aleksandar Karadjordjevic proclaimed the existence of the Kingdom of Yugoslavia on 1 December. Two years later, in 1920, the Treaty of Rapallo set relations on a concrete footing. The Italian Kingdom would gain Istria, Lussin, Cres, Lastovo and Zadar, uncontested by

18   Tanner, M., *Croatia: A History from the Middle Ages to the Present Day*, p.121.

the Yugoslavs.[19] These regions would join Trieste under Italian control, and as a result the final step in the *Risorigmento* was completed. The historical clock in Dalmatia had been turned back to 1797 by Rapallo, with the Italian Kingdom coming to rest as a victorious power.

The central spine of this book has not just been the tale of how Italy overcame its archnemesis to reclaim the maritime empire that Venice had bequeathed it. It has principally been the documentation of the fortunes of the *Regia Marina*, and within that body the creation of the space for the MAS to exist and then their actions upon their formation. So what happened to the *Regia Marina* after 1918? As part of the peace treaty at the end of the war, the Italian Kingdom's now illustrious navy received the vast majority of Habsburg vessels. On 9 November 1918, it was granted all ships still at Pola.[20] In February 1919, this force was joined by the 6,265-ton armoured cruiser SMS *Kaiser Karl VI*, whilst on 23 March that year, the surviving dreadnought SMS *Tegetthoff*, which Luigi Rizzo had failed to sink on 10 June 1918, also joined the *Regia Marina*. The two *Erzherzog* class battleships SMS *Erzherzog* and SMS *Franz Ferdinand* also became part of the Italian fleet, alongside the light cruiser SMS *Spaun* and two *Tatra* class destroyers, SMS *Balaton* and SMS *Tatra*. Three torpedo boats – 80T, 86F and 92F – also joined the Italian navy. A victory parade showing off their considerable spoils to the world was undertaken on 25 March 1919. Yet all of their impressive haul was scrapped, save the *Tegetthoff*, which was kept for sentimental reasons, even though it was rapidly becoming obsolete. The light cruiser *Spaun* was also retained and refitted. The granting to Italy of the whole former naval allocation to the Yugoslav nation removed Yugoslavia's potential to become a maritime power to rival Italy. In consequence, Rome returned to considering the French *Marine Nationale* as its primary enemy in the Mediterreanian. The Italian MAS boats would enjoy much attention in the post-war period. Throughout the inter-war years, intense interest was heaped upon the concepts developed within the unit, with particular intrigue surrounding the underwater attack on the SMS *Viribus Unitis*. The MAS squadrons would survive the lean inter-war years with surprising resilience, but their continued existence served only to lead them down a path which would see the unit write its own far darker legend. As the clouds of fascism began to engulf the Italian Kingdom in the two decades that followed 1919, the actions of the MAS squads would take a truly terrible turn. For after the Italian armistice with the Allies in 1943 following the invasion of Italy, the Italian aristocrat Junio Valerio Borghese, disobeying the order of his king to aid the Allies, delivered the MAS units over to the Germans. During the remainder of the war, they were primarily engaged in anti-partisan activity, committing atrocities throughout German-controlled Italy and frequently collaborating with the Waffen SS.

19   Tanner, M., *Croatia: A History from the Middle Ages to the Present Day*, p.121
20   Dodson,. A., *Spoils of War: The Fate of Enemy Fleets after the Two World Wars*, pp.24–26.

Bibliography

Printed Sources

Akhavan, J., *The Chemistry of Explosives* (London: Royal Society of Chemistry Publishing, 2011).

Alberini, P. & Prosperini, F., *Uomini della Marina: 1861–1946: Dizionario Biografico* (Roma: Ufficio Storico della Marina Militare, 2015).

Anderson, F., *Crucible of War: The Seven Years' War and the Fate of the Empire in British North America* (New York: Vintage, 2001).

Aube, T., *La Guerre Maritime et les Ports Militaires de la France* (Paris: Revue des Deux Mondes, 1882).

Badsey, S., *The Franco-Prussian War 1870–1871* (Oxford: Osprey Publishing, 2003).

Bagnasco, E., *I MAS e Le Motosiluranti Italiane 1906–1966* (Roma: Ufficio Storico della Marina Militare, 1967).

Ballantyne, I., *The Deadly Trade: The Complete History of Submarine Warfare, From Archimedes to the Present* (London: Weidenfeld & Nicolson, 2018).

Bassett, R., *For God and Kaiser: The Imperial Austrian Army 1619–1918* (London: Yale University Press, 2015).

Botti, F., *Il Pensiero Militare e Navale Italiano dalla Rivoluzione Francese alla Prima Guerra Mondiale (1789–1915), Volume II* (Roma: Stato Maggiore dell'Esercito Ufficio Storico, 2000).

Botti, F., *Il Pensiero Militare e Navale (1789–1915), Volume III Tomo II* (Roma: Ufficio Storico dello Stato Maggiore dell'Esercito, 2010).

Bourguet, E., *Les Ruines de Delphes* (Paris: 1914).

Bouvier, F., *Bonaparte en Italie 1796* (Paris: 1899).

Braddock, J., *A Memoir on Gunpowder* (London: J.M. Richardson Publishing, 1832).

Cary, E., *Dio's Roman History in Nine Volumes* (London: William Heinemann Ltd, 1957).

Chalkley, A., *Les Moteurs Diesel Type Fixe et Type Marine* (Paris : Dunod et Pinat Éditeurs, 1919).

Clark, C., *Iron Kingdom: The Rise and Downfall of Prussia, 1600–1947* (London: Penguin Publishing, 2017).

Clark, C., *The Sleepwalkers: How Europe Went to War in 1914* (London: Penguin Publishing, 2013).

Colarizi, S., *Storia del Novecento Italiano* (Milano: Mondadori, 2013).

Collins, R., *Early Medieval Europe: 300–1000* (London: Palgrave, 1999).

Cook-Branfill, R., *Torpedo: The Complete History of the World's Most Revolutionary Naval Weapon* (Barnsley: Seaforth Publishing, 2014).

Crawley, R., *The History of the Peloponnesian War by Thucydides* (London: J.M. Dent & Sons Ltd, 1950).

Cuccu, L., *Storia della Burocrazia Italiana: Dalla Riforma Cavour alle Riforme Bassanini* (Cagliari: L'Universale, 2018).

D'Amato, R., *Republican Roman Warships 509–27BC* (Oxford: Osprey Publishing, 2015).

D'Annunzio, G., *La Beffa di Buccari* (Milano: I Fratelli Traves, 1918).

Davey, J., *In Nelson's Wake: The Navy and the Napoleonic Wars* (London: Yale University Press, 2015).

Davidson, J., *The French Revolution: From Enlightenment to Tyranny* (London: Profile Books, 2017).

Declare, J., *Histoire de la Chimie* (Paris: Imprimerie Gauthier-Villars Et C, 1920).

Desmond, K., *The Guinness Book of Motorboating: Facts, Feats and Origins* (Enfield: Guinness Superlatives Ltd, 1979).

Detroyat, L., *L'Intervention Francaise au Mexique* (Paris: Amyot Edituer, 1868).

Disney, A.R., *A History of Portugal, and the Portuguese Empire: From Beginning to 1807* (Cambridge: Cambridge University Press, 2009).

Dodson, A., *Spoils of War: The Fate of Enemy Fleets after the Two World Wars* (Barnsley: Seaforth Publishing, 2020).

Ecorchon, F., *Le Moteur Diesel et ses Derives : Traite Theorique et Pratique* (Paris: Librairie, 1929).

Engel, P., *The Realm of St Stephen: A History of Medieval Hungary, 895–1526* (London: Continuum International Publishing Group, 2005).

Fairbank, J.K. & Goldman, M., *China: A New History* (Cambridge: Harvard University Press, 2006).

Fenby, J., *The History of Modern France: From the Revolution to the War on Terror* (London: Simon & Schuster Publishing, 2015).

Figuier, L., *Les Merveilles de la Science ou Description Populaire des Inventions Modernes* (Paris: Jouvet et C Éditeurs, 1870).

Fontin, P., *Guerre et Marine : Un Essai sur L'Unite de la Defense* Nationale (Paris: Berger-Levrault Éditeurs, 1906).

Frezet, J., *Histoire de la Maison de Savoie: Tome Troisième* (Torino: De L'Imprimerie, 1827).

Galibert, L., *Histoire de la République de Venise* (Paris: Paris, 1850).

George, G., *Histoire de la Grèce Depuis les Temps les Plus Recules Jusqu'à La Fin de la Generation Contemporaine d'Alexandre le Grand: Tome 5* (Brussels: A. Lacroix Verboeckhoven et Éditeurs, 1867).

Glenny, M., *The Balkans 1804–2012: Nationalism, War and the Great Powers* (London: Granta Books, 2017).

Goldsworthy, A., *The Fall of Carthage: The Punic Wars 265–146BC* (London: Weidenfeld & Nicolson, 2003).

Guilbaud, T., *Les Explosifs Actuels* (Paris: Éditions & Libraire, 1916).

Hastings, M., *Catastrophe: Europe Goes to War, 1914* (London: William Collins Publishing, 2013).

Hennebert, E., *L'Artillerie* (Paris: Libraire Hachette, 1887).

Henry, V., *Explosions et Explosives* (Paris: Berger-Levrault, 1916).

Herwig, H., *The First World War: Germany and Austria-Hungary, 1914–1918* (London: Arnold Publishing, 1997).

Hett, W.S., *Aristotle: Problems, Books XII–XXXVIII* (London: William Heineman Ltd, 1957).

Ivetic, E., *Storia dell'Adriatico: Un Mare e La Sua Civilta* (Bologna: Il Mulino, 2019).

Jablonski, J., *Getting Clear on the Basics: The Fundamentals of Technical Diving* (High Springs: Global Underwater Explorers, 2001).

Jackson, P., 'The Fleuss Apparatus', *Historical Diver*, Vol. 10, Issue 2 (2002).

James, L., *The Rise & Fall of The British Empire* (London: Abacus Publishing, 1998).

Jezierski, L., *Combats et Batailles du Siege de Paris: Septembre 1870 a Janvier 1871* (Paris: Garnier Frères, 1872).

Jones, W. & Ormerod, H., *Pausanias' Description of Greece with an English Translation* (Cambridge: Harvard University Press, 1918).

Kern, I., *Actions des MAS Italiens en Adriatique Pendant la Grande Guerre et Reactions des Autrichiens* (Paris: Ecole de Guerre Navale, 1935).

Konstam, A., *British Ironclads 1860–75: HMS Warrior and the Royal Navy's Black Battlefleet* (London: Osprey Publishing, 2018).

Konstam, A., *European Ironclads 1860–75: The Gloire Sparks the Great Ironclad Arms Race* (London: Osprey Publishing, 2019).

Kramli, M., *Austro-Hungarian Battleships and Battleship Designs: 1904–1914* (Szeged: Belvedere Meridionale, 2021).

Lacey, R., *Inside the Kingdom* (London: Arrow, 2010).

Leier, M., *Bakunin: The Creative Passion* (New York: Thomas Dunne Books, 2007).

Lepre, A. & Petraccone, C., *Storia D'Italia Dall'Unita a Oggi* (Bologna: Il Mulino, 2008).

Lincoln, B., *The Romanovs: Autocrats of All the Russians* (New York: Doubleday Publishing, 1983).

Londres, A., *Pecheurs de Perles* (Paris: Albin Michel Editeur, 1931).

Macintyre, D., *Jutland* (New York: Norton & Company, 1958).

Mahan, A., *The Influence of Sea Power upon History: 1660–1783* (Boston: Little, Brown & Company, 1890).

Mansfield, P., *A History of the Middle East* (London: Penguin Publishing, 1991).

Matt, F., *Le Siege de Paris* (Paris: Maison et C Éditeurs, 1871).

Meunier, R., *La Guerre Russo-Japonaise Historique, Enseignemernts, par le Chef D'Escadron D'Artillerie Brevete* (Paris: Berger-Levrault Editeur, 1906).

Moigno, F., *Recherches sur les Agents Explosifs Modernes et Sur Leurs Applications Récentes* (Paris: Gauthier-Villars, 1872).

Molinari, E. & Quartieri, F., *Notices sur les Explosifs en Italie* (Milan: U. Hoepli, 1913).

Molnar, M., *A Concise History of Hungary* (Cambridge: Cambridge University Press, 2001).

Montipo, G., *La Vita di un Modenese Tra i 30 della Beffa di Buccari* (Udine: Gaspari, 2020).

Morris, J., *History of the US Navy* (North Dighton: J.G. Press, 2003).

Musarra, A., *Medioevo Marinaro: Prendere il Mare Nell'Italia Medievale* (Bologna: Il Mulino, 2021).

Musatti, E., *Storia d'un Lembo di Terra: Venezia ed i Veneziani* (Padova: 1882).

Nansouty, M., *Les Merveilles de la Science: Moteurs* (Paris: Bovin Éditeurs, 1910).

Noppen, R., *Austro-Hungarian Battleships, 1914–1918* (New Vanguard series, 193) (Oxford: Osprey Publishing, 2012).

Norwich, J., *A Short History of Byzantium* (London: Penguin Publishing, 1998).

Norwich, J., *Sicily: A Short History from the Ancient Greeks to Cosa Nostra* (London: Murray Publishing, 2015).

Norwich, J., *The Popes: A History* (London: Vintage Publishing, 2012).

O'Hara, V., Dickson, D. *et al.*, *To Crown the Waves: The Great Navies of the First World War* (Annapolis: Naval Institute Press, 2013).

Paine, L., *The Sea and Civilization: A Maritime History of the World* (London: Atlantic Books, 2015).

Paixhans, H., *Nouvelle Force Maritime et Application de Cette Force a Quelques Parties du Service de L'Armee de Terre* (Paris: Bachelier Libraire, 1822).

Pecout, G., *Il Lungo Risorgimento: La Nascita dell'Italia Contemporanea (1770–1922)* (Torino: Bruno Mondadori, 1997).

Philippe, J., *D'Annunzio* (New York: Viking Press, 1973).

Pipes, R., *Russia Under The Old Regime* (London: Penguin Publishing, 1974).

Poma, S., *L'Italia in Guerra: La Grande Storia degli Italiani del Regno 1896–1943* (Cagliari: L'Universale, 2020).

Rainero, R. & Alberini, P., *Le Forze Armate e la Nazione Italiana* (Rome: Ufficio Storico della Difesa, 2003).

Roberts, A., *Napoleon the Great* (London: Penguin Publishing, 2015).

Roberts, J., *The Battleship Dreadnought* (Oxford: Osprey Publishing, 2001).

Rodger, N.A.M., *The Command of the Ocean: A Naval History of Britain 1649–1815* (London: Penguin Publishing, 2005).

Rodger, N.A.M., *The Safeguard of the Seas: A Naval History of Britain 660–1649* (London: Penguin Publishing, 2004).

Rottauscher, M., *With Tegetthoff at Lissa: The Memoirs of an Austrian Naval Officer 1861–66* (Solihull: Helion & Company Ltd, 2010).

Saviano, R., *Gomorrah* (London: Picador, 2019).

Scott, D., *Leviathan: The Rise of Britain as a World Power* (London: Harper Press, 2013).

Smith, I.B., 'The Impact of Stephen Hales on Medicine', *Journal of the Royal Society of Medicine*, Vol. 86 (June 1993).

Sondhaus, L., *The Great War at Sea: A Naval History of the First World War* (Cambridge: Cambridge University Press, 2014).

Sondhaus, L., *The Naval Policy of Austria-Hungary, 1867–1918: Navalism, Industrial Development and the Politics of Dualism* (West Lafayette: Purdue University Press, 1994).

Steerk, M., *Guide Pratique de la Fabrication des Poudres et Saltpetres* (Paris: Librairie Scientifique Industrielle et Agricole, 1866).

Stone, N., *The Eastern Front 1914–1917* (London: Penguin Publishing, 1998).

Sumption, J., *Trial by Battle: The Hundred Years War, Vol. I* (London: Faber & Faber Publishing, 1990).

Tanera, C., *De La Dynamite et De Ses Applications Pendant le Siege de Paris* (Paris: Librairie Pour L'Art Militaire et Les Sciences, 1871).

Tanner, M., *Croatia: A History from the Middle Ages to the Present* Day (London: Yale University Press, 2010).

Taylor. A.J.P., *The Habsburg Monarchy 1809–1918* (London: Penguin Publishing, 1948).

Taylor. A.J.P., *The Struggle for Mastery in Europe: 1848–1918* (Oxford: Oxford University Press, 1954).

Taylor, J., *Futurism* (New York: Doubleday & Company, 1917).

Thomas, N., *Armies in the Balkans 1914–18* (Oxford: Osprey Publishing, 2001).

Thompson, M., *The White War: Life and Death on the Italian Front, 1915–1919* (London: Faber & Faber, 2008).

Ular, A., *La Revolution Russe: La Dynastie et La Cour, La Bureaucratie, Le Regime Witte* (Paris: Paris, 1903).

Vann, R., Denoble, P. *et al.*, *Rebreather Forum 3 Proceedings* (Durham: PADI, 2014).

Watson, A., *Rings of Steel: Germany and Austria-Hungary at War, 1914–1918* (London: Penguin Publishing, 2014).

West, J., *Marcello Malpighi and the Discovery of the Pulmonary Capillaries and Alveoli* (2013).

West, J., *Torricelli and the Ocean of Air: The First Measurement of Barometric Pressure* (Bethesda: Physiology, 2013).

Wilson, P., *The Holy Roman Empire: A Thousand Years of Europe's History* (London: Penguin Publishing, 2016).

Woodgate, W., *Boating* (London: Longmans, Green & Co, 1888).

Zamoyski, A., *Phantom Terror: The Threat of Revolution and the Repression of Liberty 1789–1848* (Glasgow: William Collins, 2015).

Electronic Sources

About Biglietto <https://www.baglietto.com/about-baglietto/>

Camuffo History <https://www.camuffo.it/en/history/>

Index